HOW TO FORGIVE
ANYONE FOR ANYTHING

Discover the Freedom to Live, Laugh, and Love Again

FREDERICK HERMANN

How To Forgive Anyone For Anything

© 2016 Frederick Hermann

Scripture quotations are from the following sources:

ISBN-13: 9781537687117
ISBN-10: 1537687115

I DEDICATE THIS BOOK
TO MY MOTHER AND FATHER,
my extended family and friends, and all those individuals
whose wisdom, understanding and encouragement helped me
to persevere in writing this devotional.

Special thanks to the joyful individuals of The Carmelite
Monastery of St. Joseph -- without their living dedication
and prayerful inspiration this book would never have seen the
light of day.

I also wish to thank all the people I have met who have forgiven more than their fair share of sorrows. They wonderfully
demonstrate by quiet example how genuine forgiveness truly
sets us free.

Thanks to Carol Campbell and Mary Wainscott for their
editorial assistance, and Sister Maria Battista for proofreading
with her eagle eyes and red pen.

PREFACE

❖ ❖ ❖

T HE MORE I learn about forgiveness, the more I realize that we cannot forgive alone; we need God's help to do it.

I am convinced that forgiveness bestows healing on those who give it and receive it. The lack of forgiveness imprisons and impoverishes our souls, while the gift of forgiveness enriches and ennobles us beyond our wildest imagination.

I am writing this sitting outside a rustic wooden cabin nestled by a peaceful lake. Surrounding me is a dense green forest filled with whispering leaves, chirping birds, and vibrant wildlife. A bumblebee buzzes around a bright red flower. The soft hooting from two unseen owls echoes across the lake, "Who, who, who cooks for you?"

My soul is nourished by this hushed silence, tranquil solitude, and the blessings of life. My two faithful dogs are curled up at my feet and sleeping comfortably. They always seem to be most serene when I am writing, as if they enjoy it more than I do.

Hidden in this secluded place deep in the heartland, my cabin sits near the shore of the lake on a point of land that slopes gently into the water, sending out ripples like a quill pen dipping into a blue inkwell.

I like to write facing the lake so I can see the sunlight glinting and flashing on the water, sparkling like diamonds before my eyes. I wait patiently to become mindful of God's presence and he illuminates my soul.

Such is the light of truth that I wish to reflect to you. It is a labor of love that I find humbling, inspiring, and fulfilling.

I have given and received many offenses in my life, so I have experienced the intense struggle to give and receive forgiveness. Now I wish to share with you what I know is desperately needed and readily available to completely heal broken hearts and hurting souls.

I hope this book inspires you to seek forgiveness as if you were seeking a pearl of great price.

Pearls are formed when an irritant, such as a grain of sand, works its way into the soft interior of an oyster. The oyster's natural reaction is to cover the irritant with a smooth coating to protect itself. Layer upon layer of this coating is deposited until a lustrous, iridescent pearl is formed.

True forgiveness is like a pearl: it is irritating, and it takes time, but it creates something rare, exquisitely beautiful, and extremely valuable. You will find the forgiveness you desire when you dive deep into the depths of love.

I pray for the wisdom to write in a way that is helpful to heal your wounds and bring new light and life to you in unexpected ways.

O Lord, come to our assistance. Teach us how to forgive others, ourselves, and you -- so that we may live, laugh, and love again!

Frederick Hermann
Lake Innsbrook

Before you the whole universe
is like a grain from a balance,
or a drop of morning dew
come down upon the earth.

But you have mercy on all,
because you can do all things;
and you overlook sins
for the sake of repentance.

For you love all things that are
and loathe nothing that you have made;
for you would not fashion what you hate.

How could a thing remain,
unless you willed it;
or be preserved,
had it not been called forth by you?

But you spare all things,
because they are yours,
O Ruler and Lover of souls

- WISDOM 11:22

THE LORD IS CLOSE

❖ ❖ ❖

The Lord is close to the brokenhearted.

- PSALM 34:19

YOU DO NOT have to live very long in this life before you experience a personal offense, a betrayal, or an injury. Naturally you may feel confused, resentful, or angry. In the midst of your frustration, take a moment to reflect on the fact that *the Lord is close to the brokenhearted.* God is near you always, but he is especially close to you when you are feeling broken or disheartened. He wants you to know that he is right there beside you when you need him most. Rest in his care, take comfort in his presence, and be healed by his love. Allow him to guide you peacefully through the forest. As you travel along the leafy path, look up and see the protective canopy of branches arching overhead. Can you feel God reaching out to you, embracing you, restoring your soul? *He heals the brokenhearted and binds up their wounds.*

⁓

Pray: O Lord, I am sometimes blinded and confused by my circumstances. Thank you for being by my side to comfort me and guide my way ahead.

BLESSED ARE YOU

❖ ❖ ❖

*Blessed are you when they insult you and
persecute you and utter all kinds of evil against
you falsely because of me.*

- MATTHEW 5:11

WAIT A MINUTE, you say, how is that again? How can I be blessed when people insult me and persecute me? This does not make any sense! You are correct; we cannot understand this with our natural minds. It only becomes clear as we begin to see things supernaturally. As we gradually allow ourselves to listen to the wisdom of God, we begin to see things in a whole new light. Jesus clearly says *rejoice and be glad, for your reward will be great in heaven.* In some mysterious way, when we are offended in this life, we may rejoice, knowing that it generates a greater reward in heaven. We may receive our reward partially in this life, but God will give it to us fully in heaven.

Pray: O Lord, it is hard for me to understand your wisdom. When I am offended, help me to believe that I am blessed.

DO NOT BE SURPRISED

❖ ❖ ❖

*Beloved, do not be surprised that a trial by
fire is occurring among you, as if something
strange were happening to you.*

- 1 PETER 4:11

WHEN SOMEONE OFFENDS us, we often feel ambushed, shocked and surprised. We didn't see it coming! But Peter reminds us that we should not be surprised when we suddenly find ourselves in a trial by fire. After all, we live in a fallen world surrounded by sinners, so we should expect others to sin against us. But God is in control; nothing surprises him. Remember God does not cause our suffering but he allows it sometimes in order to bring about a greater good. At this moment, you may not be able to imagine something good coming out of your circumstances, but God is silently working behind the scenes on your behalf, so be patient. *Rejoice to the extent that you share in the sufferings of Christ, so that when his glory is revealed you may also rejoice exultantly.* Rather than lamenting our cruel fate, we should rejoice because we are being tested and improved by fire. Jesus learned wisdom by his sufferings. We are sharing in the sufferings of Christ. Someday we will rejoice!

Pray: O Lord, help me to remember that I should not be
surprised by evil. I believe you allow my trials by fire to refine
my soul. Help me to rejoice today knowing that I share in the
sufferings of Christ.

OUR FATHER

❖ ❖ ❖

Our Father, who art in heaven, hallowed be thy name.

- MATTHEW 6:9

MANY TIMES IN life we are tempted to think suffering proves that God does not exist or that he is far away, aloof and uncaring. Nothing could be further from the truth. How do we know? Jesus teaches us to pray to God as *Father*, Abba, a familiar greeting akin to saying "Daddy". As a perfect Father to us, God is not careless, as we often fear. Rather he is close at hand, caring deeply for our well-being and nurturing us throughout our lives. We can trust him in all situations to make everything right. We can rest in his embrace as a child sleeps blissfully in the arms of a parent. Notice how Jesus did not instruct us to say "My Father" but emphasized "Our Father" because we do not live in isolation. In God's kingdom we experience his fatherhood as members of big happy family. This should remind us to recognize that all people are children of God. This makes it easier to treat others accordingly. Even when people disrupt the family of God and reject the will of our loving Father, we can still pray for them and show them God's mercy.

Pray: O Lord, I thank you for revealing yourself to me as a loving, caring Father. I delight in reminding myself that I am a member of huge family destined for eternal happiness.

THY KINGDOM COME

❖ ❖ ❖

Thy kingdom come, thy will be done,
on earth as it is in heaven.

- MATTHEW 6:10

THE SINS OF this world are so painful that we sometimes feel overwhelmed. Like dense clouds that block out the sun, our grief and sadness may darken our days. We wonder if God really cares. We are tempted to think life on earth is only filled with meaningless suffering and that we must wait until we get to heaven for relief. The truth is we do not have to wait. We can pray as Jesus taught us for God to start our heavenly experience here on earth. *Thy Kingdom come, thy will be done, on earth as it is in heaven.* We can help God accomplish his heavenly plan by cooperating in all that we do, say, and pray. We can begin to rejoice today because God promises to give us many blessings here and now, in the land of the living. His blessings may come in disguise so we may not recognize them as gifts. We may suffer many setbacks. But we believe in God's goodness, so we believe all our failures contain the seeds of God's blessings. We believe we will soon see these seeds sprout and grow, making our desert bloom with lush fruit and bright flowers.

Pray: O Lord, I thank you today for allowing me to help you accomplish your divine plan to make heaven on earth.

OUR DAILY BREAD

❖ ❖ ❖

Give us this day our daily bread.

- MATTHEW 6:11

D O YOU SOMETIMES feel as if you are wandering alone in a desert? Are you anxious and wondering how you will possibly survive? When the Israelites turned away from God and got lost in the desert, they grumbled and complained that God had abandoned them. But God sustained them by miraculously raining down plain bread (manna) from heaven every night. God provides for us in the same way. Every morning we arise to find new bread. Every day dawns with God reminding us in new ways of his presence and his goodness. God delights to surprise us daily with evidence of his loving abundance. Jesus teaches us to pray for this daily nourishment to remind us that all good things come to us from God. God gives us the strength to plow the field and plant the seed, but it is he who waters the earth and causes the sprouts to grow, so the harvest belongs to him. We grind the grain and bake the bread but without God we have nothing. God is our nourishment, the Bread of Life, the Eucharist. All that we are and everything we receive belongs to God, so our gratitude mirrors his love and knows no bounds.

Pray: O Lord, thank you for giving me your daily bread. Help me to nourish others who are starving for your love.

FORGIVE US OUR TRESPASSES

❖ ❖ ❖

And forgive us our trespasses,
as we forgive those who trespass against us.

- *MATTHEW 6:12*

PERHAPS THE BIGGEST challenge we face in our lives is learning how to ask for forgiveness and how to forgive others. Jesus teaches us how to ask forgiveness for our sins. We simply pray to God with a humble heart and ask to be forgiven. In other situations, we are assured of God's unconditional love, but here we find a necessary condition to his love: we are forgiven only *as we forgive those who trespass against us.* God reveals a direct connection between his forgiving us and our forgiving others. You may protest that your sins are completely unrelated to the more grievous sins committed by others against you. Yet God lovingly insists that his forgiveness of us is absolutely dependent upon our forgiving others. Why is this so? In his infinite wisdom God wants us to realize that he cannot fill our hearts with his love until we have first emptied them of anger and bitterness. He also wants us to learn that we cannot forgive others by ourselves: we need his strength that we receive in prayer.

Pray: O Lord, help me to delight in forgiving others
as much as I delight in receiving forgiveness from you!

LEAD US NOT INTO TEMPTATION

❖ ❖ ❖

And lead us not into temptation, but deliver us from evil.

- MATTHEW 6:13

IN THIS PRAYER we acknowledge our weakness and need for help when it comes to fighting temptation. We are all tempted at times to be angry, resentful, and bitter. These are natural human emotions that are ignited by sins against us. The evil one gleefully fans these flames to separate us from one another and alienate us from God. Yet God calls us to ascend to a higher level. God sent the Holy Spirit to empower us to soar above our weakness by forgiving others. Yet we pray every day for divine assistance to steer us clear of temptation. On those days when God does allow temptation into our lives, we remember that it is only to give us an opportunity to strengthen our faith. He will assuredly deliver us, when we ask him in prayer, from all evil. With the Holy Spirit as our protector and guide, we find ourselves swiftly delivered from all our difficulties and ordeals.

Pray: O Lord, help me avoid all temptations, strengthen me to resist what I must endure, and deliver me from all evil.

New Life Every Morning

❖ ❖ ❖

The steadfast love of the Lord never ceases, his mercies never come to an end; they are new every morning.

- Lamentations 3:22

Beloved, see how the love of the Lord is steady and unceasing toward you and his entire creation. He delights in renewing all things with the dawn of each day. Only God can love us perfectly, as no human can. Does this help you believe that his mercies are never-ending in your life? Why is he so loving and merciful when we are undeserving? Because he created us, he is our Father. We are his children, so he wants what is best for us: he wants to gather us up in his loving arms and heal us in every way, now and forever.

Pray: O Lord, I believe I am renewed by your love. Help me overflow your loving mercy and forgiveness to others!

BE ANGRY BUT DO NOT SIN

❖ ❖ ❖

*Be angry but do not sin; do not let the sun set
on your anger, and do not leave room for the devil.*

- *EPHESIANS 4:26*

IT IS OKAY to feel angry. Anger is a natural emotion in response to an external threat or offense. Anger helps us preserve, protect and defend ourselves and others. Even the smallest child displays loud and vehement protests against whatever is negligent or unfair. Our anger against injustice proves that we possess the idea of perfect justice. On a deeper level, our anger proves that God exists, because our recognition of the imperfect would be impossible without an inborn conception of the perfect. So anger is a good and God-given gift. The problem occurs when we allow our anger to get out of control. Then we start thinking about retaliation, retribution, and revenge. *A fool gives full vent to anger, but the wise quietly holds it back.* We are wise when we practice patience, forbearance, and self-control. The best way to develop these virtues is to forgive others and reconcile with them before the sun sets every day. Get in the habit of being slow to anger and forgiving others before the end of the day. Whom do you need to forgive at this moment? Release your anger and forgive that person before sunset today, then rest in God's loving embrace and sleep in heavenly peace.

⌐

Pray: O Lord, help me learn how to let go of my anger
and forgive others by the end of the day, every day!

UNDERSTANDING ANGER

❖ ❖ ❖

*You have heard that it was said to those of ancient times,
'You shall not murder'; and 'whoever murders shall be liable
to judgment.' But I say to you that if you are angry with a
brother or sister, you will be liable to judgment.*

- MATTHEW 5:21

EXTREME ANGER IS like murder. If we do not renounce
our anger, it spreads like cancer out of control, darkening
our thoughts and poisoning our feelings. Our angry words,
thoughts and emotions can be just as deadly as guns, knives
and bombs. We can kill self-esteem in other people, ruin their
reputation, or destroy their peace of mind. Without realizing
what we are doing, we can become so angry with others that we
murder them in our minds and assassinate them in our hearts.
Jesus says extreme anger is equal to murder and puts our souls
in danger. Our anger may even make us more guilty in God's
eyes than the person who offended us! *All who hate a brother
or sister are murderers, and you know that murderers do not have
eternal life.* We need to forgive others for their trespasses against
us and confess our anger in every form it takes. God will calm
us down, give us peace and self-control, fill us with his healing
love, and lead us to eternal life.

⌒

Pray: O Jesus, help me forgive others and release my anger
into your healing hands. Replace my anger with your love!

Vengeance Is Mine

❖ ❖ ❖

Dearly beloved, avenge not yourselves…
vengeance is mine; I will repay, says the Lord.

- Romans 12:19

You need not be angry, you need no revenge, for God will right all your wrongs. When bad things happen in our lives, our natural tendency is to insist on immediate justice. Those who wrong us may appear to go unpunished, but God has them in his sights. He is weighing them in his perfect scales of justice and their day in his court will come soon enough. If they repent of their wrongs he is merciful and will forgive them for all their sins, just as he has forgiven you. *If we acknowledge our sins, he is faithful and just and will forgive our sins and cleanse us from every wrongdoing.* However, if they do not repent, they will suffer the fearful consequences of their choice to separate themselves from his mercy. In any case, God will repay us for all that has been stolen from us, so let us release our anger against all the wrongdoers we hold captive so grievously and mercilessly. Let us pity them instead, for they are poor souls indeed. We can pray that they see the light and experience the love of God.

⁓

Pray: O Lord, I release all the prisoners of my anger into your hands, for I know you judge everyone perfectly.

TURN THE OTHER CHEEK

❖   ❖   ❖

You have heard that it was said,
'An eye for an eye and a tooth for a tooth.'
But I say to you, offer no resistance to one who is evil.
When someone strikes you on your right cheek,
turn the other one to him as well.

- MATTHEW 5:38

MUST YOU REALLY turn the other cheek? Does this show weakness, excuse evil, and encourage it? Yet Jesus clearly says you must turn the other cheek and *hand him your cloak as well.* How can we understand this saying? The way of the world has always been to show strength and eliminate adversaries, but history proves this tactic spirals out of control like a wildfire. To control this escalation, the Judaic law advocated retribution equal to the injury: *an eye for an eye.* Jesus goes further by urging against resistance or revenge against offenders. We may understand this teaching as an encouragement to be patient and always forgive everyone in every circumstance. Nevertheless, we may have recourse to legal remedies or reasonable action in some situations, as Jesus did when he threw the moneychangers out of the temple. And of course we must defend ourselves against threats to our lives or the lives of innocent people. Yet Jesus showed us that there are times when we are called to truly give no resistance to those who would crucify us.

⤵

Pray: O Jesus, give me the patience and wisdom to know how to turn the other cheek, always forgiving others!

LOVE YOUR ENEMIES

❖ ❖ ❖

You have heard that it was said,
'You shall love your neighbor and hate your enemy.'
But I say to you, love your enemies,
and pray for those who persecute you.

- MATTHEW 5:43

SURELY THIS TEACHING by Jesus to *love your enemies* struck his listeners like a thunderbolt. Indeed it strikes us today as absurd and outrageous! Yet Jesus insists and goes even further, saying *pray for those who persecute you.* Preposterous and impossible! Why does Jesus say this? He wants to take you outside yourself, above and beyond your limited and selfish view of the world. He wants to open the doors of your heart to receive his life-changing love, see others as he sees them, and show you how to experience life in a whole new way. As soon as we attempt to love our enemies, we are flooded with the realization that God loves all humankind, *for he makes his sun rise on the bad and the good, and causes rain to fall on the just and the unjust.* When we love our enemies, we experience God's intimate, infinite love for us. Then it dawns on us that we are children of our heavenly Father and that he loves us all with an everlasting love.

Pray: O Jesus, open my eyes and soften my heart. Help me learn to love my enemies with your divine love!

BE PERFECT

❖ ❖ ❖

Be perfect, just as your heavenly Father is perfect.

- MATTHEW 5:48

THIS SEEMS LIKE a preposterous thing for Jesus to say. How can anyone to be perfect? Yet Jesus calls us to strive for perfection. We are each called to be a saint! We must reach for the ideals given to us by our heavenly Father and embodied in his son Jesus. As we endeavor to follow in the footsteps of Jesus by loving our enemies and praying for them, we imitate what Jesus commanded and obtain God's grace to succeed. Our exertions alone will not suffice; we must confess our sins to God and be washed clean. Then God engulfs us with his supernatural grace and empowers us to live the virtuous life he ordains for us. With God's help, each of us can forgive others as God forgives us, leave our sins behind, and excel in living the perfect virtues of faith, hope and love. As we grow in spiritual maturity and let God ripen our special gifts, we smile inwardly as we contemplate the fact that all saints were once sinners. As we humble ourselves and invite Jesus to live in our hearts more each day, he welcomes us into the ultimate life of the Trinity, in whom we gradually experience ever more of the perfect love of the Father, the Son, and the Holy Spirit.

Pray: O Jesus, I welcome you into my heart. I know I am not perfect, but I am made perfect by your infinite love!

Running Toward The Goal

❖ ❖ ❖

I have not yet reached my goal, and I am not perfect.
But Christ has taken hold of me. So I keep on running
and struggling to take hold of the prize.

- Philippians 3:12

I F YOU FALL, get up. Do not be discouraged when you stumble, my beloved, as you invariably will, but rather let Christ take hold of your hand and raise you up again. While you are called to be perfect, as your heavenly Father is perfect, remember the Saints were once sinners who stumbled. You are not yet perfect, but Christ who lives in you is perfect. If you fall and bruise your elbow or skin your knee, arise like a Saint-in-training and continue the race. If you injure others during the race, ask them for forgiveness. If others injure you, forgive them at once and proceed forward. Let no power on earth dissuade or discourage you from running the race that is before you and reaching your divine goal. With Jesus holding you up and giving you wings on your heels, run like the wind. If you cannot run, then walk; and if you cannot walk, then pray your way ahead. *I forget what is behind, and I struggle for what is ahead. I run toward the goal, so that I can win the prize of being called to heaven.*

Pray: O Jesus, pick me up when I stumble and fall down.
Help me to run my race with humility and joy!

How To Rebuke And Reconcile

❖   ❖   ❖

If your brother sins against you,
go and tell him his fault between you and him alone.
If he listens to you, you have won over your brother.

- MATTHEW 18:15

HAVE YOU EVER wanted to know the best way to rebuke someone who has offended you? Listen to Jesus tell you the right steps. First you go directly to that person, face to face if possible, and speak to him privately. How many of us fail to take this first step! How many friendships are lost, relationships estranged, and marriages disbanded because one party simply abandoned the ship? It is easy to criticize, denounce and condemn an offender from a safe distance. It is proof of superior virtue to speak the truth in love, and if he listens, you have converted an enemy into a friend! Of course this pleases God. Jesus says, *if he does not listen, take one or two others along with you.* Then if he refuses to listen to them, *tell the church.* If he refuses to listen even to the church, then Jesus allows you to let go of that person and *treat him as you would a Gentile or a tax collector*, meaning cautiously as you would an unbeliever or a dishonest person. Every step of the way, your goal is not to rebuke but to reconcile, just as Jesus seeks not to condemn us but to save our souls.

⌐

Pray: O Jesus, help me follow your steps to speak the truth in love. Help me learn to rebuke and reconcile if possible!

The Lord Hears

❖ ❖ ❖

The righteous cry out, the Lord hears
and he rescues them from all their afflictions.

- Psalm 34:18

IN THIS BEAUTIFUL verse we learn several things. First, if we want God to hear us, we must be righteous. That means we must be in a right relationship with God; he must be the most important person in our lives. Second, we learn we must ask God for his assistance. God knows what we need but he wants us to cry out in humble prayer so that *we* know how much we need him! Third, our Lord listens to us. We may not think God cares about us but he hears our every word. Fourth, God rescues us. Like a lifeguard he rushes to our aid when we are in distress. We may wonder why he is taking so long to appear, but he is always near. He is our heavenly lifesaver. Fifth, God rescues us from all our afflictions. Some of our afflictions? No, *all* our afflictions. Who is at work to deliver us from all our troubles? God is at work, our Creator who can do all things. Our Lord who created the entire universe out of nothing is continually at work behind the scenes creating a new reality for us. *Many are the troubles of the righteous, but the Lord delivers him from them all.*

Pray: O Lord, come to my assistance, make haste to help me.
I trust you are rescuing me from all my afflictions!

WALK HUMBLY WITH GOD

❖ ❖ ❖

He has shown you, O mortal, what is good.
And what does the Lord require of you? To act justly
and to love mercy and then walk humbly with your God.

- MICAH 6:8

WHEN AN OFFENSE hurts deeply, God can use the hurt to remind us that we are mortal. This raises our gaze higher, beyond this present life, to our eternal life, where God showers us with his goodness, justice and mercy. In return, God requires us to act justly and to love mercy towards others. While it may be difficult to love a person who has offended us, we love the mercy we show towards that person, because it is the same mercy God has shown to us. While we know God's mercy, other people may only experience our mercy. When we show God's mercy, we know the special joy that comes with humility, then we can walk humbly in peace with God.

Pray: O Lord, let the hurts I have received raise my gaze to you and your perfect justice. Help me to act justly and to love mercy toward others so that I may walk humbly at your side today. I like being at your side!

You Have Everything You Need

❖ ❖ ❖

God...has blessed us with every spiritual blessing."

- Ephesians 1:3

AN OFFENDER MAY steal something precious from you. It may be your health, wealth, reputation, a relationship, or your peace of mind. But it's important to remember that God has blessed you with every spiritual blessing - meaning everything you need to accomplish his will in your life. Meditate on this: you lack nothing that you need to fulfill your destiny. If you feel deprived of something or someone precious, offer your sorrow freely into God's loving hands. God provides everything and everyone in your life, so you can safely give it all back to him, knowing that you will always have every spiritual blessing you need for your journey.

Pray: O Lord, I give you thanks for promising to give me every spiritual blessing I need to accomplish your holy will in my life. I will not feel deprived and pitiful but rather replenished and bountiful because of your love every day.

OUT OF DEATH INTO LIFE

❖ ❖ ❖

Do not be surprised, brethren, if the world hates you.
We know that we have passed out of death into life,
because we love the brethren. He who
does not love abides in death.

- 1 JOHN 3:12

SOMETIMES IT SEEMS that others hate us. This is not surprising because we live in a fallen world with broken people. The most loving response we can give to hateful people is to love them as God loves them, and pity them because they do not know the love of God. We pity hateful people because those who cannot love abide in death. We know that we have passed out of death into life when we desire to love those who hate us. We have risen above the world when we use love to conquer hate. When we love those who hate us, we are showing them the love of God. Indeed, we are never more like God than when we show them his love. How can we do this? Because we have experienced God's supernatural love. Love has transformed us, raised us up, and filled us to overflowing. Now we know what it means to be reborn, renewed, and alive in Christ.

⌣

Pray: O Lord, help me to experience your love
more deeply every day. Fill me to overflowing so that
I may show your life-giving love and mercy to others.
I want to help others journey from death into new life.

BE KIND TO ONE ANOTHER

❖ ❖ ❖

*Be kind to one another, tenderhearted, forgiving
one another, as God in Christ forgave you.*

- *EPHESIANS 4:32*

WHOM DO YOU need to forgive? Perhaps a family member, a friend, or a stranger hurt you. Maybe someone continues to say and do things to offend you. Do you hold onto the past and nurture grudges about things that were said years ago? Forgiveness is the key to healing these relationships. In fact, nothing happens without forgiveness. When people are unkind to you, be kind in return. If people are hard-hearted, show them what a soft heart is like. When others do not deserve your mercy, be merciful anyway, for this is the way God treats you. He is kind to you, tenderhearted and forgiving. God heals you with his mercy, now go and do likewise. Heal others with your mercy, whether they ask for it or not. You will experience the mysterious healing connection between forgiving others and receiving forgiveness from God. You will discover how forgiveness heals both yourself and the one you forgive.

Pray: O Lord, teach me how to be kind, tenderhearted,
and forgiving toward others as you have been to me!

RECEIVE AND GIVE FREELY

❖ ❖ ❖

You received without paying, now give without being paid.

- MATTHEW 10:8

THE BEST GIFTS in life are free. We cherish free gifts such as kindness, friendship, encouragement, and love. But perhaps the most powerful gift we can give and receive is mercy. Giving and receiving mercy changes our lives; it renews our hearts, relieves our minds, and restores our souls. There is no better gift to receive from God than his forgiveness and he wants to continue giving it to us every day of our lives. While God's redeeming mercy does not cost us anything, it cost him the death of his only son. Yet God restored his son to new life, and now he restores us to new life by forgiving our sins. God offers us his marvelous forgiveness freely but with one condition; we must offer this same forgiveness freely to others. That which we have received without cost, we must turn around and give without cost. God pours his love into us until our cups overflow. This is what it means to be Christ-like.

Pray: O Jesus, as you freely bestowed forgiveness upon me, help me desire to freely give it to others!

ASK SOMETHING OF ME

❖ ❖ ❖

God said, "Ask something of me and I will give it to you."

- I KINGS 3:5

I F GOD ASKED you this question, as he asked Solomon, how would you answer? If you are troubled because somebody offended you, how would you reply? Would you ask for justice or revenge against the offender, or health and wealth for yourself? Solomon replied, "*Give your servant... an understanding heart to judge your people and to distinguish right from wrong.*" God was so pleased with this wise and humble request that he gave Solomon the most understanding heart of anyone who ever lived. Then God said, "*In addition, I give you what you have not asked for, such riches and glory that among kings there is not your like.*"

⤳

Pray: O Lord, help me to look past my hurts and pains. Instead, give me an understanding heart to see beneath the surface of things so that I may judge your people rightly and show them your mercy and forgiveness.

EVERYTHING WILL BE REVEALED

❖ ❖ ❖

Do not fear them, for there is nothing concealed that
will not be revealed, or hidden that will not be known.

- MATTHEW 10:26

WHAT A HAPPY thought that we do not need to fear any-one! People who offend us often do so in secret. They may shroud their actions in darkness so that no one knows about their offenses. When confronted about their hurtful ways, some people deflect, deny or excuse their actions. How can people be so audacious and hard-hearted? Instead of apologizing to us and asking for our forgiveness, certain individuals skillfully repudiate our witness, refuse to acknowledge the truth, and deny any responsibility for a tragedy. This can be more hurtful than the original offense because it makes us feel betrayed, unrecognized and abandoned. It can tempt us with the idea that we are disconnected, isolated, and alone. But Jesus says we need not fear *for there is nothing concealed that will not be revealed, or hidden that will not be known.* The day will come, as surely as the sun rises in the east, when the light of God's truth will illuminate everyone and everything. In that day darkness will be as midday, all errors will be corrected, and all wrongs will be made right.

Pray: O Lord, I rest in your promise that all things will one day be brought into the healing light of your infinite love.

IN HIS IMAGE

❖ ❖ ❖

God created mankind in his image;
in the image of God he created them;
male and female he created them.

- GENESIS 1:27

I F YOU WANT to know the most profound truth about yourself, you must know that you were created in the image of God. You look like your parents, of course, but you resemble God even more. When God created the universe, he created you *in his image.* So in many mysterious ways you are like God! You are not God, but you are godlike. You carry within yourself supernatural qualities that are truly divine. Your outrage against evil proves that you possess a divine awareness of God's perfect good. Created as a man or woman, you are self-evidently made not to exist alone, for your own sake, but rather to relate to others in self-giving love; thus you reflect God's existence in a perfectly loving relationship between the three persons of the Trinity. God gave you free will to act freely, as he does, intelligence to communicate, as he does, and a soul to live and love forever, as he does. God also created you with the holy healing ability to forgive others, as he forgives you. You are never more like God than when you forgive others.

⌐

Pray: O Lord, I am astonished to think that you created me in your image. Help me to understand this profound truth!

ARE YOU SUFFERING?

❖ ❖ ❖

Are any among you suffering? They should pray.
Are any cheerful? They should sing songs of praise.

- JAMES 5:13

WE MAY HAVE to endure some suffering caused by others while we wait in joyful hope for the coming of our Savior. This type of suffering can be frustrating because we did not ask for it and we do not want it. Suffering caused by others is usually not fair. Often there is nothing we can do about it. We think we are powerless and useless. Like Job in the Old Testament, we find ourselves sitting on an ash heap. Jesus knows all about this kind of suffering. Having suffered as we suffer, at the hands of others, Jesus knows exactly the right remedy for those who suffer. *They should pray.* Seek out a quiet corner in your house or your heart right now and take the time to pray. Talk to God. Listen to His voice in the quiet of your soul. Deepen your relationship with your Creator who makes everything right. When you become cheerful again, as you surely shall, remember to turn to God and *sing songs of praise.*

⌐

Pray: O Lord, when you allow me to suffer, teach me to pray.
When you bring me good cheer, teach me to praise.

CONSIDER IT ALL JOY

❖ ❖ ❖

My brothers and sisters, whenever you face trials
of any kind, consider it nothing but joy.

- JAMES 1:2

J OY IN THE midst of suffering? That sounds utterly absurd, completely impossible, hopelessly idealistic! How can we find joy in the midst of trials such as deception, disfunction, depression, divorce, disability, disease, or death? Only by faith can we see suffering in a new light. This light is the love of God that penetrates the darkness of our mind and illuminates the cavernous cathedral of our soul. God does not cause our suffering but he allows it for reasons beyond our comprehension, yet we know that he always brings about something better in the aftermath as with Jesus' resurrection. Sometimes God allows our suffering to be so severe that it strips us of all we once cherished and deprives us of everything that made life worth living. In our desolation we may turn to him all the more completely and abandon ourselves more utterly to his divine providence. God shines the light of faith in our hearts, infuses us with perseverance, and provides us with joy in the midst of our suffering. Gradually our darkness dissolves into dawn and we see the face of Christ. *Let perseverance be perfect, so that you may be perfect and complete, lacking in nothing.*

Pray: Dear Lord, I consider all my suffering to be joyful because I know you have a perfect plan for everything!

COME TOWARD THE LIGHT

❖ ❖ ❖

*The light came into the world, but people preferred
darkness to light, because their works were evil.*

- JOHN 3:19

ONE OF THE hardest things to understand is why people do
bad things. Individuals can be shockingly arrogant and
cruel. How can people be so mean and inconsiderate, especially
when we want to love them? Why are people so hard-hearted
and selfish? Jesus gives us the answer very clearly if we listen.
Jesus says He came to bring the light of God's love into the
world, *but people preferred darkness to light.* But why would anyone prefer darkness to light? *Everyone who does wicked things
hates the light and does not come toward the light, so that their
deeds may not be exposed.* In the same way a cockroach scurries
away from light, evildoers scurry away from truth. Wickedness
and shame seek the cloak of darkness. *But those who do what is
true come to the light, so that it may be clearly seen that their deeds
have been done in God.*

Pray: O my Jesus, shine the light of your truth into
every corner of my life. Illuminate my soul with
the light of your love so that I may reflect it to others.

SERVING OTHERS BY SUFFERING

❖ ❖ ❖

The Son of Man did not come to be served but to serve
and to give his life as a ransom for many.

- MATTHEW 20:28

WHATEVER OFFENSE YOU are suffering from right now, as difficult or unlikely or unwelcome as it may seem, you may see it as part of your destiny. If you truly "offer up" your suffering to Jesus, it places you at the service of all people, including your offender. Just as Jesus willingly came to serve others by suffering and giving up his life as a ransom for them, you may join your sufferings with Jesus to serve others as a living sacrifice. Gradually you will understand Jesus' healing words: *Whoever wishes to be great among you shall be your servant.*

Pray: O Lord, I thank you for allowing this suffering
in my life because it teaches me humility and gives me
the heart of a servant, a loving heart like yours.

HEARING GOD'S PROMISES

❖ ❖ ❖

*Son though he was, he learned obedience
from what he suffered.*

- HEBREWS 5:8

GOD ALLOWED HIS son to suffer and die on the cross. Why does a good God allow suffering? This is a great mystery, requiring our most devout faith and ardent trust. We know that God used his son's death to redeem our souls. Then God raised his son from death to new life. He promises to do the same for us, if we believe in him. Jesus learned obedience to his Father during his suffering. Obedience means "listening" in Latin. So Jesus learned to listen to his Father. What did Jesus hear? He heard the comforting promises of his Father.

Pray: O Lord, in the midst of my suffering, help me to
be humble and quiet, so that I may listen to your promises
of new life, and hear your whispers of eternal love.

MORE PRECIOUS THAN GOLD

❖ ❖ ❖

It was good for me to be afflicted, in order to learn your statutes.
The law of your mouth is more precious to me than heaps of silver
and gold.

- PSALM 119.71

WHILE GOD DOES not want us to suffer, he sometimes allows it and he promises to bring about a greater good. While we wait for that "greater good" we can put our affliction to good use by letting it deepen our understanding of God's statutes, his ways, his laws. *He must increase, but I must decrease.* In our pain we are surprised to discover that God's wisdom is more precious than silver and gold. Why? Because it enriches us far more than earthly fortune. Suffering can take us to lofty places where the mind and heart would not willingly go in comfort. In these places that are strange to us, but familiar to Jesus, we are purified by the divine compassion, empathy, and wisdom of God.

⌒

Pray: O Lord, I accept the difficult afflictions you have
allowed in my life. While I do not understand completely,
I trust it is for a "greater good" in me and for others.

How Often Must I Forgive?

❖ ❖ ❖

Peter approached Jesus and asked him, "Lord, if my brother sins against me, how often must I forgive him? As many as seven times?"

- *Matthew 18:21*

I⎯T's hard enough to forgive someone once. But what if a person continues to sin against us many times? If someone is that cruel, reckless or careless about causing suffering, surely there must be a limit to how often we must forgive? Jesus answers clearly: *I say to you, not seven times but seventy-seven times*. In other words, we must keep forgiving that person continually for an unlimited number of times. We may legitimately separate ourselves from that person to protect ourselves, but we must never stop forgiving. This seems so unfair does it not? Yes, to our way of thinking. But this is the way God freely forgives us, with an inexhaustible love, day by day. Let us then imitate the saints who prayed for their persecutors. While the stones of our enemies cover our bodies with wounds, let us practice forgiveness toward them daily to extinguish the flames of anger and unbelief. We can do this for the love of God, with his supernatural assistance, and in this way we shall win his forgiveness for our own sins too.

Pray: O Lord, I cannot forgive a person who continually sins against me. Please give me the power of your sacred heart so that I may forgive others the way you forgive me.

Eye Has Not Seen

❖ ❖ ❖

Eye has not seen, and ear has not heard...what
God has prepared for those who love him.

- I Corinthians 2:9

WHEN WE FRET about those who have wronged us and wonder why they prosper, it seems as if there is no justice in the world. God promises perfect justice. But we may not see it with our natural eyes or hear it with our natural ears. We may witness God's justice come to fruition today or we may have to wait patiently until we get to heaven. As we wait upon our Lord to make things right, we may meditate on the fact that God has prepared everything marvelously, and that our lives are in his loving hands right now and forever, in ways we have not yet seen or heard, beyond our wildest imagination.

Pray: O Lord, I am fretting about the lack of justice
in the world and in my life. Strengthen my faith in you,
increase my loving trust in you, help me to believe that
you are working out a splendid plan for my life.

FORGIVE US OUR TRESPASSES

❖   ❖   ❖

Forgive us our trespasses,
as we forgive those who trespass against us.

- MATTHEW 6:12

I F YOU ARE experiencing difficulty forgiving someone, meditate on the wisdom in this verse. This is the response Jesus
gave to his followers when they asked him how to pray. In
words that are as clear as a ringing bell, Jesus says we must
first admit our own need for forgiveness. Then he quickly adds
that our forgiveness is connected to the way we forgive others
who trespass against us. If we want forgiveness for our sins,
we must forgive others for their sins. If you and another person are dying in a dry desert, can you accept water at an oasis
without giving some to the other person? Jesus is teaching us
something very profound. Offering and accepting the water of
God's mercy are inseparable. Giving and receiving forgiveness
are connected. Forgiveness springs forth in the desert from the
same oasis.

⌐

Pray: O Jesus, help me to understand this great truth.
Forgive us our sins, as we forgive others.

IF YOU FORGIVE OTHERS

❖ ❖ ❖

If you forgive others their transgressions,
your heavenly Father will forgive you.

- MATTHEW 6:14

SOMETIMES WE FIND ourselves confronted by another person who offends us, perhaps repeatedly, but has not repented. How are we supposed to forgive a person who does not deserve it? Here Jesus gives us the best possible reason, which in some cases is the only possible reason: because the result is that *your heavenly Father will forgive you.* You may legitimately protest that this is not about you, and that you did nothing wrong in this situation! Nevertheless, Jesus explains that you must indeed forgive others for their sins in order to receive God's forgiveness for your sins. This is a great mystery. Perhaps this is God's way of getting our attention and turning us in his direction to seek his help.

Pray: O Lord, help me to understand that when
I forgive others, you simultaneously shower me
with your forgiveness.

IF YOU DO NOT FORGIVE OTHERS

❖ ❖ ❖

But if you do not forgive others, neither will your Father forgive your transgressions.

- MATTHEW 6:15

JESUS HAS JUST taught us that when we forgive others, God forgives us. Now he explains that the opposite is also true. If we do not forgive others, God will not forgive us. But wait a minute, you may object that you did nothing to offend that person! You may even have tried your best to extend love but received only contempt in return! All the same, Jesus admonishes us that we must indeed forgive others or we will not receive God's forgiveness for our sins. While our sins may have nothing to do with the present situation or the person who offended us, God still connects our sins with the sins of others. All sin is against God. As we judge others, so may we expect to be judged.

Pray: O Lord, I never want to hinder or obstruct
your forgiveness of my sins. Thank you for assuring me that
when I forgive others, you forgive me!

FIRST BE RECONCILED

❖ ❖ ❖

*When you are offering your gift at the altar,
if you remember that your brother or sister has something
against you, leave your gift there before the altar and go,
first be reconciled, and then come and offer your gift.*

- MATTHEW 5:23

To show us the supreme importance of reconciliation, Jesus says that if we remember someone with whom we have a conflict, disagreement or dispute, we should actually depart from the church and try to reconcile with that person! It may mean writing a note, making a phone call, visiting the person, or saying a prayer. It may be impossible to reconcile with that person, but at least we must try. We must do something. Then we may return to our church and offer our gifts to God without hypocrisy. We may rest easy in the knowledge that we have done our best to reconcile with that person just as God does everything he can to reconcile us with himself. Why does Jesus require this action? It is simple. The love of reconciliation is the gift we offer on the altar.

Pray: O Lord, thank you for reconciling me with you. Give me the courage to reconcile with others!

WHENEVER YOU ARE DISTURBED

❖ ❖ ❖

Whenever you stand praying, forgive, if you have
anything against anyone; so that your Father also
who is in heaven may forgive you your trespasses."

- MARK 11:25

WHEN YOU SEEK peace in prayer, you may be disturbed by
memories of past offenses by others (or yourself). These
intrusive thoughts are most unwelcome! You are tempted to
despair that God will not allow you to find peace and quiet.
But this is natural. When the wind calms down, the waves on
the lake disappear, so you notice the smallest ripples. To find
peace, Jesus counsels you to forgive the person. Whenever you
are troubled by ripples or waves of bad memories, whether you
are standing, sitting, walking, or praying, just forgive. As often
as you are disturbed, once a day or a hundred times a day, simply forgive. Soon your lake will become smooth as glass and
reflect the face of God.

Pray: O Lord, whenever I am disturbed by memories
of a past offense, I will say "I forgive you" repeatedly
until I receive your peace.

MOMENTARY LIGHT AFFLICTION

❖ ❖ ❖

*For this momentary light affliction is producing for us
an eternal weight of glory beyond all comparison.*

- 2 CORINTHIANS 4:17

OUR PAIN IS never in vain. Even though we cannot perceive it, our suffering is producing good things. When we offer our trouble up to God, he joins it with Jesus on the cross, then good things happen. God knows our suffering; he is right there with us, every step of the way. As we hang on our cross, Jesus is hanging there with us. With every breath we take, Jesus is breathing with us. While it may seem to us that our suffering is unbearable, Jesus helps us to bear it. Just when we feel we cannot endure any more pain, Jesus smiles at us reminds us that our discomfort is only a temporary, light burden, producing for us an incomparably wonderful weight of glory, now and eternally.

⌒

Pray: O Lord, help me to realize that all my sufferings
are in your loving hands. I trust that you are mysteriously
joining me with your son Jesus on the cross in order to produce great wonders like his resurrection.

Mourning Into Dancing

❖ ❖ ❖

You changed my mourning into dancing.

- Psalm 30:12

ONE OF THE hardest things to accept when someone offends us is not just the offense itself; it's that it throws us into mourning for a loss of our joy in life. We mourn what has been taken from us. We grieve what we have lost. In this darkness we lament the loss of light, of lightness, of our natural desire to dance. We see children skipping merrily on the sidewalk and think, "I was once like that." At times like this we must remind ourselves that God has promised to be with us always, especially when we are brokenhearted and hopeless. Rest assured that God always brings new light into darkness. Then like the Psalmist we will give thanks to God as we praise him. *You took off my sackcloth and clothed me with gladness.*

⌒

Pray: O Lord, I trust you in my darkness to bring me
into a new dawn. I know you will restore my joy
and make me dance again.

THEY REPAY ME EVIL FOR GOOD

❖ ❖ ❖

They repay me evil for good; my soul is desolate.
Yet I, when they were ill, put on sackcloth, afflicted myself
with fasting, and sobbed my prayers upon my bosom.

- PSALM 35:11

I T IS A sad fact of life in our fallen world that some people respond to our goodness with evil. Yet such people oppose us and fill us with sadness. They cause our souls to be desolate. We reach out in love, yet we are repaid with hate. We reach out in friendship and conciliation, but they react with enmity and aggravation. The psalmist in the verse above teaches us how to deal with such people. Although they are ill and in need of a dose of humility, the psalmist puts on sackcloth to do penance in their place. When others afflict him with desolation, he afflicts himself with fasting for their good. When others cause him sadness and should rightly repent of their sins, he forgives them and sobs his prayers with tears in his eyes. We can do the same. God will use our sackcloth, fasting, tears, and prayers to save souls and renew the world. One day we will see this with perfect clarity and rejoice. *Then my tongue shall recount your justice, and declare your praise, all the day long.*

Pray: O Lord, help me accept the sadness in my life caused by others. Use my sorrow to transform me and save souls!

HEALING PAINFUL MEMORIES

❖ ❖ ❖

Lo, I am about to create a new heavens and a new earth;
the things of the past shall not be remembered
or come to mind.

- ISAIAH 65:17

EVEN WHEN WE forgive someone who offends us, we can still be troubled by the memory of the offense. Even though we are able to forgive, we cannot forget. No matter how hard we try, the hurtful memory may surface again and again. But we do not need to be distressed because God assures us that he *makes all things new.* At this very moment, deep in your mind and heart, God is washing your mind clean, healing your memories, and restoring your heart. Let God gently and exquisitely create you anew. Soon you will completely forget the pain of your past. *There shall always be rejoicing and happiness in what I create.*

⌐

Pray: O Lord, I rejoice in knowing that you are gradually healing my painful memories and deeply restoring my joy.

BECOMING A NEW CREATION

❖ ❖ ❖

Whoever is in Christ is a new creation.

- 2 CORINTHIANS 5:17

WHEN WE HURT one another, we are reminded that we are all flawed human beings living in a fallen world. We all need to be born again in Christ. This a great gift, available to everyone. When we accept this gift, our sins are washed away so completely that we are *a new creation.* This gives us an entirely new perspective on life. It empowers us to think with the mind of Christ and see others with the eyes of God. Gradually we see sinners as they really are, poor lost souls, and we are more easily able to forgive them for their trespasses against us. We pity others because we see how their sins separate them from God. Our sins once separated us from God, but now *the old things have passed away; behold, new things have come.*

Pray: O Lord, I praise you for making me a new creation. Show me how to be your eyes and ears, hands and heart!

DARKNESS BEFORE DAWN

❖ ❖ ❖

My God, my God, why have you forsaken me?

- MATTHEW 27:46

SOMETIMES OUR DESOLATION is so intense that it feels as if God has forsaken us. At times like this, we know how Jesus felt on the cross when he cried out to his Father. When God feels distant, the pain is almost unbearable. The worst part is feeling alone, confused, and abandoned. But God promises that he is never closer to us than when we need him most. He assures us that he wants to save us. *Whoever calls my name will surely be saved.* If we embrace our cross and wait patiently, he will surely come to our assistance to save us at an unexpected hour, in a surprising way.

Pray: O Lord, in my darkness and confusion, I call your holy name. Help me to wait patiently for your healing hand and loving words. Rescue me with the dawn of new life!

THE MINISTRY OF RECONCILIATION

❖ ❖ ❖

All this is from God, who has reconciled us to himself through Christ, and given us the ministry of reconciliation.

- 2 CORINTHIANS 5:18

I T IS NOT easy to forgive others. It goes against our prideful, selfish, fallen nature. In our natural state of mind, we want to get back at the other person somehow. Revenge seems sweet. Vengeance appeals to our primitive desire for payback. When we think more deeply, we realize that God has forgiven our sins and reconciled us to himself so how can we refuse to forgive others? God has shown us the way forward; he has given us *the ministry of reconciliation.* God actually empowers us to minister to others on his behalf! *We are ambassadors for Christ, as if God were appealing through us.* They may not know God, but we can show them the gift of his forgiveness. We can show others the love of God and help to reconcile them with him for the eternal good of their souls. *We implore you on behalf of Christ, be reconciled to God.*

⁓

Pray: O Lord, thank you for forgiving my sins and reconciling me to you. Help me to show your forgiveness to others and reconcile them to you too.

Reconciling The World

❖   ❖   ❖

God was reconciling the world to himself in Christ,
not counting their trespasses against them and entrusting
to us the message of reconciliation.

- 2 CORINTHIANS 5:19

EVERY DAY GOD is reconciling us closer to himself. How does he do this? It is a supernatural mystery in Christ. God sent his only begotten Son to suffer and die on the cross to pay for our sins, so he no longer counts our trespasses against us. He has forgiven and forgotten our sins. He draws us near and embraces us with his perfect love. All we need to do is accept his gift of forgiveness and we are good to go! But his gift contains more than just forgiveness. God entrusts to us *the message of reconciliation,* meaning he wants us to deliver to others the good news of forgiveness of sins. God empowers us to offer his forgiveness to others. We may not feel like forgiving others, but we can do it by letting God work through us.

Pray: O Lord, I thank you for forgiving my sins and trusting me to forgive others. Help me to deliver your message of forgiveness to others and reconcile the world.

AMBASSADORS FOR CHRIST

❖ ❖ ❖

So we are ambassadors for Christ,
as if God were appealing through us.

- 2 CORINTHIANS 5:20

WHEN SOMEONE HURTS us, we usually feel diminished, but actually we are empowered. We have been given great power as *ambassadors for Christ* to forgive that person. We may not feel powerful but we are indeed. All we have to do is let God work through us. God can work through our weakness and brokenness. Why? Because we are more inclined to invite God to help us when we feel weak. When we cannot do it by ourselves, we can let go and let God do it. Then he will appeal to others through us! We become his ambassadors to others. Just as God has forgiven us, he gives us the power to forgive others. With our spoken words and hidden prayers, we can say to others *we implore you on behalf of Christ, be reconciled to God.*

⌐

Pray: O Lord, I invite you to work through my weakness. I want you to flow through my words, deeds, and prayers so that I may show others your loving forgiveness.

He Answered Me

❖ ❖ ❖

*I sought the Lord, and he answered me
and delivered me from all my fears.*

- Psalm 34:4

WHEN OUR LIVES are adversely affected by someone else, we fear things will never be the same. We want things to be as they were before. We are afraid of living with our brokenness. To make matters worse, God may seem far away. On our own, we do not know which way to turn when everything seems so unfamiliar. This is precisely the time to seek the Lord. God knows your every move; he hears your every word; he cherishes your every thought. Wait for God and he will certainly answer you in a quiet time. He may not make things as they were before, but he will deliver you from all your fears and show you how to live in a new and better way. *Look to him that you may be radiant with joy.*

⌣

Pray: O Lord, I seek you now with all my heart.
Deliver me from my fears and make me radiant with joy.

LOOKING INTO THE HEART

❖ ❖ ❖

God does not see as a mortal, who sees the appearance.
The Lord looks into the heart.

- 1 SAMUEL 16:7

WHEN WE EXPERIENCE wrongdoing we are tempted to condemn the perpetrator. How could someone do something so terrible? We are quick to guess a person's motives and convict him or her outright. We are severe in our condemnation and liable to think the worst. But we need not trouble ourselves endlessly in this way. After all, we do not know the whole story. We see only the outward appearance. God alone looks into the human heart. God only knows what is motivating a troubled soul. So the next time we are inclined to denounce troublemakers, let us remember that while their actions may condemn them, we see only their outward actions. God is the only one who sees into the heart. Only God can fix a troubled heart.

⁓

Pray: O Lord, I know that I can only see the surface.
I want to see into the heart and fix what is broken.

My Ways Are Higher

❖ ❖ ❖

As the heavens are higher than the earth,
so are my ways higher than your ways,
my thoughts higher than your thoughts.

- ISAIAH 55:9

SOMETIMES FORGIVING SEEMS impossible. The hurt is just too much. We know God wants us to forgive, as we have been forgiven, but we just cannot do it. It does not seem fair. After all, the other person does not deserve it! Doesn't forgiveness just allow evil to continue? In our confusion and frustration, our strength fails. Now we are at the great crossroads, the great "turning point." Now that we admit we cannot do it alone, God will rush to help us. God has been waiting to help us, he has been willing to help us, and he has been wanting to help us. In our exhaustion, we turn our eyes upward, towards heaven, and see the stars twinkling above. We realize that God's ways are higher than our ways. We can give everything up to God.

Pray: O Lord, I find great relief in knowing that
your ways are infinitely higher than my ways.
I gladly trust your thoughts and rest in your design.

INFINITELY FAR AWAY

❖ ❖ ❖

*As far as the east is from the west, so far has he put
our transgressions from us.*

- PSALM 103:12

HOW FAR IS the east from the west? It is farther than scientists can measure and more distant than we can imagine. God wants us to know that he has removed our sins and cast them infinitely far away. In other words, God's mercy removes our sins completely. God has disconnected and obliterated our transgressions. Our sins are out of sight, out of mind, gone forever and ever. We are washed clean. This is good news, isn't it? How liberating! Let us rejoice in the mercy of God. Let us put our newfound freedom to good use by extending God's mercy to others. Since we have been set free, let us liberate others as well. *The Lord is kind and merciful.*

Pray: O Lord, I cannot fathom your mercy. All I can do
is rejoice in your forgiveness, give you thanks,
and give your mercy to others.

FILLED WITH COMPASSION

❖ ❖ ❖

*While he was still a long way off, his father caught sight
of him, and was filled with compassion. He ran to
his son, embraced him, and kissed him.*

- LUKE 15:20

IN THIS PARABLE Jesus tells how the prodigal son finally comes to his senses and returns home. The young man is starving, ragged, and filled with remorse for his dissolute lifestyle. His father catches sight of his son a long way off, proving that he has been patiently waiting for his son's return. Instead of being angry, his father is *filled with compassion* and runs to embrace his long-lost son! All is forgiven, reunion is sweet, now is the time for celebration. Jesus wants us to realize that this is exactly how our heavenly Father feels compassion towards us. As soon as we turn towards him, God runs towards us, embraces us, and kisses us.

Pray: O Lord, I have been far away from you,
but now I am glad I returned. Your loving kindness is
so overwhelming; I wish I had never left your side!

A POOR REFLECTION

❖　❖　❖

Now we see but a poor reflection as in a mirror;
then we shall see face to face. Now I know in part;
then I shall know fully, even as I am fully known.

- 1 CORINTHIANS 13:12

WHEN WE ARE injured by others, we may be filled with a thousand questions. Our minds work overtime trying to make sense of the situation. Why did that person act that way? What was the motivation? Why didn't I see this coming? How should I react? Why did God allow this to happen to me? Saint Paul reminds us that we see only a poor reflection of things in this life, as in a broken mirror. Have you ever tried to see your reflection in a broken mirror? It's hard to do, isn't it? Someday we will see God face to face, then we will understand everything. Now we can only know partially, but eventually we will know fully.

Pray: O Lord, I am content to see things in this life
only as a poor reflection in a broken mirror. Let me
reflect the light of your forgiveness to others.

RENEWED EACH MORNING

❖　❖　❖

*The Lord's acts of mercy are not exhausted, his compassion
is not spent; they are renewed each morning.*

- *LAMENTATIONS 3:22*

LET'S FACE IT, forgiving others is exhausting. Whether it's for
a onetime offense or a continuing offense, we usually find
that we have to forgive over and over again. Over time it can
wear us out. Nothing seems to change. What is the answer? We
need to release the person. We need to give the person to God.
He knows how to deal with the person when we do not. God
has an inexhaustible supply of mercy and an unlimited amount
of compassion. Every morning of every day God renews his
love to us. He makes the sun rise to shine on lost souls. He
makes the rain fall on our dry and thirsty land. He renews our
strength. He reaches out to sinners and saints alike.

⁓

Pray: O Lord, whenever I need new strength, I know I can
give my troubles to you. I trust you to renew me and others
every morning with your mercy and compassion.

DO NOT FEAR

❖ ❖ ❖

Do not fear, for I have redeemed you;
I have called you by name; you are mine.

- ISAIAH 43:1

WHEN WE ARE fearful of other people or anxious about their actions, we need only turn our attention to God. The more we focus on God, the sooner we lose sight of our fears. As we listen to God's wisdom, our fears vanish. God wants us to live fearlessly! To be sure we hear this message loud and clear, he encourages us to be fearless 365 times in the Bible! What is the basis for our courage? Because God has created us. He has redeemed us. He has called us by name. We realize God is in charge, guiding us and protecting us. As we meditate on these great truths, we discover his peace and serenity. We listen to God calling our name as he whispers *you are mine.*

Pray: O Lord, whenever I come into your holy presence, my fears vanish and I am filled with supernatural courage!

I WILL BE WITH YOU

❖ ❖ ❖

*When you pass through waters, I will be with you;
through rivers, you shall not be swept away.*

- ISAIAH 43:2

W E NEED NOT fear any person or any event. No matter how threatening our foes or the circumstances of our lives may appear, we can face everything courageously. No matter how stormy the seas, we will pass through the rough waters. How is this possible? Because our Creator is right there beside us, every step of the way. *I will be with you,* he promises. Imagine walking calmly through a burning building with Jesus at your side, holding your hand, guiding your way to safety. *When you walk through fire, you shall not be burned, nor will flames consume you. For I, the Lord, am your God.*

Pray: O Lord, how wonderful it is for me to know
that you are always near me, by my side, protecting
and guiding me all the days of my life.

I Am Doing Something New

❖ ❖ ❖

Remember not the events of the past, the things
of long ago consider not. See, I am doing something new!

- Isaiah 43:18

S OMETIMES WE GET stuck in the past, remembering hurtful words and deeds. This behavior prevents us from moving forward. God wants us to forget all those painful experiences. If we are preoccupied with the past, we cannot see the amazing beauty of the present. God will heal our troubled memories completely when we simply turn our attention to him. God's new plans will outshine all our problems! Look around, see the child skipping alongside his mother, hear the geese honking overhead, feel the warmth of your fingers folded in prayer, see the sun rising in the east! *Now it springs forth, do you not perceive it?*

⌐

Pray: O Lord, I want to look forward and not backward, up and now down, and rejoice in your new work every day.

TIMES OF REFRESHING

❖ ❖ ❖

Therefore repent and return, so that your sins may
be wiped away, in order that times of refreshing may
come from the presence of the Lord.

- ACTS 3:19

WHEN WE STRUGGLE to forgive others, it often means we need to repent of sins in our own lives. That is a bitter pill to swallow, but it quickly heals our spiritual afflictions. The good news is God guarantees that when we acknowledge our sins and return to him, he will rush to embrace us and wipe away all our sins. How can we resist such a loving Father? The moment we turn toward him, he hurries to embrace us. He has been waiting for us all along! In God's holy presence, life returns to normal and every day is a quiet celebration of his love. Finally, we can relax and enjoy *times of refreshing.*

Pray: O Lord, I am glad you run to meet me and embrace me. I am humbled and renewed by your loving kindness.

GOD WILL ANSWER

❖ ❖ ❖

When you pray, God will answer.

- ISAIAH 58:6

SOMETIMES GOD SEEMS far away, doesn't he? We feel alone in our hurt. We may be tempted to think he does not care about us. We pray but nothing happens. Where is God? He is right next to us, watching over us, listening to our prayers. When we fold our hands, God hears every word we say, every sigh, and every wish. More to the point, he will answer. God always gives us an instant response to every prayer — his answer is either yes, no, or not now. Listen for his voice in the silence of your heart. God likes to speak in a hushed, whispering voice to a heart that is waiting and still. Like a loving parent, God knows what is best for us. *Be still and know that I am God.*

Pray: O Lord, I am praying for an answer. Help me
to believe that you always listen to all of my prayers
and that your answer is always best for me.

HERE I AM

❖ ❖ ❖

You'll call out for help and I'll say, 'Here I am.'

- ISAIAH 58:9

WHEN YOU PRAY to God for help, which would you rather have, an answer to your prayer or God's presence at your side? In the bedtime story when Aladdin rubs an enhanced lamp, a magic genie appears to do his bidding. Real life is much better. When we pray to God, he says, *'Here I am.'* That's better than any fairy tale! Now we can relax in his presence, we can take a deep breath, we can breathe again. Now we can listen to our Creator, the great 'I AM.' His words are comforting, but somehow just knowing he is near is better than anything he says. When we are near to God, everything just seems right and all is well. We say this prayer knowing God is at our side: *O Lord, come to my assistance. Make haste to help me.*

Pray: O Lord, whenever I pray, even though I may not feel your presence, I know you are right here by my side.

A Better Plan

❖   ❖   ❖

I know the plans that I have for you, says the Lord,
plans for your welfare and not for calamity, to give you
a future and a hope.

- JEREMIAH 29:11

WHEN OUR LIVES have been turned upside down by an offense, we may think we will never recover. But God assures us that he has a better plan in place. We may not see it taking shape yet, but He is working behind the scenes in a hidden way. He may have allowed something that seems like a calamity, but that is not the end of the story. He wants us to know that his plan is for our welfare, for our happiness, and for a bright future. He wants to fill us today with joyful hope. God promises that he will make things even better than they were before, just as he did for his son Jesus. As we are filled with His promises to replace our sadness with happiness and holiness, God is also giving us the opportunity to deepen our faith.

Pray: O Lord, I thank you for your promise that you have
a better plan for my life, a plan to make everything new.
I wait in joyful expectation as your plan unfolds!

HEAR MY VOICE

❖ ❖ ❖

*Evening, and morning, and at noon, will I pray,
and cry aloud: and He shall hear my voice.*

- PSALM 55:17

CAN WE EVER have too many assurances that God hears our prayers? Perhaps the reason he reminds us so often is that he really, really wants us to believe it. Whenever we need God to help us forgive others or ourselves, he wants us to be certain that he hears our prayers at any time of day. He wants us to have absolutely no doubt that he is listening when we pray — in the morning, at noon, or in the evening. Do we believe this? It will change our lives. God wants us to have the certain expectation that he is present, closer to us than we are to ourselves, all the time. Our God is an alert sentinel in the watchtower who never sleeps; he wants us to rely on him. *Then you will call upon Me and come and pray to Me, and I will listen to you.*

⌒

Pray: O Lord, help me to believe you listen to all my prayers, all the time. If I ever doubt you, remind me!

WITH ALL YOUR HEART

❖ ❖ ❖

You will seek Me and find Me when you search
for Me with all your heart.

- JEREMIAH 29:13

I F YOU AS if like you have tried everything but failed to find God's will in your life, do not give up seeking now. Many people give up just before the finish line. You are closer to success than you realize. There is one more thing to try that is guaranteed to succeed. Ready? Listen now; God does not say that you will find him when you seek him casually or half-heartedly. You will find God only when you search *with all your heart.* As Jesus declares, *You shall love the Lord, your God, with all your heart, with all your soul, and with all your mind. This is the greatest and the first commandment.* Remember when you were young and desired something for your birthday so much that you could think of nothing else? God wants you to desire him that way, with childlike enthusiasm. Then you will find him. To your surprise, you will discover that he has been ardently seeking you more passionately than you have been seeking him; he has been waiting for you all along. *I will be found by you, declares the Lord, and I will restore your fortunes.*

Pray: O Lord, I yearn to discover you with all my heart.
I wait in joyful hope to find you in an unexpected moment!

Woe To Those

❖ ❖ ❖

Woe to those who call evil good and good evil.

- *Isaiah 5:20*

Sometimes we are injured by a person who is so rude and disrespectful that we can hardly believe it. While normal people can be simply careless or thoughtless, others act so far outside the bounds that they seem downright evil. They growl and roar like lions. With them around, up is down and down is up. They often do not face the consequences of their actions. They decrease our faith in humankind. God says *woe* to them. Rather than allowing hell-raisers to disillusion us, we must hold fast to what we know is good and right. We must turn evildoers over to God and pray for them because they have separated themselves from God's love. *Their root will be as rottenness, and their blossom go up like dust.*

Pray: O Lord, I refuse to listen to others call evil good. Instead I hold fast to you and pray for their repentance.

Do Not Be Anxious Or Worried

❖ ❖ ❖

You are anxious and worried about many things.
There is need of only one thing.

- Luke 10:41

IF YOU ARE anxious and worried about many things today, listen to this solution. One day Jesus visits Martha's home. Martha burdens herself *with much serving* while her sister Mary sits quietly at Jesus' feet *listening to him speak.* When Martha complains, Jesus explains that she is needlessly anxious and worried about many things. *There is need of only one thing. Mary has chosen the better part and it will not be taken from her.* Can we learn from Jesus? We are often anxious and overstressed by many troubles, most of our own making and some caused by others. We may quickly rediscover God's peace and tranquility by quieting ourselves in prayer and listening for the voice of Jesus. We may visit a nearby chapel or simply kneel at our bedside. When we listen to Jesus, he will comfort us with soothing reassurance that he is with us. Certainly there is a time and place for daily chores and serving others, but first we must listen at the feet of Jesus. If you are anxious and worried about many things today, remember you need only one thing — the peace of Jesus that no one can take from you.

Pray: O Jesus, I know you want to relieve me of all my anxiety and worries. In quiet prayer I listen for your peace.

HUNGER AND THIRST

❖ ❖ ❖

Blessed are they who hunger and thirst
for righteousness, for they will be satisfied.

- *MATTHEW 5:6*

WHEN WE ARE distressed, we hunger and thirst for things to be made right again. Have you ever been really hungry and thirsty? Your stomach growls and your mouth is dry and parched. Your body craves food and drink. Even a morsel of food or a drop of water would taste delicious! Until you find relief, you cannot think of anything else. Jesus says we are blessed when we hunger and thirst in this way for justice and righteousness. Righteousness means a right relationship with God. The mere fact that you desire righteousness shows you have "God within you." The good news is that when you hunger and thirst for God, he promises that he will personally satisfy you.

⌒

Pray: O Lord, I hunger and thirst for you.
I am waiting for you to satisfy me soon!

Do Not Be Afraid

❖ ❖ ❖

Teacher, do you not care that we are perishing?

- Mark 4:38

SOMETIMES OUR LIVES get dark and turbulent. The angry waves threaten to overwhelm us as they threatened to overwhelm the disciples in their boat during the storm. Like Jesus sleeping in the boat, God does not seem to care about our emergency. If God is good, why doesn't he help us in our time of distress? In the nick of time, Jesus arises and calms the sea. Then he speaks to the cowering disciples. *Why are you afraid? Have you no faith?* Clearly we are in no danger when Jesus is with us. He is with us every second of every day. Faith in him is the answer to all our fears.

Pray: O Lord, who are you that even the wind and the sea obey you? With you by my side, I will fear no storms.

BE KIND TO EVERYONE

❖ ❖ ❖

Let us beset the just one,
because he is obnoxious to us...
merely to see him is a hardship for us.

- WISDOM 2:12

ONE OF THE hardest things to understand is why some people oppose us for no apparent reason. They may set themselves against us even though we have done nothing wrong to them. We may have their best interests at heart but they insist on hostility. We may even love them. Why can't we win them over? It may be simply because our goodness offends them. Our very innocence is a reproof to their waywardness. Our righteousness is a silent rebuke to their stubbornness. We can expect some people to oppose us for the same reason they opposed Jesus. *But they erred; for their wickedness blinded them. They did not know the hidden counsels of God... nor discern the innocent souls' reward.*

⌣

Pray: O Lord, help me to always respond to
difficult people with your love and compassion.

THE CAUSE OF CONFLICT

❖ ❖ ❖

What causes wars, and what causes fightings among you?
Is it not your passions that are at war in your members?

- JAMES 4:4

To discover the reasons for our conflicts, we need only look in the nearest mirror. Within our minds and hearts, our selfish desires fight and compete for supremacy, making us disordered in all our ways like leaves tossed in the wind. Then our prideful passions become inflamed at the slightest spark or offense by someone else, and before we know it we are carrying blazing torches at midnight to burn down the houses of our adversaries. *You desire and do not have; so you kill. And you covet and cannot obtain; so you fight and wage war.* Truly we live in a fallen world with contentious minds and wounded hearts. We live on a great battlefield with the virtues of good and the vices of evil arrayed on opposing sides. How shall we make peace within our fevered souls and reconcile our heated conflicts with others? *You ask and do not receive, because you ask wrongly, to spend it on your passions.* We must begin by asking God to forgive us and heal us of our selfish passions. Then we must heal others with forgiveness. By God's mercy we will find peace and tranquility again.

⁓

Pray: O Lord, I am tired of conflict. Heal me of all my conflicting passions and help me to become a peacemaker!

IDENTIFYING YOUR REAL ENEMY

❖ ❖ ❖

For our struggle is not against flesh and blood.

- EPHESIANS 6:12

WHEN PEOPLE ARE hostile toward us, we can endlessly analyze the psychology of their motives or we can face the deeper reality of the existence of evil in the world. Our true struggle is not against other people, but rather *against the rulers, authorities, and powers of this dark world and against the spiritual forces of evil in the heavenly places.* While the modern world dismisses this idea of the devil as a medieval superstition, Holy Scripture clearly confirms the reality of evil spirits who oppose us. It is actually a relief to understand this fact because it explains the implacable hostility that has beset, besieged, and beleaguered all humankind throughout history. Accepting the reality of evil helps us to see clearly behind the shifting scenes of anger, conflict and war that flash before our eyes. God gives us a supernatural power to see deeper and recognize his ultimate plan to eliminate the dark forces that lead people astray. Gradually we understand the underlying reasons why we struggle to live in peace among misguided people who insist on opposing us. But we need not be afraid, for Jesus has conquered the devil. We may pray with confidence and serenity for God's kingdom to come. If you look carefully, you can see his kingdom has already begun to appear.

⌐

Pray: O Lord, I take courage in knowing you are with me in all of my struggles and that victory with you is assured!

STAND YOUR GROUND

❖ ❖ ❖

*Therefore put on the full armor of God, so that when
the day of evil comes, you may be able to stand your ground.*

- EPHESIANS 6:13

GOD DOES NOT leave us defenseless against evil. He instructs us to put on his armor to guarantee our victory in the battle. What is this armor? It is specially made for us. We gird our loins with truth, put on the breastplate of righteousness, shoe our feet with the gospel of peace, take up the shield of faith, the helmet of salvation, and the sword of the Spirit. What formidable warriors we are now, how invincible with the help of our God! Imagine riding into a fierce battle with the sure knowledge in advance that you will victorious! *You can quench all the flaming arrows of the evil one.*

Pray: Heavenly Father, I thank you for providing me
every protection I need to win every battle.

RESIST THE DEVIL

❖ ❖ ❖

Resist the devil, and he will flee from you.

- JAMES 4:7

BELOVED, DO NOT be discouraged by temptations. Simply resist the temptations of the devil and he will flee from you. See how Jesus resisted the devil when he was tempted after forty days in the desert. Satan offered Jesus all the riches of the world if only he would bow down to him, but Jesus refused. He rebuked the devil by repeating the words of his father. Then the devil fled. *Draw near to God, and he will draw near to you.* The devil appears strong, and indeed he is the ruler of this present world, but he is a coward when confronted by the mighty power of God. As a cockroach scurries away from light into darkness, the devil will flee from you when God is at your side. It takes time and effort to believe this truth, but soon you will be convinced beyond the shadow of a doubt. Remember you cannot do this alone; you must ask God to help you. He will make you more than a conqueror because his son Jesus has vanquished the devil and conquered the world. *Humble yourselves before the Lord and he will exalt you.*

Pray: O Lord, the nearer I am to you, the more clearly
I can see, and the better I can resist evil with your power!

WHEN LIVING FEELS LIKE DYING

❖   ❖   ❖

*If this is the way you will deal with me, then please
do me the favor of killing me at once, so that I need
no longer face my distress.*

- NUMBERS 11:15

BELOVED, SOMETIMES LIVING can be so painful and difficult that it feels like dying. In a desolate season, you may feel beleaguered, pursued, or hopeless. You may be so miserable that, like Moses, you have considered suicide and asked God to end your life. In fact, part of you really is dying, or has died, or will die as a result of the injury you have received. You may need to die to your desire for health, wealth, a cherished dream, or a relationship with a loved one. If it is God's will, let it go, place it all in his hands. Allow forgiveness to flood your heart, heal you, and lead to new life in Christ. Jesus died from his injuries caused by the sins of all humanity. He could have lashed out in anger and called down the wrath of God to annihilate his offenders. Instead he chose to forgive us and offer up his life as a sacrifice to pay for our sins. What is it that you are being called to sacrifice today? Face your sacrifice, embrace it, then let it go. Imagine holding it in both of your hands and freely offering it up to God, who smiles, wipes away your tears, and receives it in his hands. Then hear God whisper in your ear that you need not worry, for he will take care of everything. *Behold, I make all things new.*

Pray: O Lord, guide me through this darkest night. I offer
everything to you. I trust you to make all things new!

A Fortified City

❖ ❖ ❖

Do not be terrified on account of them... for I am the one who today makes you a fortified city, a pillar of iron, a wall of bronze, against the whole land.

- Jeremiah 1:18

HAVE YOU EVER seen a castle or fortified city? Built on high ground, it is always securely surrounded by high walls to keep enemies out. Guards keep watch in towers and soldiers patrol the ramparts. No matter what happens outside the walls, inside everyone is safe. The villagers carry on with life normally. Every day they draw fresh water from the wells, milk the cows, collect eggs from the henhouse, and grow ripe red tomatoes in the gardens. All is well. We sleep soundly and fear no one for a good reason; God has fortified us. Life is good when God makes us a fortified city with pillars of iron and walls of bronze.

Pray: O Lord, I know that I do not need to worry about any adversary because you have made me a fortified city. Thank you for giving me a safe place to live with you.

THEY SHALL NOT PREVAIL

❖ ❖ ❖

They will fight against you; but they shall not prevail
against you, for I am with you, says the Lord,
to deliver you.

- JEREMIAH 1:19

You CANNOT EXPECT to go through life without making a few enemies. Even Jesus, the perfect man, had enemies; so you should not be surprised if some people dislike you. God says they will fight against you. They may use harmful words or deeds, gossip or lawsuits, lies or neglect. As much as you might wish to avoid a fight, it is sometimes beyond your control. In these situations, God promises that *they shall not prevail against you.* This is an encouraging promise, but you may wonder how it is possible. Your adversaries may seem to have the advantage. They might appear to have the upper hand. God provides the answer. *I am with you, says the Lord, to deliver you.*

⌐

Pray: O Lord, I would rather have you by my side than
all the armies of the world. I know you are with me today.

THE LORD IS MY SHEPHERD

❖ ❖ ❖

The Lord is my shepherd, I shall not want.

- PSALM 23:1

IF YOU ARE angry at God for any reason, perhaps you need a clearer picture of him. Have you ever seen a shepherd with his sheep? He patiently tends them as they graze serenely in the field. He herds them together towards verdant pastures to help them find the most nutritious green grass. He guards them from foul winds, fierce storms, and dangerous predators. In the same way, the Lord is our Shepherd. He looks out for us, looks over us, and stays always nearby. With him in our midst, we shall not want. We need to cast away our preconceptions of God and see him more clearly for who he really is. He is our everyday protector, ever-present provider, and ever-sure guide. He is not our enemy, adversary, or foe. We delight to discover that God is our loving Father, living Fountain, and loyal Friend. If we wander off far away from him, as we often do, and become lost or injured by a predator, God rushes to our rescue, binds up our wounds, hoists us up on his shoulders, and carries us swiftly back home. With God as our Shepherd, there is nothing we shall want.

⸱⸱⸱

Pray: O Lord, help me to see you clearly. I want to know who you are in truth; show me your loving kindness today!

HE RESTORES MY SOUL

❖ ❖ ❖

*He makes me lie down in green pastures. He leads
me beside still waters; he restores my soul.*

- PSALM 23:2

WHEN WE ARE running too fast, going in the wrong direction, or worrying about too many things, God makes us lie down. If we are too prideful, self-serving, or unforgiving, God makes us pause for our own good. He slows us down to help us wise up. He speaks to us quietly to calm us down, and makes us lie down in green pastures. Sometimes in his wisdom he makes us lie down by allowing us to break a leg, catch the flu, or suffer a broken heart. We may protest in anger and frustration at this unexpected delay because we want to pursue our own desires! But if we trust that God seeks and allows only what is best for us, we will find that his plan is best. While we may scoff that God is making us lie down in a desolate desert with a scorching sun, we soon discover that it was only a temporary stopping point on our journey to lie down in verdant green pastures beside fresh still waters. As we drink deeply from these cool waters of grace, we grow in confidence and trust in the presence of our Shepherd, and then we begin to relax and praise his holy presence. *He restores my soul.*

Pray: O Lord, help me to find rest in green pastures. I want you to lead me beside still waters and restore my soul!

He Leads Me In Right Paths

❖ ❖ ❖

He leads me in paths of righteousness for his name's sake.

- Psalm 23:3

WE ARE LIKE sheep in one obvious way; we have a tendency to wander off and get lost in the woods. We want to follow our own path, chart our own course, and do things our own way. The problem is we do not always know what direction is best. This is true with forgiveness too; we try to do it our own way but find ourselves lost in frustration and tangled in the thorn bushes of resentment. Fortunately, we have a loving Shepherd who will lead us in the right pathways. God will show us what to do, what to say, and how to make everything turn out okay. His paths are not ours, his ways are often unknown to us, but if we trust him to guide us we will soon discover that he knows the surest direction home. God will sometimes lead us along rocky roads that hurt our feet and wound our knees. On the way we may expect to encounter difficult people with harsh voices and stony hearts who push us aside and rush headlong in the opposite direction. As we sit forlorn on the side of this path of righteousness we discover the brightly-colored flowers of forgiveness growing all around us. We did not notice these tender shoots before, but now we do. We smell their fragrance and pick a few to give to others.

Pray: O Lord, I trust you to lead me in the right direction. Guide me on the paths of righteousness. Show me the way!

I Will Fear No Evil

❖ ❖ ❖

Even though I walk through the valley of the shadow
of death, I will fear no evil; for thou art with me.

- Psalm 23:4

ONE DAY YOU are merrily waltzing in a sunny meadow with flowers everywhere. Then a bad experience makes you feel as if you have been plunged into a valley of deep darkness. Everything seems cold and desolate. The people you trusted may have betrayed you. God seems distant. In the twilight, familiar places seem foreign, and shadows dance in strange shapes. Death and despair seem near. What are you to do? Instead of hiding in the hollow of a tree or cowering in a gloomy cave, keep walking. Even if the path is twisted or treacherous, keep walking without fear. How is this possible? Because God is right there at your side. As you walk, keep reminding yourself, *I will fear no evil; for thou art with me.* How would you live your life differently if you were truly fearless?

⌇

Pray: O Lord, help me to live fearlessly.
With you by my side, I can do it -- starting today!

A Comforting Rod And Staff

❖ ❖ ❖

Thy rod and thy staff, they comfort me.

- Psalm 23:4

IF YOU RESENT the way your life is going right now, maybe you are a lost sheep and do not realize it. To guide his sheep to the best pastures, a shepherd carries a crook. This is a long wooden stick with a pointed rod on one end and a curved staff on the other end. The shepherd uses the straight rod to prod the sheep forward, if they are lagging behind, and the curved staff to pull the sheep out of thorn bushes and ravines. If you think of yourself as a sheep and God as your shepherd, you can see how comforting his presence can be. Rather than resenting the way God is prodding you one way with his rod today and pulling you another way with his staff tomorrow, be grateful for his tender loving care and perfect guidance. Instead of resisting God's rod and staff, welcome his nudgings and tuggings as daily reminders of his constant presence. *He leads me in paths of righteousness for his name's sake.*

⌐

Pray: O Lord, when I do not know the way, it comforts me to know that you are pushing and pulling me the right way!

My Cup Overflows

❖ ❖ ❖

You set a table before me in front of my enemies.

- PSALM 23:5

A T TIMES WE encounter people who set themselves in opposition against us. They may be bombastic and intimidating or deceptive and subversive but their opposition is unsettling. Some people resist all attempts at conciliation because they relish their anger and fan the flames of a fight. It seems impossible to find peace in the midst of such conflict or serenity in the face of such adversaries. Yet to our surprise we discover fearlessness and peace of mind when we place ourselves in God's hands. God sets an ordinary table before us even in the presence of our enemies. He pulls out a chair, sits us down, and then joins us at the table. The brightness of his holy presence keeps our enemies away as a campfire keeps the wolves at bay. As we eat, drink and converse with him, our worries melt away and we relax in the mystery of his presence. Extending his hand to bless us, he relieves our troubled minds, pours out his sublime confidence, and engulfs us with his Spirit that helps us love and forgive all humankind. *You anoint my head with oil; my cup overflows.*

Pray: O Lord, I delight to discover that you truly give me confidence and peace in the midst of all of life's storms.

GOODNESS AND MERCY FOLLOW ME

❖ ❖ ❖

*Surely goodness and mercy shall follow me
all the days of my life.*

- PSALM 23:6

HAVE YOU EVER seen a flock of baby ducks following their mother? No matter where she goes, the little ducklings waddle behind her, quacking loudly to always remind her that they want to find her. This is how God sends goodness and mercy to follow us all the days of our lives. When we accept his loving presence, God gives us his loving kindness every day. Like baby duckling following us everywhere, God's goodness and forgiveness are ever-present. No longer do we struggle to forgive others, God, or ourselves. No more do we doubt the essential goodness of God. Always and in every situation he constantly reminds of his holy presence. With his goodness and mercy following us all the days of our lives, we enjoy our adventure until we reach our ultimate destination. *I shall dwell in the house of the Lord forever.*

Pray: O Lord, thank you for following me wherever I go. Help me forgive others and show them your goodness too!

LED BY THE SPIRIT

❖ ❖ ❖

*Jesus was led up by the Spirit into the wilderness
to be tempted by the devil.*

- MATTHEW 4:4

SOMETIMES WE FEEL lost in the wilderness and beset by adversaries. Jesus had the same experience. Notice how the Holy Spirit led Jesus into the wilderness, so the Holy Spirit was quietly present with Jesus during his entire ordeal. The point of the ordeal was not to make Jesus suffer; it was to provide Jesus an opportunity to prove his faith against his adversary. The adversary is very clearly identified: it is the devil himself. Three times the devil tempted Jesus. Each time Jesus rebuked him by using God's words from scripture. If we resist temptation, with Jesus as our example, we can expect the same result. *Then the devil left Him; and behold, angels came and began to minister to Him.*

Pray: Holy Spirit, I trust you as you lead me through this desert experience in my life. Help me resist the temptation to despair and send your angels to minister to me.

THE BOY WAS CURED

❖ ❖ ❖

*Jesus rebuked the demon, and it came out of him,
and the boy was cured instantly.*

- *MATTHEW 17:14*

IF SOMEONE IN your life seems hopelessly lost, listen to this
story. A man begs Jesus to cure his epileptic son. The boy
suffers terrifying seizures that cause him to fall into campfires
and lakes. When Jesus rebukes the demon, it comes out of the
boy and he is instantly cured. How shall we understand this
story? Did the boy have epilepsy or a demon? Apparently he
had both. When the disciples ask Jesus why they were unable
to cast out the demon, he says it is because they lack faith and
that *this kind does not go out except by prayer and fasting.* Jesus
explains that even a little bit of faith can move mountains. *If
you have faith the size of a mustard seed, you will say to this mountain, 'Move from here to there,' and it will move; and nothing will
be impossible for you.*

⌐

Pray: O Lord, help me to pray for people who have medical
problems or spiritual troubles. Increase my faith
in your ability to cure them from all their afflictions.

THE LAMB OF GOD

❖ ❖ ❖

Behold the Lamb of God who takes away
the sin of the world!

- JOHN 1:29

THIS IS WHAT John the Baptist shouted when he saw Jesus coming towards him in the middle of the desert. John was poorly dressed in *clothing of camel's hair with a leather belt around his waist, and his food was locusts and wild honey.* John knew he did not have the light within himself, but that did not stop him from bearing witness to the light. When John finally saw Jesus approaching, his poverty allowed him to recognize Jesus! Here at last John faced the long-awaited savior *who takes away the sin of the world!* You may be feeling poor right now, in your wallet, your heart, or your soul, weighed down by the sin of the world. Be like John the Baptist, earnestly seeking the light of Christ, living as if you have already received his forgiveness, and proclaiming the good news of his mercy.

Pray: O Jesus, I am not worthy to untie your sandal,
but I rejoice because I recognize you every time
I see someone forgiving worldly sins.

BLESSED ARE THE MERCIFUL

❖　❖　❖

Blessed are the merciful, for they shall receive mercy.

- MATTHEW 5:7

WHEN JESUS SPOKE these words in his sermon on the mountain, his listeners were surely baffled. Jesus contradicted the prevailing idea of justice that required retribution. What did he mean? To be merciful means to show forgiveness and compassion to those in need. Jesus is saying that we need to be merciful and forgive others, even if they do not ask for it or deserve it. When we forgive others, we are blessed in the eyes of God because we are demonstrating the same mercy God shows to us. If we wish to receive God's mercy for our sins, we must offer his forgiveness to others. This action puts us in a right relationship with God, in harmony with his perfect will. This allows us to receive God's blessings that make us truly happy and holy.

Pray: O Lord, I thank you for showing me
the divine connection between forgiving others
and receiving your forgiveness.

BE MERCIFUL

❖ ❖ ❖

Be merciful, just as your Father is merciful.

- LUKE 6:36

AGAIN, JESUS STUNS his listeners by encouraging them to forgive others the same way God forgives. This seems impossible, outrageous, preposterous! After all, we are not God! It is hard enough for us to forgive on our own. How can we be expected to forgive the same way God forgives? This is a hard teaching but it is true: by ourselves we cannot forgive others. We are too weak. We simply do not have the strength within ourselves. We need God's help. When we realize this, we come to a great turning point in our lives. In humility we must turn to God and ask his help. We must allow God to work through us. Since God is love, he will use us as a channel of his love to reach others. To our surprise, God overflows his love though us and showers his mercy upon others. This is his Holy Spirit in action.

⌒

Pray: O Lord, I humbly admit that I cannot forgive alone.
But I delight in the realization that you can channel
your forgiveness through me to others.

THROWING STONES

❖ ❖ ❖

*Let the one among you who is without sin
be the first one to throw a stone at her.*

- JOHN 8:7

A WOMAN CAUGHT in adultery is dragged by a crowd to
Jesus. A poor woman is she indeed, to be so shamed by
her friends and neighbors who might be expected to help her.
But the rowdy crowd expects Jesus to condemn her to death
according to the law of Moses. Jesus calmly bends down and
writes in the sand with his finger. What was he writing? Perhaps
the word *mercy*. Then Jesus suggests that whoever is without
sin should cast the first stone. At this the crowd settles down
and becomes quiet. *They went away, one by one, beginning with
the elders, until Jesus was left alone with the woman.* How quick
are we to judge? How certain are we of our condemnation? We
must remember that one day we will stand before Jesus. On
that day of judgement, will we need mercy?

⌒

Pray: O Jesus, help me to remember that you did not come to
condemn the world. You came to set the world free!

NEITHER DO I CONDEMN YOU

❖   ❖   ❖

Woman, where are they? Has no one condemned you?
She replied, No one, sir.
Jesus said, neither do I condemn you.

- JOHN 8:11

WHY DID THE murderous crowd disperse? Because Jesus reminded them of their own sinfulness. Anger subsides and gentleness returns when we reflect on our own failures. Every single person in the crowd went home in humility. There is not one person among us who is without sin. Jesus then reminds the woman that he does not condemn her. Imagine this woman's relief! Facing certain death by stoning just seconds earlier, she is now free to continue living her life. Perphaps she will live with greater humility as a result of the experience, but she will certainly live with a greater love of her neighbors and a deeper devotion to Jesus. She now knows very well that his mission in life is to set sinners free. To encourage her newfound freedom, Jesus encourages and empowers her with gentle words: *Go and do not sin again.*

Pray: O Lord, I am heartily sorry for having offended thee.
I promise with the help of your grace to amend my life.

DO NOT CONDEMN

❖ ❖ ❖

Do not condemn, and you will not be condemned. Forgive, and you will be forgiven. Give, and it will be given to you.

- LUKE 6:37

HOW EASY IT is for us to condemn others! After all, we can see their faults so clearly! Their faults are on display like black flags on a flagpole and we are more than happy to raise the flags high so everyone else can see them flapping the wind. We need to remember that we have plenty of shabby flags and ragged clothes neatly folded in our own drawers. How would we like to have our dirty linen run up the nearest flagpoles? Jesus cautions us strongly not to condemn others or we will be condemned too. The good news is that if we forgive others, we will be forgiven. See the connection? Forgiveness is a gift from God, given to all of us equally. If we give this gift of forgiveness to others, we will surely receive it in return. *Give, and it will be given to you.*

⌐

Pray: O Lord, instead of condemning others, help me learn how to give them the same gift of forgiveness you gave me.

A GOOD MEASURE

❖ ❖ ❖

A good measure, pressed down, shaken together
and running over, will be poured into your lap.
For with the measure you use, it will be measured to you.

- LUKE 6:37-38

WHEN YOU BAKE a delicious birthday cake, you need a good measuring cup. If you use too little flour, eggs, or milk it ruins the cake. The same is true when you judge others. Here Jesus says that if you are severe in judging others for their sins, the same severity will be used to measure your sins. If you are vindictive toward others, you may expect the same treatment. On the other hand, if you are forgiving, merciful and generous to others, you can expect the same from God. So fill your measuring cup with patience, kindness and hope. God will shake up these loving ingredients until they overflow into every area of your life.

⸱⸱⸱

Pray: O Lord, thank you for showing me how
to fill up my cup of life with exactly the right ingredients.
I want my cup to overflow with your love.

MERCY TRIUMPHS OVER JUDGEMENT

❖ ❖ ❖

*Speak and act as those who are going to be judged
under the law of freedom, for judgement without mercy
will be shown to anyone who has not been merciful.
Mercy triumphs over judgment.*

- *JAMES 2:12*

DO YOU CRITICIZE others? You are free, of course, to say and do whatever you wish. But if you are inclined to gossip about others or judge them, reflect on the fact that you will one day face judgement by God. For the good of your soul, remember God will judge you in exactly the same way as you judge others. Are you kind, forbearing, and compassionate? Or are you harsh, critical, and derogatory? Do you look for the good in people or are you a fault-finder? Do you build people up or do you tear them down to make yourself look better in comparison? Be careful of how you speak and act because one day you will face judgement too. On the day of your judgement, when you stand before God, he will show you the same severity you have shown others. If you have shown no mercy, you will be judged without mercy. But if you have shown mercy toward others, God will show mercy to you, for *mercy triumphs over judgement.* Let God be the judge of others in your life.

⌣

Pray: O Lord, help me to stop criticizing and judging others.
I want to show mercy as I hope to receive mercy.

MY REWARD IS WITH GOD

❖ ❖ ❖

*I thought I had labored in vain, for nothing and
for naught spent my strength, yet surely the justice due
to me is with the Lord, and my reward with my God.*

- *ISAIAH 49:4*

WHAT IF YOU knew, beyond the shadow of a doubt, that everything taken from you is not lost, but in fact has been stored up for you as a reward in a safe place? When our lives are devastated, everything we have worked for may seem ruined. A lifetime of building may suddenly look like rubble strewn on the ground. How can we forgive someone for such causing such desolation? There is only one way: we must turn our eyes upward, towards God. We must trust that God is good despite all evidence to the contrary. He is doing justice in His own way and time. Nothing is lost. God is storing up for us a reward far greater than our present suffering. When we receive our reward, in this life or in heaven, it will make our present sufferings seem miniscule. In the meantime, let us be grateful that God's creation is perfectly just and balanced. *My reward is with my God.*

Pray: O Lord, when everything I have worked for seems lost,
I choose to believe that you are storing it all up behind the
scenes and will give it back to me multiplied.

When Life Seems Hopeless

❖ ❖ ❖

*He believed, hoping against hope...and was fully
convinced that what God had promised he was able to do.*

- Romans 4:18

SOMETIMES PEOPLE DASH our hopes on the rocks of life. Our dreams may be shattered. We feel marooned on a desert island. Like a solitary survivor of a shipwreck, our plans for the future have sunk in pieces to the bottom of the ocean. What shall we do? God wants us to keep believing in him. Even when life seems hopeless, God wants us to *hope against hope.* That is what our faith in him is all about. When we cannot see God or feel his presence, we can still rest in the confidence that he is in control. Despite all the evidence to the contrary, God still has a plan for our lives. He has promised to make all things work out for the best. We may be hurting and bewildered, but we can still allow ourselves to accept the mystery of God's plan. God has promised that our new life, while it may look very different from our old life, will be much better for us. Whatever God promises, he is willing and able to fulfil. He will do it.

⁓

Pray: O Lord, while I do not see my future clearly,
I trust your plan as it unfolds. I trust your promise
that all will be well.

A Cheerful Giver

❖ ❖ ❖

God loves a cheerful giver.

- 2 Corinthians 9:7

J UST AS A parent delights when a baby returns a smile or a child makes a birthday card to present to his or her parent, God loves it when we give something cheerfully. God should know about gift-giving: he gave us his only begotten son Jesus! Jesus is another good example of giving cheerfully: he willingly gave up his life as a sacrifice on the cross to save us from our sins. What are you being called to give up today? It is easy to give a birthday card to a friend, but what about something you cherished that has been painfully torn away from you by someone else against your will? Perhaps it is a relationship, your health, your wealth, or your peace of mind? Whatever it is, instead of giving it up to God begrudgingly, trust that God has allowed your current situation in order to bring about a greater good. He is sadder for your loss than you are. Release your loss into his loving hands, but do it cheerfully, as he gave his son Jesus to die for you. Remember that God gave everything to you in the first place, including life itself, so you are just returning it to the rightful owner. Let God bring about his greater plan.

Pray: O Lord, I know you love a cheerful giver. Give me more grace today to give you all my losses cheerfully.

A Hundred Times More

❖ ❖ ❖

*Everyone who has given up houses or brothers or sisters
or father or mother or children or lands for the sake of
my name will receive a hundred times more,
and will inherit eternal life.*

- MATTHEW 19:29

WHEN WE STRUGGLE to forgive someone, the reason is often because that person has deprived us of something or some-one we valued. We are naturally angry and resentful. We cannot give up what was taken away from us. Although our loss is now in the past, we struggle to let it go in the present. If only we knew that somehow we could get it all back, even if it meant waiting until some future time, we would be able to let it go for now. The good news is that Jesus said everyone who gives up anything, no matter how valuable, whether it is loved ones or possessions, will receive *a hundred times more!* Think about that! The key is not just letting go of your losses, Jesus says, but giving them up *for the sake of my name.* Offer up your sufferings to Jesus and let him pay you back a hundred times more. Part of your payback is that you will be empowered with the freedom to forgive. Better yet, Jesus promises that you *will inherit eternal life.*

Pray: O Lord, I offer up to you all my pain and suffering.
Convert it into forgiveness and gratitude for eternal life.

TRIALS FOR EVERYONE

❖ ❖ ❖

No trial has overtaken you that is not common to everyone.

- I CORINTHIANS 10:13

IN THE MIDST of a disappointment or betrayal, the most natural reaction is for us to cry out, "Why me?" Our setbacks may seem irreversible and our lives may have changed permanently. We think God has singled us out for suffering while the rest of the world goes on its merry way. No one else seems to suffer the way we do. Our anger may even be tinged with fear since it seems we face an unknown path that no one has ever travelled before. The words of Saint Paul give us a new perspective. He says that our current trials are not new, and our sufferings are not unique - quite the contrary. The circumstances we face are common to everyone. Throughout history, people have experienced similar trials and tribulations. The crosses God allows us to be given have been shouldered by many people before us and will be born by many others after us. We are not alone. Let us pick up our crosses and carry them valiantly together, helping each other.

⌒

Pray: O Lord, I realize I do not carry my cross alone.
Help me to see the crosses others carry so I can help them and
let them help me.

NOTHING TOO MUCH TO BEAR

❖　❖　❖

*God is faithful, and he will not let you be tried beyond
your strength, but with the trial he will also provide the
way out so that you may be able to endure it.*

- 1 CORINTHIANS 10:13

PART OF THE reason we get so angry and resentful toward other people is because we think they have made our lives unbearable. The disappointment or suffering they have caused us may feel overwhelming. We think our current trial is beyond our ability to endure. Nothing could be further from the truth. God promises us that he will not let us be tried beyond our strength. In the midst of your difficulties *he will also provide the way out so that you may be able to endure it.* Take courage in your current trial, knowing that God is providing all the strength you need to get through it. Moment by moment, you are receiving the grace and power you need. God is never early or late; he is always right on time. Hold fast to your faith that God's timing is best. In this way you will pass through your trial. Rely on God's strength and he will show you the way.

⤳

Pray: O Lord, I take heart in knowing that you will never give me anything beyond my ability to endure. Thank you for giving me your strength at the perfect time.

MY CHOSEN ONE

❖ ❖ ❖

Here is my servant whom I uphold,
my chosen one with whom I am pleased.

- I Corinthians 10:13

WHEN WE ARE beset by trials, temptations, and tests, we struggle to sustain our confidence. Especially when we do not see the path ahead clearly, we may fear that God has left us alone to work everything out. On the contrary, all the answers to our worries are in God's hands. When we quiet ourselves, we find the source of our strength. We begin to hear God's voice. To our delight he says *here is my servant whom I uphold.* When we seek to serve God, he promises to uphold us. When we strive to become God's servants, he sustains and supports us in our daily lives. God is placing his hand on your shoulder and calling you by name, *my chosen one with whom I am pleased.*

Pray: O Lord, help me to believe that you are pleased
with me even when I fall short. Uphold me as I try
my best to serve you.

A BRUISED REED

❖ ❖ ❖

A bruised reed he shall not break,
and a dimly burning wick he will not extinguish;
He will faithfully bring forth justice.

- ISAIAH 42:3

H AVE YOU EVER been pushed to your breaking point? You feel so beaten that you know you have reached your limit. You may think, "I just cannot take it anymore!" Hang on, help is coming. God is near and his promise is clear. God may allow you to be burdened by a great weight, but not enough to buckle you. Stretched thin and taut as a rubber band, you will not snap. Bruised and bent like a reed, you will not snap. Burned out like a smoldering candle wick, you will not be extinguished. No matter how bad your situation gets, God will protect you and keep you safe in his arms. Why is God allowing you to experience such an extreme trial? You may not know the ultimate answer until you get to heaven, but the immediate reason is all good: God wants to turn you more perfectly in his direction; he wants you to run more earnestly into his loving arms. Gradually you will see the miracle of your mind transforming, your heart reforming, and your soul conforming to his perfect will. *He will faithfully bring forth justice.*

⌐

Pray: O Lord, I take courage in knowing
that matter how bad my circumstances get,
you will not let me be broken if I rest in your arms.

DARKNESS INTO LIGHT

❖ ❖ ❖

I will lead the blind on a way they do not know;
by paths they do not know I will guide them.

- ISAIAH 42:16

P EOPLE ARE BLIND in many ways. When someone offends
you and does not repent, that person is blind. When you
offend someone else and do not repent, you are blind. In all
cases involving unforgiveness, there is blindness. Wherever
there is an absence of mercy, there is a lack of sight. How frustrating when we cannot make people see how hurtful they are!
But how can a blind person be expected to see? Only God can
lead the blind, open their eyes, and guide them along the right
paths. Let us pray for others and ourselves that God will help
us see the light. *I will turn darkness into light before them, and*
make crooked ways straight.

Pray: O Lord, I ask you to lead others to the light
of your divine life. Cure the blindness in myself
and in others so we see your light clearly!

A Light To The Nations

❖ ❖ ❖

*It is too small a thing that you should be my servant...
I will also make you a light of the nations.*

- Isaiah 49:6

Your destiny is not small when you seek to serve the Lord. When you seek to serve him above all others, he will ask you to love and forgive others. When you forgive others, you become one of his favorite servants. But wait a minute, that is too small. God has a much bigger, brighter future in store for you. *I will also make you a light to the nations.* When you truly forgive others, God will make you a shining example to many people. You may not realize it but you powerfully influence other people by your humility, gentleness, and love of neighbor. After seeing your example, a husband may go home and quietly apologize to his wife. A son may forgive his estranged father. A pastor may preach a more effective sermon on forgiveness to his congregation. Let me use you, God says, *so that My salvation may reach to the end of the earth.*

Pray: O Lord, I want you to use me however you like.
If I can be of any service to you, I am content!

He Emptied Himself

❖ ❖ ❖

Though he was in the form of God, he did not
count equality with God a thing to be grasped.
He emptied himself, taking the form of a servant,
being born in human likeness.

- Philippians 2:7

W HEN LIFE TAKES a turn for the worse, our natural reaction is to protest. We rebel. We think we could do a
better job than God in running the world. In contrast, consider the humility of Jesus. There he is, sitting in heaven, enjoy-
ing a perfect existence as a member the Holy Trinity. God asks
him to go to earth and be born in human likeness. Rather
than grasping his own divinity in protest, Jesus humbly accepts
the will of his Father, empties himself, and comes to earth as
a servant to all. Can we imitate this example Jesus gives us?
Rather than grasping our rights and preferences, can we empty
ourselves and accept the will of our Father in our present circumstances? Without question, this is a difficult challenge. It
goes against our nature to become a servant, but it is easy to
serve when our Master is God. *Even the Son of Man came not to*
be served but to serve.

⁀

Pray: O Lord, instead of grasping my desires, I want
to empty myself, become your servant, and do your will.

He Humbled Himself

❖   ❖   ❖

He humbled himself and became obedient unto death,
even death on a cross.

- Philippians 2:8

A GREAT TEMPTATION is to think God is depriving us for no good reason. Then we get so focused on our grievances that we cannot forgive. In our grief, we are stretched further and we fear we will break. To banish the clouds of fear, Jesus showed us his supreme example of humility. He completely accepted the will of his Father. He trusted the will of his Father by offering his entire life as a living sacrifice. He became obedient all the way unto death. Our Father may not be asking us to be obedient unto death at this very moment, but he will someday, so we do well to practice being obedient in the little things. Can we really offer up our lives as living sacrifices to God? In small ways and large, can we truly make every thought and action a sacrifice? *Thy kingdom come, thy will be done.*

Pray: O Lord, give me the grace to accept your will.
I want to give you everything you ask of me today.

THY WILL BE DONE

❖ ❖ ❖

Thy will be done, on earth as it is in heaven.

- MATTHEW 6:10

To sweep away pride, anger and resentment, this is the most powerful prayer. You will be surprised how quickly it ushers in humility, contentment, and gratitude. It swiftly conforms our thinking to God's way of thinking. Many people assume everything that happens is God's will, but that's not true. Abuse, neglect, and adultery are not his will. God allows bad things to happen because he has given us free will and we often choose the wrong path. But we know that if we love him above all others, he will make all our crooked paths straight. God turns bad into good, sickness into health, and darkness into light. Expect it in your life! God's will is to remake things perfectly here on earth as they are in heaven. When we pray *thy will be done,* we are helping God's kingdom to come.

Pray: O Lord, I thank you for showing me how to
pray with joyful expectation that you are making everything
perfect on earth as it is in heaven.

ALL THINGS WORK FOR GOOD

❖ ❖ ❖

We know that God causes all things to work together
for good to those who love God, to those who are
called according to His purpose.

- *ROMANS 8:28*

I MAGINE TOSSING ALL your hurts, sufferings, resentments, and embarrassments into a red velvet bag. Pretty heavy, isn't it? Now shake the bag, open it carefully, and see the contents miraculously transformed into brightly colored ribbon-wrapped gifts. What a surprise! Your name is handwritten on each present with a tag "from God." This is not a dream; this is the reality God promises each of us when we love Him. Everything God promises is already true in his eternal plan. We may have to wait a minute or a lifetime to see our gifts but they are already ours. It may seem hidden to our eyes, or impossible at this moment, but *God causes all things to work together for good.* Not some things, *all things.* This is God's message to us in the life of his son Jesus. God allowed his son to be crucified, but then He caused a greater good in the resurrection. Everyone thought the death of Jesus was the worst thing that could possibly happen, but God caused it to be transformed into the best gift in history.

～

Pray: O Lord, I believe you cause *all things* to work together
for good. I love your miraculous gifts!

YOU WILL RECEIVE POWER

❖ ❖ ❖

You will receive power when the Holy Spirit comes
upon you, and you will be my witnesses.

- ACTS 1:8

MOST OF US share a frustrating experience of trying to forgive others and failing many times. We feel powerless to do what God is asking us to do. Then we begin to get angry with God for asking us to do the impossible. We are indeed correct that he is asking us to do something that is impossible for us alone. God wants us to turn to him for help. Where we have failed, he will succeed. He promises to send us the Holy Spirit to give us power beyond our natural abilities. If we are lacking power, we need to stir up the Holy Spirit within us. How? Repeat this ancient prayer often to invite the Holy Spirit to come alive in your heart: *Veni Sancte Spiritus* - Come Holy Spirit. How do you know when you have the Holy Spirit? Just as Jesus' disciples knew, you will too. Among other signs, you will notice a new supernatural power to forgive. This is a great mystery.

Pray: Come Holy Spirit, send forth your sacred healing power and the heavenly radiance of your light.

THE SPIRIT OF TRUTH

❖ ❖ ❖

I will ask the Father, and He will give you another Helper,
that He may be with you forever; that is the Spirit of truth,
whom the world cannot receive, because it does not
ssee Him or know Him.

- JOHN 14:16

WHEN JESUS TOLD his disciples he was leaving them, they became afraid and asked how to find the way without him. We know exactly how the disciples felt, do we not? Often God seems absent or far away. We fear the future because we do not see the path ahead. But Jesus assures us that he will not leave us alone. *I will not leave you orphans.* Jesus says his Father is sending us a Helper, named the Spirit of truth, to be with us forever. Jesus here reveals the reality of three persons in the Holy Trinity - Father, Son, and Spirit. While our Father is in heaven, and his son Jesus sits at his right hand, the Holy Spirit resides deep in our hearts. Most people cannot receive this invisible Spirit because they do not believe the Spirit exists. We believe the Spirit is a real person and resides intimately with us. We can feel the presence of this Helper deep within our hearts. *You know Him because He abides with you and will be in you.*

Pray: Come Holy Spirit, stir my heart with flames of love. Be my Helper, show me the truth, be with me forever.

THE HOLY SPIRIT

❖ ❖ ❖

God's love has been poured into our hearts
through the Holy Spirit who has been given to us.

- ROMANS 5:5

WHO IS THE Holy Spirit? God has revealed himself as three persons in one: the Father, the Son, and the Holy Spirit. These three persons coexist eternally in a perfect life-giving relationship. This is how we know God is love, because love always seeks to give itself to another. So it makes sense that God is not a solitary, self-centered being but rather a family of three loving, self-giving persons. As the Father gazes upon his Son, and the Son gazes back at his Father, they breathe a mutually delightful sigh of love. This eternal sigh is the divine wind, the Holy Spirit, the third person of the Trinity. This is the same Spirit of love that Jesus breathed upon his disciples to give them supernatural power, and it is similar to the breath that God breathed into Adam's nostrils to give him life. Once you have received this divine breath of love, this mysterious Holy Spirit, you will find yourself forgiving and forgetting as easily as inhaling and exhaling.

⸎

Pray: Come Holy Spirit, into my life, stir up my gifts, banish
all strife. I want your loving power
to work through me to forgive others.

HE WILL TEACH YOU

❖ ❖ ❖

*The Counselor, the Holy Spirit, whom the Father will
send in my name, he will teach you all things, and bring
to your remembrance all that I have said to you.*

- JOHN 14:26

REMEMBER THE PERSON who gave you the best advice when you were young? Who was it and what did he or she say? Now think of a time when you really needed good advice but could not find it. You were seeking a good friend, confidant, or spiritual director but no one appeared. That probably hurt. God has sent you the perfect Counselor, the Holy Spirit, to dwell in your heart all the time. *He will teach you all things.* Whenever you need guidance, the Holy Spirit is near. You may hear him speaking to your heart in a quiet time, in prayer, or when reading Scripture. Sometimes he will surprise you by providing the answers you seek during an unexpected moment with unlikely people. Be on the lookout for messages from your ever-present Counselor, the Holy Spirit, as he speaks to you every second of your life. If you cannot hear him, listen more carefully in greater silence. Gradually you will learn to hear him everywhere, in everyone and in everything, except where there is sin.

Pray: Come Holy Spirit, teach me all things. I believe
I can hear your wisdom whenever I listen with all my heart.

THE FRUIT OF THE SPIRIT

❖   ❖   ❖

The fruit of the Spirit is love, joy, peace,
patience, kindness, generosity,
faithfulness, gentleness, and self-control.

- GALATIANS 5:22

As we know a peach tree is healthy when fruit appears on its branches, you know you are healthy when you display the fruit of the Holy Spirit. You are healthy when you forgive others with *love, joy, peace, patience, kindness, generosity, faithfulness, gentleness, and self-control.* Are you healthy in these ways today? If not, ask the Holy Spirit to come alive in you right now. Humble yourself, become the soil in which the Holy Spirit can sprout and grow. Bear the fruit of the Holy Spirit and be nourished. Grow the divine fruit of the Holy Spirit for your own sake and for the sake of others. Gradually you will find yourself blossoming with new fruit. You will receive a newfound ability to respond to others with gentleness and compassion. Your response-ability will nourish others in ways that will confuse and delight them. Your fruit will bring them closer to God.

⁓

Pray: Come Holy Spirit, bring forth in me your heavenly fruit. I want to be nourished and help others to grow.

My Peace I Give You

❖ ❖ ❖

Peace I leave with you;
my peace I give to you;
not as the world gives do I give to you.

- John 14:27

I T IS NATURAL for us, when someone ruins our peace of mind, to try to regain the peace we had previously. While it may be possible to reclaim our old peace, it is more likely that God is using this experience to take us on a journey to a higher place with even greater peace. We want to go back to the familiar place, but God wants to show us something new and better. We seek the peace of the world, but that peace is fragile and fleeting. Jesus wants to give us his peace which is much stronger and more enduring. What is this peace Jesus wants to give us? It is the delightful peace that does not depend on other people, our limited perspective, or unpredictable circumstances. With the peace of Jesus we can fly high above the dark and stormy clouds of our everyday cares and anxieties into pure light. Jesus offers us peace that is out of this world and surpassing our understanding. When we accept the peace Jesus gives us, we hear him speak clearly to us. *Let not your hearts be troubled, neither let them be afraid.*

Pray: O my Jesus, I thank you every day for giving me your peace, your tranquility, and your serenity.

GREATER WORKS THAN JESUS

❖ ❖ ❖

Amen, Amen, I say to you, whoever believes in me
will do the works that I do, and will do greater ones than these...
And whatever you ask in my name, I will do.

- JOHN 14:12

H OW WOULD YOU like to have the ability to perform miracles like Jesus and heal people in every way? Think about one person in your life right now who needs healing. In what specific way would you like to heal that person? Jesus promises that *whoever believes in me will do the works that I do, and will do greater ones than these.* How is this possible? The keys are having faith and asking in His name. This means praying *thy will be done.* If it is God's will for someone to be healed, and you ask in Jesus' name, God will heal that person. You may or may not see the result, but if it is God's will, it will happen. Healing always occurs according to God's perfect timing. Do not be surprised if you gradually realize that the person God wants to heal is you. Remember, Jesus said that compared with physical healing, the forgiveness of sins is a much greater miracle! *If you ask anything of me in my name, I will do it.*

Pray: O Jesus, I ask you to help me forgive myself
and others of all our sins. I ask you to heal us
in your holy name, Amen.

BORN OF THE SPIRIT

❖ ❖ ❖

The wind blows wherever it pleases. You hear its sound,
but you cannot tell where it comes from or where it is
going. So it is with everyone born of the Spirit.

- JOHN 3:8

LIKE A SAILOR who waits for the wind and catches in his sails, we must wait for the Holy Spirit to fill our hearts with joy and mercy. At times we feel impatient and adrift at sea, lacking any wind to sail onward. On other days the wind becomes a frightening storm, a howling hurricane threatening to dash our hopes on the rocks and sink our tiny ship. As faithful sailors we always know what to do. When we are windless, we know the Holy Spirit wants us to be still and know that He is still with us. When the wind blows hard, we know it is time to come about and sail into the wind, into Him. We cannot control the wind, but we can allow the Holy Spirit to help us adjust our sails to reach our destination. When the storm blows too hard, and sailing becomes impossible, we know the Holy Spirit wants us to release the tiller and run free with the wind at our back. Through it all, if we abide in prayer and trim our sails with confidence, the Holy Spirit will surely fill us with hope. Whether the Holy Spirit seems absent and motionless, or gusting and stormy, we pray always for guidance and direction. The Holy Spirit may not blow when and where we please, but if we allow ourselves to be born anew every day, he will certainly guide us safely to the harbor where we belong.

Pray: Come, Holy Spirit, fill my sails with your divine breath of love. I trust you to guide me to your safe harbor.

HE DIED FOR ALL

❖ ❖ ❖

*He indeed died for all, so that those who live might
no longer live for themselves but for him who for
their sake died and was raised.*

- 2 CORINTHIANS 5:14

WHY DID JESUS have to die for us? Because God's perfect justice required a payment for our sins, He sent his only son to die on our behalf, as a sacrifice to atone for our sins. Because Jesus was perfect, his death satisfies the demands of God's perfect justice and opens to us the gates of eternal life. If Jesus had not died for our sins, God's justice would have required us to die instead. Jesus balances the scales of justice to give us eternal life. What a gift! How can we possibly repay this debt? We can express our gratitude by living selflessly as Jesus did. We can live sacrificial lives for Jesus and for others. What sacrifice is God asking you to make today? What is God asking you to give up, to forgive, to release, to patiently endure? This is the meaning of offering your life as *a living sacrifice*. Sometimes it hurts. Can you offer yourself as a living sacrifice? Do it today and watch God raise you up.

Pray: O Lord, I thank you for dying for my sins. I offer my life as a living sacrifice to you in return. Raise me up!

YOU ARE THE TEMPLE OF GOD

❖ ❖ ❖

Do you not know that you are the temple of God,
and that the Spirit of God dwells in you?

- 1 CORINTHIANS 3:16

I F YOU ARE feeling lonely, neglected or abandoned, meditate on the fact that you are never alone. Friends and acquaintances may hurt you or desert you, but the Spirit of God is always with you. You are God's beloved child, whom he loved enough to create by breathing his life into you! You may not believe it, but you are a sacred temple of God. The Spirit of God actually dwells in you. Take a deep breath right now as you count to three, then exhale as you count to four. Do you feel yourself relaxing? Do it again. Your breath is the breath of the Holy Spirit, the Third Person of the Trinity. The Holy Spirit is with you, breathing new life into you every moment of every day. It is the Holy Spirit who inspires you, sustains you, and uplifts you. He is closer to you than you are to yourself. He knows you more intimately than you know yourself. Breathe deeply and enjoy the comforting companionship of the Holy Spirit in your life.

Pray: Come Holy Spirit, stir up your love in my heart, make me more aware of your intimate divine presence.

PEACE BE WITH YOU

❖ ❖ ❖

When the doors were locked, where the disciples were,
for fear of the Jews, Jesus came and stood in their
midst and said to them, 'Peace be with you.'

- JOHN 20:19

OFTEN WE LOCK the doors of our hearts and minds because we fear other people. Fearful of what our adversaries may do or say, we barricade ourselves behind closed doors hoping to stay safely out of the way. We hide in prisons of our own creation. After Jesus' crucifixion, the disciples locked themselves in a room and cowered in fear of the murderous crowds in the street. Their beloved master was dead. Then, to their astonishment, Jesus appeared in their midst! He was not dead after all, but miraculously alive! The first words from his lips banished their fears. *Peace be with you.* Just as Jesus appeared to the disciples, expect him to appear to you in an unexpected moment. No locked door can keep him out. He wants to enter into your barricaded heart today. Open your arms and invite him into your life. Hear Jesus whispering to you softly. *Peace be with you.*

⌒

Pray: O Jesus, I invite you into my life today. Calm my heart and mind with your presence. Bring me your peace.

So I Send You

❖ ❖ ❖

Jesus said to them again, 'Peace be with you.
As the Father has sent me, so I send you.'

- John 20:21

To make sure the disciples realized he was empowering them to live without anxiety or fear, Jesus repeated his greeting. *Peace be with you.* Now they could relax with the knowledge that God was with them! Imagine the disciples sighing with relief and regaining their composure. Jesus had fortified them with his peace, the peace that surpasses all understanding. Now they were ready for anything. They could take on the whole world! That is precisely what Jesus had in mind as he gave them their new instructions. *As the Father has sent me, so I send you.* Having unlocked their courage, Jesus now sends them forth to proclaim the good news of the forgiveness of sins, the resurrection of the dead, and the life of the world to come. Be prepared for Jesus to send you forth with the same purpose. Jesus knows just how to use your talents.

Pray: O Jesus, give me your peace and courage that surpasses understanding. Send me forth to do your will.

RECEIVE THE HOLY SPIRIT

❖ ❖ ❖

He breathed on them and said to them,
'Receive the Holy Spirit.'

- JOHN 20:22

NOTICE HOW JESUS gave the Holy Spirit to the disciples. *He breathed on them.* This is similar to the way God breathed life into Adam in the Garden of Eden. What is this holy breath, this sacred wind? This is the Holy Spirit, the mutual love between the Father and the Son, expressed as a simultaneous sigh of delight. This sigh of mutual love is so creative and powerful it proceeds forth eternally as a Person; the third Person of the Trinity. This is the Holy Spirit that Jesus breathed into his disciples and into you. Think about the divine origin of your breath when you speak, yawn or sneeze. The next time you feel the wind on your face or hear the rustling breeze of the leaves in the trees, let it remind you that the Holy Spirit surrounds you. Let your lungs be filled with the breath of Jesus. Receive the Holy Spirit into the unfathomable depths of your soul. The Holy Spirit is your best friend and closest companion. He guides, protects, empowers and directs you all the days of your life. Now you can forgive as Jesus forgives.

Pray: Come Holy Spirit, inspire me with your breath of life.
As I inhale and exhale, I think of you and thank you.

THE LIGHT OF THE WORLD

❖ ❖ ❖

I came into the world as light.

- JOHN 12:46

WHEN THE DARKNESS of sin enshrouds, us we need to turn toward the light. Are you stumbling around in darkness today because of sin? It may be caused by the sin of others, or perhaps it is because of your own sin. Whatever the cause, look for the light. No matter how faint or dim, turn toward the light. If you cannot see any light, but only darkness, calm yourself and look again with the eyes of faith. Jesus is the light of the world; he came to dispel the darkness of sin, fear and shame. *I came into the world as light.* Turn to Jesus, walk toward the light, he is waiting with open arms. Bask in his light, be bathed in his glow, let him wash away all your sin and unforgiveness forever. The light of Jesus is pure light, eternal love, illuminating your mind and renewing your spirit. *Whoever believes in me may not remain in darkness.* Go to Jesus and live in the light of love.

⌐

Pray: O Lord, I see your light, I turn toward you now. Dispel all my darkness with your holy light.

I Did Not Come To Condemn

❖ ❖ ❖

I did not come to condemn the world but to save the world.

- JOHN 12:47

THE WORLD IS full of condemnation. We are quick to judge one another for transgressions large and small. We criticize neighbors, denounce strangers, and damn all offenders to hellfire. Friends become enemies and spouses become antagonists. Families are estranged, groups are alienated, and nations are torn asunder. Where does it stop? Jesus said *I did not come to condemn the world but to save the world.* Jesus does not want to condemn you; he wants to save you. We are all drowning in criticism, judgement and denunciation, but Jesus is our ever-ready lifeguard who plunges into the raging waters to rescue us with forgiveness, pardon, and new life. If you are feeling condemned today, by others or yourself, you are listening to the wrong voices. Stop listening to the voices of the world and hear the voice of Jesus instead. If you are struggling with a spirit of unforgiveness, you are struggling with the spirit of the world. Rest in the Holy Spirit instead. Wherever there is condemnation, there is sin. Wherever there is forgiveness, there is the love of God.

⌒

Pray: O Jesus, I am so grateful that you did not come to condemn but to save! Help me learn to love as you do.

IT WAS VERY GOOD

❖ ❖ ❖

God saw all that he had made, and it was very good.

- GENESIS 1:31

THE DEEPEST TRUTH about life is that God originally created everything perfect. Our world is so full of sorrow and disappointment that we are tempted to despair. Yet it was not always this way. In the beginning God created the entire universe out of pure love and *it was very good.* Read this again. When God looked down upon his creation, what did he think? That it was merely good? No, that it was *very good.* Originally everything was perfect. Imagine a perfect world. Adam was perfect, Eve was perfect, the entire universe was in perfect harmony. Sadly, we lost that perfection through the disobedience of our first parents, and we continue to lose our way because of our own disobedience, but Jesus came to show us the way home. Jesus has redeemed all who believe in him. He is in the process of renewing each and every one of us. He wants to restore us to our original state of perfection. Sometimes it hurts when Jesus bends our crookedness to make us straight. If we allow Jesus to do his wonderful work in us, he will reform us and remake us into the saints we are meant to be. God wants us to be *very good.*

Pray: O Lord, help me to do everything I can to help you redeem the world. Transform me, reshape me, refine me!

My House Of Sacrifice

❖ ❖ ❖

*The Lord appeared to Solomon during the night and
said to him: I have heard your prayer, and I have
chosen this place for my house of sacrifice.*

- 2 CHRONICLES 7:12

WE WANT GOD to hear our prayers, and we believe he hears every prayer, but we need to be prepared to accept his answers. In this verse God hears the prayer of King Solomon and responds, *I have chosen this place for my house of sacrifice.* Solomon expected rain, harvest, and health, but God decided to allow drought, locusts, and pestilence to ravage the land and people. Sometimes we pray for blessings but God responds by asking for sacrifice! Could it be that God wants to bless us by depriving us for a season? We know God transforms all sacrifices into blessings. God asks Solomon to continue to walk in faith, in spite of his suffering, and promises him a noble reward. *I will establish your royal throne.* How is God asking you to accept a sacrifice in your life today?

Pray: O Lord, I praise you even when you ask me to make sacrifices because I know they produce eternal blessings.

I Will Forgive Their Sin

❖ ❖ ❖

If my people who are called by my name humble themselves, and pray and seek my face, and turn from their wicked ways, then I will hear from heaven, and will forgive their sin and heal their land.

- 2 Chronicles 7:14

IN THE MIDST of our trials, in the middle of our sufferings, if we humble ourselves and seek God, he will find us. When we get down on our knees and seek the face of God in prayer, he promises to hear us, wash away our sins in the ocean of his forgiveness, and heal our land. Are you willing to be humble today? Kneel down now, wherever you are, and ask God to help you turn away from your wicked ways. Thank God for hearing your prayer and forgiving your sin. Can you feel yourself being cleansed and healed deep in your soul? Even if you cannot feel it, you can still believe it. Now that you have received God's healing, overflow that same forgiveness to others.

Pray: O Lord, thank you for forgiving my sins and healing my soul. Help me to forgive others in the same way!

YOUR CONSOLATIONS DELIGHT MY SOUL

❖ ❖ ❖

When my anxious thoughts multiply within me,
your consolations delight my soul.

- PSALM 94:19

HAVE YOU NOTICED how one anxious thought multiplies itself into many anxious thoughts? When you allow one worry about a person or circumstance to distract you, several more worries quickly appear. Before you know it, you have lost your peace. Your picnic is overrun by ants. As soon as you take your eyes off Jesus, the concerns of the world multiply within your mind. When anxious thoughts attack your peace of mind, what is the best way to regain your composure? Turn toward God. Tell God you need his peace that passes all understanding. He knows what you need, but he wants to hear you ask for his help. This opens the doors of your heart to him. Now wait for him. He will enter your heart at an unexpected moment and bring you an abundance of his blessings. One of the nicest things about waiting for God and relying on him completely, is that when you finally feel his special peace returning to calm your soul, you know exactly whom to thank. *Your consolations delight my soul.*

Pray: O Lord, I wait in joyful hope for you to deliver me from my distress. I know all your blessings arrive on time.

DO NOT BE TROUBLED

❖ ❖ ❖

Jesus said to his disciples:
Do not let your hearts be troubled.

- JOHN 14:1

AT THE MOMENT of your greatest distress, Jesus will comfort you. For example, when Jesus informs his disciples that he is leaving them, he also reassures them. *Do not let your hearts be troubled.* He wants them to be at peace always, regardless of their circumstances. Notice that Jesus says it is within our power to be serene. We need not be passive and helpless; rather we can actively direct our hearts, control our emotions, and practice being at peace. When things do not go our way, we are tempted to allow our fears to cause us to worry. When something or someone causes an unwelcome change in our lives, Jesus says we can resist the inclination to be fearful or resentful. Instead, we can calm ourselves, place our hearts in God's loving hands, and prayerfully find the peace that passes understanding.

⤳

Pray: O Jesus, with you at my side, I will not let my heart be troubled by anyone or anything today.

I Am The Way

❖ ❖ ❖

Master, how can we know the way? Jesus said,
I am the way and the truth and the life.
No one comes to the Father except through me.

- John 14:5

IF WE CANNOT find it within ourselves to forgive someone, Jesus will show us the way. When Jesus informed the disciples he was leaving them, they felt lost and abandoned. They worried that they did not know the way to find him. They wanted a map, but Jesus wanted them to know he had given them something infinitely better. He had given them himself. *I am the way and the truth and the life.* Like the disciples, we want answers to our questions, but Jesus wants to give us himself instead. What would you rather have, the answers to all your questions, or the divine person of Jesus sitting at your side? When we are lost and cannot find the way, Jesus shows us the way. If we struggle to make sense of this confusing world, we turn to Jesus. In him we find the way, the truth, and new life.

⌒

Pray: O Jesus, when I cannot find the way, I put myself in your hands. With you as my guide, the way becomes clear.

WHY ARE YOU PERSECUTING ME?

❖ ❖ ❖

I am Jesus, whom you are persecuting.

- ACTS 9:5

WHEN WE EXPERIENCE persecution, we should not take it personally because all offenses are ultimately against God. Why is this so? All sin is contrary to God's will so the smallest sin offends God. Sin defies and disregards God's order for the universe. We may feel like the target of some people's cruelty and we certainly suffer the direct consequences of their actions, but we are not the target. Sinners aim at us but they hit God. We are made in the image and likeness of God, so sin strikes at the face of God. Sinners are not offending us nearly as much as they are offending God. When Paul attacked the early Christians with murderous intent, Jesus struck him with a blinding light and asked, *Saul, Saul, why are you persecuting me?* Jesus did not ask Paul why he was persecuting ordinary people. Rather, Jesus declares sin an offense against himself. *I am Jesus, whom you are persecuting.* Sin is contrary to love, and God is love, so sinners are separating themselves from God. When others hurt us, it counts as nothing compared to the fact that they destroy their relationship with their Creator. Have pity on poor sinners who separate themselves God.

⤳

Pray: O Lord, I realize all sin is ultimately against you and not me. I pray for all sinners to be reconciled with you.

POWER AND LOVE AND SELF-CONTROL

❖   ❖   ❖

For God did not give us a spirit of cowardice
but rather of power and love and self-control.

- 2 TIMOTHY 1:7

SOMETIMES OTHER PEOPLE are so mean that they diminish our courage and self-esteem. We may feel as if someone has robbed our home and stolen many valuable items, including our sense of safety and our ability to love. We may see our lives as having been cruelly turned upside down and our possessions strewn all over the floor. We may even be deprived of those things in life we most cherished. Now we are haunted by feelings of powerlessness, hatred, and unforgiveness. But God wants us to know that no one can steal his gifts from us. He has given us priceless gifts beyond the reach of any petty thief. He has bestowed upon us invaluable gifts of the spirit. God has given us *power and love and self-control.* If we do not feel powerful, or loving, or self-controlled, we need only turn to God in prayer and ask him to ignite these gifts he has hidden deep within us. Ask God to stir up his loving gifts in your soul today.

⁓

Pray: O Lord, stir up your gifts of power and love and self-control within me. Light your eternal flame of love.

THE MIGHTY HAND OF GOD

❖　❖　❖

Humble yourselves under the mighty hand of God,
that he may exalt you in due time.

- 1 PETER 5:6

WE DO NOT like to be slighted or insulted. It goes against our grain. It is natural to react with anger and indignation. We do not mind being humble when it suits us, when it is our decision. We find it easy to be humble on our own time and on our personal schedule, as when we kneel in church and pray. We can be humble when we want to be. But how do we react when humility is imposed upon us by someone else? We resent it when others put us down and try to make us feel humiliated. Who do they think they are? All our resentment fades away if we see the mighty hand of God at work. God holds us always in the palm of his hand. Nothing can reach you and no one can hurt you unless God allows the trial to pass through his fingers. God only allows us to experience hurt when it is for our good, to make us holy. Even then, he promises to exalt you in due time. *Cast all your worries upon him because he cares for you.*

⌒

Pray: O Lord, I want to accept all things in life
with humility, knowing you will exalt me in due time.

BE SOBER AND VIGILANT

❖ ❖ ❖

Be sober and vigilant. Your opponent the Devil is prowling around like a roaring lion, looking for someone to devour.

- 1 PETER 5:8

IT PAYS TO know your enemy. If we do not believe in the Devil, we will not recognize his evil stratagems in the world. While it is easy to believe in abstract evil, many think the Devil is just a medieval superstition. However, scripture is full of references to the Devil as an actual being, a fallen angel consumed with pride, envious of God and opposed to humans with an implacable hatred. When we believe in the existence of the Devil, our vision improves dramatically and we begin to see his malevolent influence in people and their actions. Not all offenders are influenced by the Devil, but some are. The Deceiver's greatest victory is to convince us that he does not exist. If we do not believe in the Devil's existence, we are surely in danger because he is *prowling around like a roaring lion looking for someone to devour.* When we can identify the Devil by his shady actions or influence, we can be sober and vigilant against his deceptions. *Resist him, steadfast in faith.*

⌐

Pray: O Lord, help me to be sober and vigilant. I will resist the Devil and seek to remain steadfast in my faith.

YOUR BROTHERS AND SISTERS

❖ ❖ ❖

Your brothers and sisters throughout the world
are undergoing the same sufferings.

- 1 PETER 5:9

ONE OF THE characteristics of suffering is that it makes us feel separated and isolated, but the truth is we are not alone. We are never alone because God is with us and we are members of a large family throughout the world who share similar experiences. We know what it feels like to experience the pain of disappointment, betrayal, disloyalty, or deception. We are united in our sufferings and we can unite our sufferings with Christ. Together we pray for each other for healing and the ability to forgive those who have trespassed against us. We find comfort and consolation in being part of our loving family. As good friends who share a common bond of life-giving love, we lift up our voices in prayer to God for the conversion of lost souls. Together we are strong and daily we shine the light of God's redeeming love into a dark and fallen world. Let us join our prayers together. We are the light of God's love to other people.

Pray: O Lord, I rejoice that I am not alone but part of a large family of brothers and sisters throughout the world.

AFTER YOU HAVE SUFFERED A LITTLE

❖ ❖ ❖

The God of all grace who called you to his eternal
glory through Christ Jesus will himself restore,
confirm, strengthen, and establish you after
you have suffered a little.

- 1 PETER 5:10

THERE IS NO way to sugar-coat it. Sin has real consequences, and when someone offends us, we suffer those painful consequences. Other people may affect us in many ways; we may experience loss of health, wealth, career, peace of mind, or relationships. How can we accept our sufferings? How can we find peace in the midst of our afflictions? The best way is to listen to God who is calling us daily to his eternal glory. If we listen carefully we can hear God's voice through his son Jesus. Can you hear his voice? Jesus is calling your name and promising that he will personally restore, confirm, strengthen, and establish you. By the power of God you are being re-created. Wait for it, watch for it, welcome it. You are being restored in Christ Jesus. You will be better than you were before.

⌣

Pray: O Lord, I thank you in advance for restoring me and making me stronger than ever by the power of your love.

I Am The Vine

❖ ❖ ❖

I am the true vine, and my Father is the vine grower. He takes away every branch in me that does not bear fruit, and everyone that does he prunes so that it bears more fruit.

- JOHN 15:1

HAVE YOU EVER seen a master gardener pruning a vineyard? He looks carefully at every vine and cuts off any branch that does not bear fruit. But he also prunes some branches that do bear fruit — causing them to bear even more fruit. Jesus does the same with us. If we are not bearing fruit, we are in danger of being completely cut off and thrown in the fire. However, Jesus may prune us even if we are bearing fruit — he knows this will cause us to grow much more fruit. So if you have been hurt by someone else, Jesus the master gardener has allowed you to be pruned. Even though it hurts, you may confidently trust the hand of your Creator. The Gifted Gardener is pruning you in order to create a greater harvest in your soul. As you bear God's new fruit to nourish yourself and others, pray for the persons who hurt you, for they are in danger of being cut off completely and cast into the brushfire.

Pray: O Lord, I trust you completely to prune my branches. Create in me a more bountiful harvest of love.

REMAIN IN ME

❖   ❖   ❖

*Remain in me, as I remain in you. Just as a branch
cannot bear fruit on its own unless it remains on the vine, so
neither can you unless you remain in me.*

- JOHN 15:4

WHEN JESUS COMPARES himself to the vine and us to the
branches, he emphasizes that we must remain in him,
as he remains in us. This makes sense because a branch receives
life from the vine, and Jesus is the source of life. As a branch
cannot survive apart from the vine, we cannot survive apart
from Jesus. *Anyone who does not remain in me will be thrown out
like a branch and wither.* A branch withers quickly when it is cut
off a vine. It dies suddenly and completely. So it is with us; if
we are cut off from Jesus, we wither and die. When something
bad happens to us, we may be tempted to blame God for not
protecting us. In our anger and disappointment we may turn
away from God and separate ourselves from him. Jesus calls us
to return to him and reconnect with his life-giving love. *I am
the vine, you are the branches. Whoever remains in me and I in
him will bear much fruit, because without me you can do nothing.*

‿

Pray: O Jesus, help me to turn to you in times of trouble. I
want to stay connected to you always.

YOU BEAR MUCH FRUIT

❖ ❖ ❖

If you remain in me and my words remain in you,
ask for whatever you want and it will be done for you.
By this is my Father glorified, that you bear much
fruit and become my disciples.

- JOHN 15:7

AGAIN JESUS EMPHASIZES the importance of remaining in him and allowing his words to remain in us. We must stay connected with him all the time, not just on Sundays or whenever we feel like it. If we want to receive life from Jesus we must abide in him, which means we must live in him, day and night. This may seem arduous or impossible, yet when we finally realize that Jesus is the true source of our life, we discover a deep desire to live in his loving presence continually. If we remain faithful, Jesus makes a surprising promise. *Ask for whatever you want and it will be done for you.* While this means asking according to his will, it still seems like an indulgent father wanting to spoil his child! Yet this is exactly what Jesus wants to do for us; he wants to bestow abundance on us so that we will become all that we were meant to be. God wants the best for us; he glorifies in blessing us. God wants you to *bear much fruit.*

⌒

Pray: O Lord, it is hard for me to imagine that you want
to give me such an abundance of blessings, but you do!

THINKING AS GOD DOES

❖ ❖ ❖

Get behind me, Satan!

- *MATTHEW 16:23*

WE MUST ACCEPT our sufferings in humility as the will of God in our lives. When Jesus announced that he must travel to Jerusalem to suffer and die, Peter protested. *God forbid, Lord!* Jesus responded with a shocking rebuke. *Get behind me, Satan!* Why did Jesus chastise his Peter so harshly? Because Jesus knew his destiny was the will of his Father. Peter's appeal to avoid suffering, while well-intentioned, was equivalent to Satan's temptation of Jesus to avoid suffering in the desert. Thus Jesus rebukes Peter. *You are not thinking as God does, but as human beings do.* Can we see ourselves as Peter, pleading with Jesus to avoid suffering? Yes of course, for we naturally desire to avoid all hardship. While this is usually a good intention, we must realize that some suffering is allowed by God for our good and for his eternal purposes. When we accept our suffering in humility, we allow God room to renew us and transform others. When Peter finally accepted Jesus as Lord, he was able to start thinking like God. Then Peter became the rock upon which Jesus could build his entire church. We must think as God does.

⸎

Pray: O Jesus, thank you for allowing my suffering. I join my suffering with yours to allow God to renew the world.

TAKE UP YOUR CROSS

❖ ❖ ❖

If any want to become my followers, let them deny themselves and
take up their cross and follow me.
For those who want to save their life will lose it, and
those who lose their life for my sake will find it.

- MATTHEW 16:24

ACCEPTING THE HURTS in our lives and forgiving others can be so difficult it feels like dying. The reason is because we really are dying in certain ways. We are being called to die to ourselves, our pride, and perhaps our hopes and dreams for the future. We are being handed a cross that we did not choose. We are being asked to carry this cross on steep paths we would rather avoid. This cross, we think, is too heavy and burdensome to carry. Why are we given this cross? Jesus explains that if we wish to follow him, we must deny ourselves and take up our cross. But why must we follow such a hard saying? The answer is one of life's greatest mysteries. *For those who want to save their life will lose it, and those who lose their life for my sake will find it.* We find the beauty and joy in life where we least expect it, in abandonment to divine providence. Jesus is our example. We can trust him and follow him.

Pray: O Lord, help me to lose myself for your sake.
Help me to carry my cross. I want to follow you joyfully!

FIRST TO THROW A STONE

❖   ❖   ❖

*Let the one among you who is without sin
be the first to throw a stone.*

- JOHN 8:7

A WOMAN IS caught in adultery and the elders stand her before Jesus in the temple area. They want to stone her according the law of Moses. They are self-righteous in their accusation and justified in their conviction. How swift is their rush to judgement! How bloodthirsty is their demand for condemnation and death! Jesus quietly kneels down and draws in the sand with his finger. What is he writing? Is he tracing the word "forgive" in the sand? Then Jesus speaks. *Let the one among you who is without sin be the first to throw a stone.* Jesus neither finds fault with the law nor excuses the prisoner's guilt. Jesus succeeds in bringing the accused woman to repentance, by showing her his mercy, and the prosecutors also, by showing them their *sins. Do not rejoice when your enemies fall, and when they stumble, do not let your heart exult.*

⌇

Pray: O Lord, instead of condemning others, let me be especially keen to repent of my own sins and become pure.

No Condemnation In Christ

❖ ❖ ❖

Neither do I condemn you. Go your way,
and from now on do not sin again.

- John 8:11

Do you hear a voice condemning you today? That is not the voice of Jesus. Are you judging others? That is not the judgement of Jesus. How easily we condemn others! Like the angry crowd condemning the adulterous woman, we demand justice! Yet when we turn our gaze within and recognize our own sins, we hang our heads in shame. One by one, our angry thoughts disperse. Gradually we return to ourselves and find peace in repentance. God assures us that justice belongs to him. Alone now with God, what about us? How will God judge our sinfulness? As he does with the adulterous woman, Jesus shows us his mercy. *Neither do I condemn you.* This is the central message Jesus brings to the world. Jesus comes not to condemn us, but to save us. We are truly happy who are not condemned but set free. Liberated by Christ's favor to us in the forgiveness of past sins, we are empowered to avoid those sins in the future and to find his path for our lives. *Go your way, and from now on do not sin again.*

Pray: O Lord, I believe in you there is no condemnation. Help me to deliver this good news to others.

GAINS AND LOSSES

❖ ❖ ❖

*Whatever gains I had, these I have come
to consider a loss because of Christ.*

- PHILIPPIANS 3:7

ARE YOU BEING asked today to give up something you cherish? Perhaps it is a person, possession, or your self-image. Would you be willing to give it up if Jesus asked you personally? As we grow in faith, Jesus gradually shows us that everything we once thought valuable is actually worthless. Compared to the supreme good of knowing Jesus, our previous successes fade into insignificance and we gladly release our tightly-held possessions. To the extent that our gains caused us to become prideful and self-centered, we now consider those gains as a loss because they prevented us from turning to God. *For his sake I have accepted the loss of all things and I consider them so much rubbish, that I may gain Christ and be found in him.* Now we can let go and let God flood us with love. Bathed in the divine light and ineffable love of Jesus, we find it easy to release others and forgive all offenses.

⁓

Pray: O Lord, nothing compares to knowing you. I gladly release all my cares and concerns into your loving hands.

FORGETTING WHAT LIES BEHIND

❖ ❖ ❖

*One thing I do, forgetting what lies behind
and straining forward to what lies ahead.*

- PHILIPPIANS 3:13

Do you ever wish you could forget the past? Forget everything that weighs you down, all the sins committed against you, and all the sins you have committed against others. Throw off all the bad memories. Start a new life, completely fresh. Believe it or not, this is possible. You can have a whole new life. Saint Paul explains how to do it. You begin by listening for the voice of God. Do you hear him softly calling your name? Be quiet now and listen. You must make it your total focus, the one thing you concentrate upon. Then you will hear the voice of the Father and you will be empowered by him to forget what lies behind. He will heal your memories and liberate you to live a new life. You will find yourself motivated to strain forward to what lies ahead. Imagine Jesus placing his hands on your head and whispering in your ear, "Forget." Now he grasps your hand and leads you forward, saying, "Let's go!" Exult as you press on toward your new goal of following him. *I press on toward the goal for the prize of the upward call of God in Christ Jesus.*

⌐

Pray: O Lord, thank you for helping me forget the past in order to focus on your upward call to new life with you.

THERE IS NO GREATER LOVE

❖   ❖   ❖

No one has greater love than this,
to lay down one's life for one's friends.

- JOHN 15:13

OUR LOVE FOR others may be measured by how much we are willing to give up for them. Are we willing to give up a little for others or a lot? What exactly are we willing to give up? Are we willing to give up our time, wealth, peace of mind, or health? When we consider how Jesus gave up everything and laid down his life for us, we discover our hearts growing softer to do the same for others. Especially when we meditate on the fact that Jesus laid down his life for us *while we were enemies*, we find a new and surprisingly peaceful ability to forgive others. Jesus calls us to love our friends and also our enemies. As Jesus is our example, we may love our enemies by laying down our lives too. This will give our enemies food for thought, a taste of God, nourishment for their souls. Just as we were converted, so may they be converted. As we were forgiven our sins, so may we show forgiveness to our enemies. God showed us the light of love, now we can show that same light to others.

Pray: O Lord, I thank you for loving me enough to lay down your life for me. I want to do the same for others.

GOD PROVES HIS LOVE

❖ ❖ ❖

God proves his love for us in that
while we were still sinners Christ died for us.

- ROMANS 5:8

ONE OF THE great turning points in life is when we realize that God has loved us always, even when we were still sinners. In fact, our sinfulness is precisely the reason he sent his son Jesus to earth to die for us on the cross - to forgive us for our sins. God proved his love for us by allowing his son to die for us while we were still his enemies. He did not wait for us to love him first. We wait for others to love us before we love them in return. We insist that others apologize before we forgive them. In contrast, God takes the initiative to make things right. God extends his love to us through Jesus as a living sacrifice to achieve the forgiveness of our sins. Now we are given the response-ability of extending God's love to others by offering ourselves as a living sacrifice. By forgiving others before they apologize, we show the world divine love and help people find God.

Pray: O Lord, you have proven your love for me beyond the shadow of a doubt. Help me show your love to others.

RECONCILED TO GOD

❖ ❖ ❖

While we were enemies, we were reconciled to God through the
death of his Son, how much more,
once reconciled, will we be saved by his life.

- ROMANS 5:10

LIKE THE MORNING mist that slowly dissipates to reveal a beautiful sunrise, our doubts disappear as we see God more clearly every day. Gradually we come to realize that he is drawing us closer to his side. As we begin to see through the haze of confusion and uncertainty against those who have trespassed against us, we discover that God has reconciled us to himself while we were still his enemies. To our delight, we comprehend that God has made us his friends. Through the death of his Son, we are forgiven and washed clean. As we stand under God with outstretched hands, he undams the endless reservoir of his mercy and engulfs us with the waters of his love. God has opened the doors of heaven and eternal life to each of us and we are free to enter. Now that we are reconciled to God by his love, how much more will be saved by having received new life in Christ! This is the greatest mystery in human history.

Pray: O Lord, I thank you for reconciling me to you. Help me to reconcile others to you by offering them forgiveness.

THE RIGHTEOUS WILL STAND

❖　❖　❖

*Then the righteous will stand with great confidence
in the presence of those who have oppressed them
and those who make light of their labors.*

- *WISDOM 5:1*

SOMETIMES WE FACE the temptation to be discouraged by other people. Their disregard, disrespect, or disdain can leave us feeling diminished and dispirited. We wonder if those who oppress us will ever relent and repent. In his infinite wisdom, God gives us peace of mind today by assuring us that we will soon stand with supreme confidence before those who have oppressed us. Our mighty God, who sees all people and all their actions, will one day balance all the scales of justice before our grateful eyes. Our eternal God, who holds the whole world in the palm of his hand, will one day gather all people to his royal court for final judgement. In that day those who made light of the labors of others will see the error of their ways. We will have the great privilege of standing with confidence on God's side, in the company of all the angels and saints, to witness this great spectacle. Let us be prepared to ask God to be merciful to our enemies and to forgive them as he has forgiven us. *Father, forgive them, for they know not what they do.*

⌒

Pray: O Lord, when I finally stand before my oppressors, give me the grace to ask you to forgive them for their sins.

He Saves Us From Our Sins

❖ ❖ ❖

She will bear a son and you are to name him Jesus,
because he will save his people from their sins.

- Matthew 1:21

BECAUSE SIN SEPARATES us from God, we have a big problem. God cannot bring us into his perfect presence unless
we are purified! But God provides the answer by sending his
beloved son to earth as a perfect living sacrifice to atone for our
sins. God chooses Mary to give birth to his son. Trusting God
in the midst of her confusion, Mary faithfully agrees. Later,
God sends an angel to explain this great mystery to Joseph. *She
will bear a son and you are to name him Jesus because he will save
his people from their sins.* Joseph humbly accepts his role and
names the child Jesus which means "God saves". So the birth of
Jesus becomes the answer to all our prayers and the solution to
all our problems by making possible the forgiveness of all our
sins. This is the central message of the entire life of Jesus: the
forgiveness of our sins.

Pray: O Lord, I am grateful beyond words for the greatest
gift of all, given by Jesus, the forgiveness of my sins.

SPEAK THE TRUTH IN LOVE

❖ ❖ ❖

Speaking the truth in love…

- EPHESIANS 4:15

O F ALL THE people you know, with whom would you like to speak the truth in love? One of the most difficult and loving things we can do for others is to tell them the truth. Especially when they are committing some kind of sin that could endanger their eternal souls, we are called to lovingly confront them and speak the truth. The alternative is to say nothing and then we share a portion of their guilt. If you are a passenger in a car and the driver is careening toward a cliff, you do not hesitate to shout a warning because both your lives depend upon it. When you hear gossip or a scandalous lie and say nothing to correct it, you abdicate your responsibility to tell the truth. If you say nothing to transgressors, you put their souls at risk and your own soul too. When you speak the truth in love, you lead all souls to heaven, especially those most in need of God's mercy. God always speaks the truth to us. When we practice speaking the truth in love, we *grow up in every way into him who is the head, into Christ.*

Pray: O Lord, give me a passionate love for your truth
so that I rejoice in speaking the truth to others with love.

WE BELONG TO GOD

❖ ❖ ❖

*We belong to God, and anyone who knows God
listens to us, while anyone who does not know God
refuses to hear us.*

- 1 JOHN 4:6

HAVE YOU EVER tried in vain to get someone to listen to you? You may have tried with all your heart, and tried to use just the right words, but failed. If that person would only listen, you are sure you could make him or her understand and be reconciled. But somehow that person turns a deaf ear towards you. Why? Perhaps he or she is unable to hear you, as someone who is paralyzed is unable to stand. Maybe he or she is simply unwilling to listen; sometimes people behave like children who prefer the sound of their own voices. In a situation like this, you may be sure of one thing; the person does not know God. Since God always listens to us, we should keep our ears open and listen to each other. If someone does not listen to you, despite your earnest appeals, you may be sure that person is not entirely listening to God either. You can tell a lot about people by whether or not they listen to you. The spirit of truth has open ears and hears everything, while the spirit of deceit has closed ears and hears nothing. *This is how we know the spirit of truth and the spirit of deceit.*

Pray: O Lord, I thank you for giving me the gift of listening.
Help me to pray for those who are deaf to you.

SHAKE THE DUST FROM YOUR FEET

❖　❖　❖

*If anyone will not welcome you or listen to your words,
shake off the dust from your feet as you leave that house
or town.*

- *MATTHEW 10:14*

HAVE YOU EVER had the unpleasant experience of knowing someone who uses you as a doormat for his or her own selfish purposes? It is no fun when someone walks all over you and leaves you mud-caked and alone. When is it okay to walk away? If you have tried repeatedly to talk with the person and explain how you want to be treated with respect, but he or she refuses to listen to your loving words, you may talk to your pastor about removing yourself from such an abusive situation. It may prompt the other person to wake up. While you can never give up praying for others, yourself or God — because God never gives up on us — there may come a time when you need to lovingly leave. *Shake off the dust from your feet as you leave that house or town.* Whether you decide to stay or leave, make it a daily habit to shake off the dust of your disgust and the dirt of your hurt. Shake free of resentment and remorse every day. Be free to love others as God loves you.

⁓

Pray: O Lord, teach me to love others as you love me,
even if I sometimes need to shake their dust from my feet.

GOD GAVE THEM UP

❖ ❖ ❖

Since they did not see fit to acknowledge God,
God handed them over to their undiscerning mind
to do what is improper.

- ROMANS 1:28

CAN WE GIVE up on someone who repeatedly offends us? In this verse God seems to give up on some evildoers who do not acknowledge him. But God never completely gives up on us as long as we are alive. He patiently waits for us with open arms. He wants us to turn back to him. We should never give up on anyone either. Nevertheless, if some people persist in their sins and refuse to acknowledge him, God will release them to do whatever they please. He will hand them over to indulge their narrow-minded cravings and become undiscerning reprobates. These sorry souls have jumped into a fearsome abyss from which not all return. When evildoers are hell-bent on following their own selfish desires, God will not condemn them to hell, but neither will he stand in their way. God does not force us to love him. After entreating them to turn back, we may follow our Lord's example and allow others to follow their wayward desires. In God's divine providence, there are none so lost as those who want to be lost, and none so found as those who wish to be found.

⌒

Pray: O Lord, I pray for the return of all the lost souls who have turned away from you to pursue their own desires.

THE WAGES OF SIN

❖ ❖ ❖

The wages of sin is death.

- ROMANS 6:23

WE MUST PITY those poor people who sin against us. Sin contains its own punishment, as surely as extinguishing a candle brings darkness. We know this is true because our daily life experience proves it. When we sin against another person, something inside us hardens and dies. Sin is life-destroying. Why is this? Because sin is contrary to God's will, it ruins our relationship with God. When we disconnect ourselves from our Creator, the source of all life, we instantly begin to die. As the branch withers when it is separated from the vine, we wither and die when we separate ourselves from God. Woe to those of us who turn away from God, for we cut ourselves off from the source of life. Happy are we who return to God, for our lives are nourished by an eternal spring of life! Only when we turn back to God can we reconnect with his life-giving love. As we live with new life every day, we grow to understand that the wages of sin is death, *but the gift of God is eternal life in Christ Jesus our Lord.*

Pray: O Lord, I pity those poor souls who have separated themselves from you by sinning against me. I pray for them to repent and turn back to you.

FILLED WITH COMPASSION

❖ ❖ ❖

While he was still a long way off, his father caught sight of him, and was filled with compassion. He ran to his son, embraced him and kissed him.

- LUKE 15:20

THE PARABLE OF the prodigal son teaches us that God loves us no matter how sinful we may have been. In this story, the wayward son finally comes to his senses and returns home. His father catches sight of him while he is still a long way off, revealing a father who is watching, waiting, longing for his son to return. Filled to overflowing with compassion, the father runs to embrace and kiss his long-lost son. The father arrives first, even before he hears his son ask for forgiveness! God waits the same way for each of us to return to him. Imagine God running down the road to greet you and embrace you with a bear hug! Hear God express his delight in your return. *Let us celebrate with a feast, because this son of mine was dead, and has come to life again; he was lost, and has been found.* Can you imagine doing this for someone who has offended you? God will empower you to forgive others even while they are still a long way off.

Pray: O Lord, fill me with your mercy and compassion
so that I may offer it to those who have injured me.

THIS MAN WELCOMES SINNERS

❖ ❖ ❖

This man welcomes sinners and eats with them.

- LUKE 15:2

OUR NATURAL INCLINATION is to shun people we find offensive, insulting or abusive. In contrast, Jesus got in a lot of trouble by spending time with the most isolated, alienated, and outcast members of society. He ate with criminals, prostitutes, and tax collectors. He mingled freely with people suffering from sickness, leprosy, and demon possession. He sought out people of all ages who were suffering from mental illness, depression, and despair. This made Jesus disreputable in the eyes of the elite. They condemned him for it and suggested he was guilty by association. He answered his critics by explaining that he came not to help the proud and haughty but rather to seek the lost. As the shepherd is keen to tend his scattered flock, Jesus welcomes sinners and eats with them.

⌒

Pray: O Jesus, I thank you for welcoming me to eat with you. Help me to welcome others to eat at your table too.

REJOICE WITH ME

❖ ❖ ❖

What man among you having a hundred sheep
and losing one of them would not leave the ninety-nine
in the desert and go after the lost one until he finds it?

- LUKE 15:4

D O YOU KNOW anyone who is a lost sheep? In this parable we learn how much God loves seeking a lost soul. When we are lost, God wants to rescue us. He is a devoted shepherd who leaves ninety-nine sheep in the desert to go after the lost one until he finds it. Do you know how passionately this shepherd loves you? Will you allow him to find you or do you prefer to hide from him? Would you rather be alone or will you allow him to return you to the safety and security of his flock? Imagine grazing peacefully in a pasture of lush green clover surrounded by friends. *And when he does find it, he sets it on his shoulders with great joy and, upon his arrival home, he calls together his friends and neighbors and says to them, 'Rejoice with me because I have found my lost sheep.'*

Pray: O Lord, I want to be found by you. Help me to seek others who are lost and return them home to you.

MORE JOY IN HEAVEN

❖ ❖ ❖

*I tell you, in just the same way there will be more joy in
heaven over one sinner who repents than over ninety-nine
righteous people who have no need of repentance.*

- LUKE 15:6

HAVE YOU EVER heard a huge crowd of people erupt with
cheering and applause? The noise is exhilarating. But
this loud ovation is merely a faint, muffled prelude compared
to the thunderous ovation in heaven that occurs when one sinner repents. When one lost soul repents, there is *more joy in
heaven than over ninety-nine righteous people who have no need
of repentance.* Imagine God dancing with delight! And it is not
only God who rejoices in the return of one humble soul. God
is joined by a great choir of angels and a multitude of saints
who raise their voices in a resounding chorus of joyful song
and praise. This divine celebration is mirrored by our personal
experience; we rejoice to high heaven when we are reunited
with a lost child, restored in a broken relationship, or reconciled to a wayward spouse. What can compare to the joy of
recovering the stolen, finding the lost, or reviving the dead?

Pray: O Lord, I know that when I turn to you, all heaven
rejoices. Help me to gently turn others toward you also.

AGAINST YOU ALONE

❖　❖　❖

Against you, you alone, have I sinned,
and done what is evil in your sight.

- PSALM 51:4

WHEN SOMEONE OFFENDS us, we naturally react with anger and resentment. We are righteously indignant. The blood rushes to our cheeks. How can a person be so mean? If we do not keep a tight rein on our anger it may gallop away like a wild horse that has jumped the corral fence. The best way to calm down is to recognize that all sin is ultimately against God. Because sin is contrary to God's will for the universe, sin disrupts the divine order of everything. While we may feel the painful effects of sin, we must remind ourselves that the other person has not offended us as much as he or she has offended God. In the fullness of time, God is the true victim, so to speak. In the midst of our pain, we may pity the poor people who offend us because we see how they have grievously offended God. Knowing this great truth makes it easier to forgive others. The same truth applies to us; when we sin against others, our offense is ultimately against God. This makes it easier for us to request and receive forgiveness from God and others. We may say to God with relief and gratitude *you are justified in your sentence and blameless when you pass judgment.*

Pray: O Lord, I know all sin is ultimately against you. Forgive me and forgive those who have sinned against you.

TEACH THE WICKED

❖ ❖ ❖

I will teach the wicked your ways,
that sinners may return to you.

- PSALM 51:15

TYPICALLY, WHEN WE are hurt by others, we want them to know how much we suffer as a result. Often we want them to get a taste of their own medicine. Alternately we yearn for someone in authority to teach them a lesson. But it may be that God wants you to be the person who teaches your offender a new way of thinking, feeling, or behaving. You may think you are the last person on earth to teach that person anything and you may be right. Nevertheless, if you pray about it, you may come to realize that God is calling you to speak truth to your offender. God wants everyone to learn his perfect ways, and he may want you to deliver his message of mercy and justice. *My tongue will sing joyfully of your justice.* Your words will either fall on deaf ears or penetrate a hardened heart, in which case the sinner will return to God. Speak God's wisdom to others without fear. *Lord, you will open my lips; and my mouth will proclaim your praise.*

Pray: O Lord, help me to know when you want me
to teach a certain sinner your loving ways of justice.
Then open my lips and give me your words of mercy.

A CONTRITE HEART

❖ ❖ ❖

My sacrifice, O God, is a contrite spirit; a contrite, humbled heart, O God, you will not scorn.

- PSALM 51:15

WHAT PARENT CAN resist a child whose eyes well up with tears? A small voice whimpering, "I'm sorry, Daddy" or "I'm sorry, Mommy" melts our heart every time and we embrace the child with love. "Do not cry," we whisper, "everything will be all right." God treats us in the same way. When we turn to God with a contrite spirit, he rushes to embrace us. As much as our pride causes us to flee from God, how much more does our humility cause God to fly to us and gather us in! Then we realize that he has been near us all along, waiting for us, yet we did not see him. He seeks us always and watches over us day and night. God is always ready to forgive us and welcome us home. Can we learn a lesson from him? Can we do the same to others who have offended us, neglected us, or caused us pain? We are never more like God than when we offer his divine unconditional mercy to other people.

⌒

Pray: O Lord, I offer you my contrite spirit as a living sacrifice. I know you find a humbled heart irresistible. Help me to show your mercy to others even when they flee.

THINGS NOT SEEN

❖ ❖ ❖

Now faith is the assurance of things hoped for,
the conviction of things not seen.

- HEBREWS 11:1

ONE OF THE biggest temptations is to think that the visible world is the only reality. According to this thinking, nothing is real unless we can see, touch, taste, smell or hear it. If God is invisible, does he really exist? Some people believe that all creation manifests the presence of a divine intelligence and proclaims the glory of our unseen God. Others insist that since we cannot prove the reality of God then he must not exist. In his infinite wisdom, rather than proving his existence to us beyond the shadow of a doubt, God calls upon us to have faith in him. This is a lifelong challenge and a profound mystery. God calls us quietly but unmistakably, in the cathedrals of our souls, to believe. He calls us to believe his promises before he makes good on them, to rejoice in his assurances that he will someday give us what we hope for, and to be grateful in advance of receiving our blessings. This is the essence of faith. It is not contrary to our reason; rather it is above and beyond our senses, illuminating our minds. Faith enables us to live joyfully in the presence of our unseen God. *The righteous person will live by faith.*

Pray: O Lord, I believe in you even when you feel far away. I delight in having faith and hope in your promises.

TO TEST YOU BY AFFLICTION

❖ ❖ ❖

Remember how for these forty years the Lord, your God,
has directed all your journeying in the wilderness, so as to
test you by affliction, to know what was in your heart: to
keep his commandments, or not.

- DEUTERONOMY 8:2

THERE ARE TIMES when we are so grievously injured by others that it seems the hurt will never end. Whether the injuries are to body, mind, heart, or soul, the pain is excruciating. We may feel closed in and cut off, isolated and alone. Years may pass with no end in sight. We question God's goodness and doubt his existence. In the midst of our desolation, God shines a bright shaft of hope into our darkness. This is a gift from God to us, assuring us that he is near. He gives us hope in spite of hopelessness, faith above reason, love without measure. We breathe a sigh of relief with the realization that God does not cause our trials and tribulations to prove our faith to him, rather he allows them in order for us to prove our faith to ourselves. Suffering refines, purifies and strengthens our faith as gold is refined by fire. God permits us to be tested by affliction for a higher good, so that we come to know what is in our hearts. In deeper faith we discover our love of God, and we glimpse the mystery of why he sent his son to suffer for us.

Pray: O Lord, I thank you for my afflictions. I know you are showing me how to share in the sufferings of your Son.

DO NOT JUDGE

❖ ❖ ❖

Do not judge, so that you may not be judged. For with the judgement you make you will be judged, and the measure you give will be the measure you get.

- MATTHEW 7:1

OUR NATURAL TENDENCY is to judge others. Most of us are keen to spot imperfections in our neighbors. We relish rushing to judgement and shouting it from the rooftops. Indeed, some of us are so critical of others and vocal in our condemnation that we sound like judge, jury, and executioner combined! Jesus cautions us against gossip, criticism and condemnation. He warns us that we will be judged by the same standards! If we show no mercy or charity to others, then neither will God show mercy to us. Does this mean we should turn a blind eye to the sins of others? Of course not. We are called to develop our moral compass. Our growth in spiritual maturity requires that we recognize the difference between good and evil. Jesus wants us to imitate him by cultivating virtue and avoiding vice, but we must not judge others rashly. *I did not come to condemn the world but to save the world.*

Pray: O Lord, help me refrain from criticizing and judging others. Cultivate in me a heart of mercy like yours.

THE LOG IN YOUR EYE

❖ ❖ ❖

*Why do you see the speck in your neighbor's eye, but
do not notice the log in your own eye? Or how can
you say to your neighbor, 'Let me take the speck out of
your eye,' while the log is in your own eye?*

- MATTHEW 7:3

HAVE YOU EVER noticed how easy it is to see the faults in other people? You can spot them instantly. Their flaws are so obvious, right? Especially when the other person's imperfections make your life miserable! Yet Jesus asks us to see things from a different perspective. Before we focus on the splinter in another's eye, Jesus wants us to look in a mirror and notice the big wooden log in our own eye. This is a hard thing to do, especially when we have been offended. We want to protest that we have done nothing wrong and we should not be accused. Nevertheless, Jesus requires us first to recognize and remove the sin in our own lives. *You hypocrite, first take the log out of your own eye, and then you will see clearly to take the speck out of your neighbor's eye.* Since we are typically most critical of sins in others that we possess ourselves, once we have removed the same sin from our lives we cease to find it so offensive in others, for we will have acquired the virtue of charity to more easily forgive that sin in them.

⌒

Pray: O Jesus, instead of criticizing other's defects, help me to
    look in the mirror and acquire more virtues myself.

IF WE ACKNOWLEDGE OUR SINS

❖ ❖ ❖

If we say, "We are without sin," we deceive ourselves,
and the truth is not in us. If we acknowledge our sins, he
is faithful and just and will forgive our sins.

- I JOHN 1:8

WE KNOW FROM painful experience that other people are sinful and need to repent. It is much more difficult to admit our own sins. In fact we are all sinful people. This is not surprising since we are imperfect people living in a fallen world. There were only two people who lived sinless lives: Jesus and Mary. We cannot deny that all the rest of us poor souls are sinners in need of forgiveness. This would be an impossible burden to carry if not for God's promise of mercy. The most wonderful truth in our lives is that if we acknowledge our sins, God is faithful and will forgive our sins. More to the point, he will *cleanse us from every wrongdoing.* Ponder this truth. Does God merely cleanse us from some of our mistakes? No, God assures us that he cleanses us from every sin. What a relief to know we are washed clean as a newborn baby!

⌒

Pray: O Lord, since I know in advance that you will forgive
every sin, I hasten to acknowledge my sins to you.

ALL HAVE SINNED

❖ ❖ ❖

All have sinned and fall short of the glory of God.

- ROMANS 3:23

JUST WHEN WE start to get comfortable with ourselves and think we are living virtuous lives, we slip and fall again. Our mistakes and the failures of others remind us of our need to turn to God for strength daily to resist temptation. Our stumbling can actually serve a good purpose; it puts us on our knees and makes us realize our dependence upon God. In this position of humility, our weaknesses make us humble and give us more compassion for others who share similar weaknesses. We may lose our indifference and discover pity for those who have offended us. We share defects, infirmities and temptations that are common to all humankind throughout history. To one degree or another, we all have feet of clay, and yet we are capable of reaching for the stars. Although we all have sinned and fall short of the glory of God, he can use our sinfulness to jolt us awake and point us in the right direction. God always points us forward but never backward, up but never down, and he always asks us to lend a hand to others. Instead of sinning and falling short of our dreams, we may practice virtue and find ourselves rising on eagles' wings toward the glory of God.

⌐

Pray: O Lord, shield and protect me against all temptation to sin. I want to grasp your hand and practice virtue.

I Was Born In Guilt

❖   ❖   ❖

Behold, I was born in guilt,
in sin my mother conceived me.

- Psalm 51:7

As we grow in spiritual maturity, we begin to understand that our sinfulness goes deeper than our own wrongdoing. We start to understand that we were born into a fallen world that is filled with imperfect people. We like to think of babies as being innocent, and in a way they are, for they have not yet sinned, yet they enter a world tainted by the sins of their parents, their grandparents, and all their ancestors back in time. How could a child not be adversely affected by such deeply ingrained sin? We begin to realize that we have all inherited this tendency to temptation and selfishness. Gradually we see the truth of the biblical account of how Adam and Eve sinned by pridefully seeking their own way and disobeying God, thereby ruining the perfect Garden of Eden in which they lived. Now we struggle to be free of their original sin. We also strain to forgive our ancestors, ourselves, and others. We cannot do it alone, but Jesus has won our freedom for us by sacrificing himself on the cross to atone for our sins. We must still struggle against sin, and this is worthy and meritorious, but Jesus has already won the ultimate victory.

Pray: O Lord, in this fallen world I need your help. Thank you for helping me learn to give and receive forgiveness.

I KNOW MY OFFENSES

❖ ❖ ❖

My offenses truly I know them; my sin is always before me.

- PSALM 51

W E KNOW WE are growing in spiritual awareness when the sins of others causes us to be mindful of our own limitations. As when a child's temper tantrum reminds us of our tendency to become angry, the offenses of other adults may reawaken memories of our own past sins. However, God does not want our sins to be always before us. He wants to relieve us of our heavy burden. He forgives us once and for all, as if it had never happened, so we need to do the same. God takes away our sins *as far as the East is from the West.* He does not want us to keep rehashing our sins or the sins of others. We need to forgive ourselves and others the way God forgives us — once and for all. God wants us to place all our sins and the sins of others in a basket and give them to him to deal with. He wants us to lay all sins at the foot of the Cross and then leave them there. He does not want us to come back to dig them up and take them home again!

⌐

Pray: O Lord, I place all my sins and the sins of others at the foot of the Cross. Thank you for forgiving everything!

CONFESS AND OBTAIN MERCY

❖ ❖ ❖

*Those who conceal their sins do not prosper, but those
who confess and forsake them obtain mercy.*

- PROVERBS 28:13

I T CAN BE frustrating to watch people who have done wrong
succeed. But rather than envy them, we should pity them.
People who commit sin in secret may prosper for a time with
worldly success, but their wrongdoing will surely find them
out someday. While they prosper on the outside temporarily,
they are crumbling on the inside eternally. They benefit their
bodies and profit their wallets but damage their hearts and dis-
integrate their souls. Like a fine house with hidden termites, a
person who conceals his or her own sins is crumbling within.
The good news is that we have a remedy. If we confess our sins
and repent of them, we will obtain God's healing mercy. God
promises to forgive us for all of our sins. No sin is too grievous
or extreme for God; he washes away all our sins as if they had
never happened. He puts them as far away from us *as the east is
from the west.* God knows all our sins, but he wants us to confess them. He wants us to acknowledge our utter dependence
on his mercy. *If we confess our sins, he is faithful and just, and
will forgive our sins and cleanse us from all unrighteousness.*

⌒

Pray: O Lord, heal all the hidden sins in my heart today.
Help me to lead others to you for the same healing!

YOUR GRIEF WILL BECOME JOY

❖ ❖ ❖

Amen, amen, I say to you, you will weep and mourn,
while the world rejoices; you will grieve,
but your grief will become joy.

- JOHN 16:20

THERE IS NO getting around it: life can be painful. Life is beautiful, to be sure, but it can also be hurtful, as when other people behave badly and cause us suffering. Then we weep and mourn for a season. We weep for the brokenness in ourselves and others. Our tears may blur our vision and cause us to think that the world rejoices while we suffer alone. Jesus tells us to expect these seasons and to be prepared to endure them as an unavoidable part of life in this fallen world. But he assures us that our grief is only for a season. As difficult as it is to imagine in our present circumstances, our grief will soon become joy. Jesus compares our suffering to the anguish of a woman in labor; when she has given birth, *she no longer remembers the pain because of her joy that a child has been born into the world.* If we offer our suffering to Jesus, he will use it to create new life in loving hearts that beat strongly for him. *I will see you again, and your hearts will rejoice, and no one will take your joy away from you.*

⁓

Pray: O Jesus, I offer all my sufferings to you as a labor of love. I know you will soon turn all my grief into joy!

I WILL COMFORT YOU

❖ ❖ ❖

As a mother comforts her child, so will I comfort you.

- ISAIAH 66:13

IS THERE A happier sight than a baby resting in its mother's arms? The baby awakes and weeps, but the mother hushes its fears and soothes its vain alarms until the baby sleeps peacefully again. God promises to comfort us like a loving mother! In the midst of our worries we may relax and trust that everything we need is near. Can you imagine God as your mother? We typically think of God as our Father but God created us male and female, in his image, so God possesses both masculine and feminine qualities. This is a great mystery. Perhaps it is easier for you to think of being comforted by Mary, the mother of Jesus. *As nurslings, you shall be carried in her arms, and fondled in her lap.* In a more visible way, all followers of Jesus are described as the Bride of Christ, so we are all called to nourish, help, and encourage each other with the love of Christ. *When you see this, your heart shall rejoice and your bodies flourish like the grass.*

Pray: O Lord, today I rest peacefully in your loving arms. Help me to nurture others and love them as you love me.

I Have Conquered The World

❖ ❖ ❖

In the world you will have trouble, but take courage,
I have conquered the world.

- John 16:33

D o you ever feel as if you are losing the battle of life? Your troubles seem to multiply and your adversaries threaten to overwhelm you. Trouble in this world is certainly unavoidable, but we can take courage because Jesus has already won the war. He informs us of this truth specifically by proclaiming his victory. *I have conquered the world.* How can this be true, you wonder, when you are still experiencing a battle? Your battle today is a minor skirmish in the aftermath of victory; Jesus has won the war. By his death and resurrection Jesus has vanquished Satan and conquered death. In the heat of your battle today you may fight fearlessly with the assurance of victory in Jesus' name. Hear Jesus calling you forward with the confidence that your victory is important for the consummation of all things into this holy hands. *I have told you this so that you might have peace in me.*

⌇

Pray: O Lord, I have complete faith, hope, and trust that you have conquered the world. I will follow you anywhere!

I Bear The Marks Of Jesus

❖ ❖ ❖

I bear the marks of Jesus on my body.

- *Galatians 6:17*

I F SOMEONE HAS hurt you physically, the wounds you suffered need not be unpleasant reminders that prevent you from forgiving. Instead of seeing your scars as something entirely negative, consider the possibility that you bear the marks of Jesus on your body. You share his injuries! Jesus was wounded by the sins of the whole world. He accepted these wounds on the cross in order to open the gates of heaven to everyone who wishes to follow him. By accepting your injuries and offering them up to God, you are sharing in the sufferings of Christ and helping to redeem the world. Can you see how this is both a responsibility and a privilege? It is also a great mystery. In the same way Jesus suffered on his cross, you are suffering on your cross. Join your pain with the pain of Jesus. Let God heal you, raise you up, and give you new life! Praise God for allowing you to help him redeem lost souls. *May I never boast except in the cross of our Lord Jesus Christ, through which the world has been crucified to me, and I to the world.*

Pray: O Lord, help me to accept my injuries and forgive those who wounded me. Turn my scars into stars!

YET WITHOUT SIN

❖ ❖ ❖

We do not have a high priest who is unable to sympathize with our weaknesses, but one who in every respect has been tempted as we are, yet without sinning.

- *HEBREWS 4:15*

WHEN WE GIVE in to temptation, and then stumble and fall, we become exasperated by our lack of progress. We feel so miserably weak in our natural human state. Though we are often strong and steadfast, at other times our human faults seem to weigh us down. We reach for the stars, then fall into the gutter. We start to blame God and wonder why he does not deliver us from our sins. We pray for deliverance from evil, but we continue to get stuck in the mud. We think God in his perfection cannot understand us with our defects. Yet God assures us that he does indeed sympathize with us in our weaknesses. How can this be? God sent his son Jesus to be born of a human mother, Mary, so that Jesus might share in our humanity. Thus Jesus was both fully human and fully divine. In his humanity Jesus was tempted *in every respect* as we are, by every sin we face in our lives, so he understands all our temptations. He wants us to bring our difficulties to him. Can you allow your failures to turn you toward Jesus? He understands you better than you understand yourself.

⌒

Pray: O Jesus, I know you understand me perfectly.
Lead me not into temptation, but deliver me from evil.

HAVE MERCY ON ME

❖ ❖ ❖

Have mercy on me, God, in accord with your merciful love;
in your abundant compassion blot out my transgressions.

- PSALM 51:3

REMEMBER A TIME in your life when you were sick but then you turned the corner and began to feel better? Perhaps your fever diminished, your stomach settled, and you felt your strength return. With a sigh of relief, you knew healing had begun. In this verse the Psalmist comes to a great healing point in his life. He is overcome with grief because of his own transgressions. He is no longer concerned with the offenses of others, rather he seeks God's forgiveness for his own sins. Notice how he approaches God with confidence. He trusts that God will smile upon him with abundant compassion and wipe away all his sins with merciful love. *Thoroughly wash away my guilt; and from my sin cleanse me.* This is the moment God has been waiting for, this is the time for healing. We cannot heal others until we have been healed. We cannot forgive others their sins until we first experience God's forgiveness of our own sins. Will you ask God to heal you? *Wash me, and I shall be whiter than snow.*

⌒

Pray: O Lord, I thank you for promising me in advance that
you delight in healing me of all my sins.

DESIGNED TO BE LIVED IN

❖ ❖ ❖

*Thus says the Lord, the creator of the heavens, who is God, the
designer and maker of the earth who established it,
not creating it to be a waste, but designing it to be lived in.*

- ISAIAH 45:15

WHEN SOMEONE HURTS us, we resent that person. If we
are honest with ourselves, we are also angry at God for
allowing the hurt in our lives. This sets up a chain reaction in
which we end up questioning whether life has any purpose.
Is life worth living? Our Lord gives us the answer we need to
hear. The answer is emphatically yes! God has lovingly created
the heavens and established the earth and given it all to us for
our benefit. He originally planned it to be a paradise for us, *not
creating it to be a waste, but designing it to be lived in.* However,
as a result of the disobedience of our first parents Adam and
Eve, our paradise was lost. But Jesus has reclaimed it; now our
glorious task is to cooperate with God in renewing the face of
the earth. Life is absolutely worth living, always and everywhere, fearlessly in all circumstances, in good times and in
bad, because all life is a gift from God! Without a doubt, God
wants us to live our lives to the fullest. One of the best ways to
live an abundant life is by forgiving others as God forgives us.

⏝

O Lord, I rejoice that you originally created the world as a perfect place to live. I want to help you recreate the world.

THE GOODNESS OF THE LORD

❖ ❖ ❖

I would have despaired unless I had believed that I would see the goodness of the Lord in the land of the living.

- PSALM 27: 13

I F WE PAY too much attention to news and gossip, we begin to lose hope in the future. When we narrow our focus to the wickedness and selfishness in this fallen world, we can quickly become depressed to the point of despair. What is the remedy? We need a shaft of sunlight to break through the dark clouds overhead. We need to pray for the gift of faith. Only when we receive the blessing of spiritual vision will we perceive the light of the Son that always shines above the clouds of doubt and despair. Ask God to let you see the world as he sees it. Gradually God will shine his light into your darkness, illuminating for you the wonders of his original creation, besmirched now by sin but daily washed clean by his goodness. Inspired by God's goodness, millions of faithful Christians like you joyfully wash the grimy face of this muddy world with the soap of mercy, the sponge of forgiveness, and the water of pure love.

Pray: O Lord, I jump for joy when I see your goodness at work cleansing people. Help me to be more forgiving!

SAY ONLY GOOD THINGS

❖   ❖   ❖

*Never let evil talk pass your lips; say only the good things men
need to hear, things that will really help them.
Do nothing that will sadden the Holy Spirit.*

- EPHESIANS 4:29

D O YOU KNOW that you can make God sad? We may not
think we can make God happy or sad but indeed we
can. As a parent is delighted with an obedient child and saddened by a disobedient one, God is gladdened or saddened by
us. In this verse Saint Paul says we make the Holy Spirit sad
by evil talk. How easy it is for us to engage in gossip, criticism, and malicious conversation! Yet this saddens the Holy
Spirit. Scandal-mongering, rumor spreading, and crude talk
injure everyone, including all the listeners and the speaker. The
tongue is indeed a powerful weapon for destruction, but it can
also be used to teach, instruct, and help other people. Try this
today; refrain from allowing any evil talk to pass your lips. *Say
only the good things men need to hear, things that will really help
them.* This will soften your heart to be more patient with the
sins of others and it will gladden the Holy Spirt.

⌒

Pray: Come Holy Spirit, guide my words and help me
say only the good things that will really help other people.

BE KIND TO ONE ANOTHER

❖ ❖ ❖

Get rid of all bitterness, all passion and anger,
harsh words, slander, and malice of every kind. In place of
these, be kind to one another, compassionate, and mutually
forgiving, just as God has forgiven you in Christ.

- EPHESIANS 4:29-32

BEFORE WE CAN forgive others, we need to get rid of our bitterness and anger toward them. We may protest that this is an impossible task because others are the cause of our anger in the first place! How can we forgive others and feel kindly towards them when they have not even apologized? Nevertheless, God calls us to a higher level of existence. He calls us to rise above our hostility and resentment. God wants us to soar above the storm clouds of malice. This is impossible for us to accomplish using our strength alone. We need to pray for his divine help. God replaces our harsh feelings with kindness and compassion. Like a bird that is learning to fly, we realize we can forgive others just as God has forgiven us. The more often we ask for God's forgiveness and receive it gratefully, the easier it is for us to forgive others.

Pray: O Lord, replace all my bitterness and anger
toward others with compassion, kindness and forgiveness.

KNOWLEDGE OF SALVATION

❖　❖　❖

You will go before the Lord to prepare his way,
to give his people knowledge of salvation
by the forgiveness of their sins.

- LUKE 1:76

THIS VERSE WAS said to John the Baptist by his father who knew that all the sufferings John would endure in his life would serve the great purpose of preparing the way for Jesus. Can you imagine how these same words might apply to you? Have you ever stopped to consider that all your trials and tribulations may be preparing you for some wonderful purpose? God can take any situation, no matter how dark, or any experience, no matter how hurtful, and turn it into something good. By faith we believe that our lives are tailor-made for us, fitting us for a special purpose: to help prepare the way of the Lord. While you may think you labor in vain or suffer in obscurity, you are growing spiritually behind the scenes. God is secretly at work in your life to help you lead other people to him. Clear away all the obstacles to God! Ask God to forgive your sins; then you will awaken to the reality of your eternal future with him. When you forgive others their sins, you give them knowledge of the possibility of their own salvation.

Pray: O Lord, I know forgiveness prepares your kingdom on earth and brings us divine knowledge of our salvation.

A New Heart

❖   ❖   ❖

*I will give you a new heart, and a new spirit I will
put within you. I will remove the heart of stone from
your flesh and give you a heart of flesh.*

- *Ezekiel 36:26*

I F YOUR HEART is breaking today for any reason, rejoice in
the knowledge that God has a new one in store for you.
God knows our human hearts are stony, flint-like and liable
to break. Like an expert heart surgeon, God stands ready to
touch your heart of stone and transform it into a new heart
of flesh, strong and healthy. No longer will you remember the
days when your heart of stone caused you pain inside your
chest and made your head throb. Your new heart will function
perfectly, softly beating day and night, pumping the blood of
pure love in your veins throughout your entire body. God will
also place within you a new spirit to guide, protect and energize
you. This is the Holy Spirit, the third member of the Trinity,
who will live quietly, prayerfully and serenely in the cathedral
of your soul. You are the temple of the Holy Spirit, a great gift
from God. *I will put my spirit within you so that you walk in my
statutes, observe my ordinances, and keep them. I will deliver you
from all your impurities.*

Pray: O Lord, thank you for removing my broken heart
of stone and replacing it with a healthy heart of flesh.

THE GOLDEN RULE

❖ ❖ ❖

Do to others as you would have them do to you.

- MATTHEW 7:12

HERE JESUS TEACHES us the Golden Rule, to treat others as we would have them treat us. This is the foundation of all the laws and prophets throughout history. How simple this is! Think how world would be transformed if everyone put this teaching into action! You desire that others should approach you with kindness, fairness, and respect: therefore treat others the same way. On the other hand, since you prefer that others not criticize, offend, or judge you, do not do these things to others. We must not return the evil done to us. This follows the great commandment, *Thou shalt love thy neighbor as thyself.* Because God created us, we are all mysteriously connected in God, so we must put others on the same level as ourselves. We must remember that everyone is entitled to the same benefit of justice that we expect for ourselves. This reflection increases our compassion, empathy, and mercy. If we fail to extend forgiveness to others, how can we expect God to extend forgiveness to us?

Pray: O Lord, thank you for teaching me the Golden Rule.
Help me to demonstrate it to others so they learn it too.

You Are Sinning Against Christ

❖ ❖ ❖

When you sin against members of your family, and wound their conscience when it is weak, you sin against Christ.

- I Corinthians 8:12

WE DO NOT usually think this way but it is true; all sins are ultimately against Christ. Why? Because God created us through Christ, so we are all connected in Christ. *All things came into being through Him, and apart from Him nothing came into being.* When we sin against another person created in God's image, we sin against our Creator. So if someone offends you, Christ is offended. Every time someone hurts you, that person lashes Christ's back with a whip. If you forgive that person, you heal Christ's wounds. Likewise, if you offend someone, you actually offend Christ. When you sin against your brothers, you add a thorn to Christ's crown. You do not want to add to Christ's suffering on the cross, do you? Certainly not. When you ask for forgiveness, you heal Christ's wounds.

Pray: O Jesus, I rejoice in washing and cleansing your wounds by asking for forgiveness and giving it to others.

We Are All Connected

❖　❖　❖

*There is but one God, the Father, from whom all things came
and for whom we exist. And there is but one Lord, Jesus Christ,
through whom all things came and through whom we exist.*

- 1 Corinthians 8:6

W E ARE NEVER alone. When we awaken to the fact that
we are connected to every other person because we share
one common Creator, our understanding of forgiveness changes
radically. We are not independent and alone, as it seems, to do
as we please. Rather we are all interrelated and interconnected
because we originated in one God. We are all brothers and sisters
in Christ; we are all related as sons and daughters of God. *Do we
not all have one father? Has not one God created us?* Our lives are
like a magnificent tapestry woven with a single divine thread. In
places the thread is broken and frayed by unkindness, yet else-
where it is bound up and repaired by a careful soul. Whether we
know it or not, we owe our existence to God. We may choose to
disobey him, but we owe our lives to God, *from whom all things
came*, and to Jesus, *through whom all things came,* and to the Holy
Spirit, by whom we are sustained. When we see this clearly, our
lives are transformed. Gradually we perceive traces of ourselves
in the fragmented lives of others and then we can start forgiving
them to heal their broken souls.

Pray: O Lord, I thank you for showing me how we are all connected in you. Help me to heal the broken connections.

WE ARE CALLED TO UNITY

❖　❖　❖

Father, that they may be one, as we are one.

- JOHN 17:22

BELOVED, DO YOU understand the deepest reality of life, that we are all connected? We are all connected because we are all created by God; we are united in sharing the same Creator. We are members of one body in Christ. Jesus wanted his followers to understand this truth above all. Three times at the Last Supper he prayed to his Father *that they may be one,* as he is one with his Father and the Holy Spirit. Jesus wants to gather us together and share his life in perfect harmony. When you understand this essential unity of all things in Christ, you can see beneath all outward appearances and past the delicate veil that covers all creation. You will see with Jesus' eyes, think with his mind, touch with his hands, and walk in his footsteps. Jesus will replace your heart of stone with a heart of flesh that will soar with the love of unity and community and break with the sorrow of division and separation. There is no better way to help unify the world than to forgive estranged people and reconcile them with yourself, with each other, and with God.

Pray: O Lord, I see that we are all connected in you. Help me always to forgive and unify others as you do!

ONE MIND, ONE HEART, ONE SPIRIT

❖ ❖ ❖

*I appeal to you… that all of you agree and
that there be no dissensions among you, but that
you be united in the same mind.*

- *1 CORINTHIANS 1:10*

IN UNITY WE find harmony, love and power. But disunity causes discord, hatred and weakness. One of the signs that we live in a fallen world is our tendency toward division; even the disciples who lived in the holy presence of Jesus argued and disagreed about who should sit at his right hand. To emphasize the supreme importance of unity, Paul spent most of his time exhorting the faithful to stop their disagreements and be unified *by being of the same mind, with the same love, united in heart, thinking one thing.* If it was so difficult for the disciples to live in peace and understanding then, is it any wonder that we still struggle to find unity today? Yet we can achieve it by forgiving one another, as we have been forgiven, and by loving one another as Christ loves us. We can live as God wants us to live, in perfect harmony, *standing firm in one spirit, with one mind, struggling together for the faith of the gospel.* When we strive to gather ourselves together and allow Christ to unify us, he blesses us with his divine grace and we experience a heavenly explosion of his infinite love.

Pray: O Jesus, please give me your mind, heart, and love. Help me to unify those who have yet to really know you!

THE MIND OF CHRIST

❖ ❖ ❖

We have the mind of Christ.

- 1 CORINTHIANS 2:16

BELOVED, IF YOU are beset by the cares and confusions of this world and you sometimes feel as if you are losing your mind, then put on the mind of Christ. You need not be weak-minded, troubled, or fearful. Instead, remember that Jesus lives in you and you live in him! He wants to give you the benefit of his wisdom, spirit, and strength to live your life to the fullest. He wants you to understand the awesome power of his mind, thoughts, and words. You know the mind of Christ when you experience the delightful, sacrificial power of forgiving others. Tap into this heavenly power, let his love excite your dormant mind, and become a channel for his mercy to others. Of course, you cannot put on the mind of Christ if you are focused on your own selfish pursuits. *Do not conform yourselves to this age but be transformed by the renewal of your mind, that you may discern what is the will of God, what is good and pleasing and perfect.* Jesus wants to draw you near and infuse you with the spirit of his love so intimately that you are transformed by divine unity and redeemed to share your life in the blessed Trinity.

⌒

Pray: O Jesus, help me put on your mind every morning to see the world anew, as you see it, with kindness and mercy!

THE WORLD DID NOT RECOGNIZE HIM

❖   ❖   ❖

*He was in the world, and though the world was
made through Him, the world did not recognize Him.*

- JOHN 1:10

N O MATTER HOW hard we try, sometimes it seems impossible to get through to some hard-headed people. They either react negatively to everything we say or they just plain ignore us. If only we could convince them that we have their best interests at heart, we imagine they would change! In the meantime, they turn a blind eye or deaf ear towards us and act as if we do not exist. It is enough to make a person feel invisible. If you have felt this way, you are not alone. People acted the same way toward Jesus. They shunned him, scoffed at him, and doubted him every step of the way. Most people did not recognize him then, and they still do not recognize him today. His enemies crucified him *though the world was made through him.* Yet he forgave them while he was on the cross. Most people today still doubt the promises of Jesus, yet he calls everyone to his side. So do not despair if some people do not recognize you and your loving intentions; take comfort in knowing that they did not recognize Jesus either.

Pray: O Jesus, thank you for helping me recognize you.
I want to forgive others to help them recognize you too.

OVERCOME EVIL WITH GOOD

❖ ❖ ❖

Do not be overcome by evil, but overcome evil with good.

- ROMANS 12:21

WE DO NOT have to live very long in this world before we are confronted by evil. Often it is something small, but occasionally it is something large. It makes us feel angry and indignant. What is the best way to deal with evil? We can retaliate with destructive words, escalate with lawsuits, or annihilate with weapons. Our Lord sets us on a different course toward peace by assuring us that we need not be overcome by evil. Instead God wants us take a radical new direction to overcome evil with good. God gives us the example of his son Jesus who chose the course of kindness, forgiveness and love. While it seems preposterous to confront a wicked world with love, nevertheless that is precisely the way of Jesus. Instead of striking back at his enemies, he absorbed their injuries in his body and trusted his heavenly Father to heal him. This served to transform many of his enemies into friends and opened the doors of heaven. This is the deep mystery of sacrificial love that Jesus used to overcome evil.

⌒

Pray: O my Jesus, as much as it hurts, I want to overcome evil with good. Help me to love and forgive all evildoers.

My Face I Did Not Hide

❖ ❖ ❖

I gave my back to those who beat me,
my cheeks to those who tore out my beard;
my face I did not hide from insults and spitting.

- Isaiah 50:6

THERE ARE TIMES when we need to stand up for ourselves against people who trouble us. Other times, guided by prayer and the counsel of faithful friends, we turn the other cheek. Can we really do this in good conscience? Yes. When we separate ourselves from an abusive person, we can accept the sad fact he or she may never change. This is an opportunity to experience humility, a chance to practice tough love, and a time to exercise our faith! Perhaps God has allowed us to suffer insults and abuse, not because he wills it or approves of it, but rather to give us an occasion to place our trust entirely in him. He promises to make all things right. If you are mistreated by some, remember Jesus was treated the same way. Surely on the cross Jesus' face was unrecognizable, covered with blood, spit and tears. As you share the humiliation experienced by Jesus, know you will share his resurrection to new life. *Then they spat in his face and struck him, while some slapped him, saying, "Prophesy for us, Messiah: who is it that struck you?"*

⌐

Pray: O my Jesus, show me when to turn the other cheek. I do not want to hide my face from others or from you.

I Have Set My Face Like Flint

❖ ❖ ❖

The Lord God is my help, therefore I am not disgraced;
Therefore I have set my face like flint, knowing that
I shall not be put to shame.

- Isaiah 50:7

How is it possible to turn the other cheek? How did the martyrs and prophets in ancient times accept their persecution without fighting back? The only way to submit to the flames and arrows of others is by putting your trust completely in God. This is not an easy thing to do. Yet with practice you can finally get to the point where you really do place yourself in the hands of your loving God. He is your protection and help in every circumstance. He gives you the power and the ability to set your face like flint. In his eyes you are not disgraced, no matter how humiliating your life may seem. God is faithful to you even when others are not. In his embrace you know that you shall never be put to shame, regardless of how others may try to insult or injure you. You fight not with weapons of malice and steel but rather with healing balms of God's love and forgiveness.

⌒

Pray: O Lord, I know you are my ever-present help in
all circumstances, protecting me from disgrace and shame.

PLANS FOR GOOD AND NOT EVIL

❖ ❖ ❖

I know the plans I have for you, says the Lord, plans for welfare and not for evil, to give you a future and a hope.

- JEREMIAH 29:11

I F THE dark clouds of disappointment have gathered over
your head and a melancholy drizzle is adding to your misery,
it may seem as if the future is bleak. You may have prayed for
hours or days or years yet heard nothing. The darkness itself
seems to mock you in silence. You may be tempted in sleep-
less desperation to conclude that God has given up on you. In
your misery you may condemn yourself and conclude that you
deserve to be deserted. Even worse, you may question whether
God exists or cares about a world so full of woe. Fear not, take
courage: God is near the brokenhearted. Into your darkness
God shines the light of his promise that he has good plans for
you. In spite of all outward appearances, he is secretly at work
on these plans. God's design for your life is for good and not
evil, for your welfare and not for woe. Out of the cinders he is
fashioning a new forest of life with tall timbers that will tower
over everything that has caused you grief. Your long spreading
branches will reach for the sky. God promises his wonderful
plan is *to give you a future and a hope.*

⤳

Pray: O Lord, I rejoice that your plan for my life
is unfolding daily for my good and not for evil.

SEEK THE WELFARE OF OTHERS

❖ ❖ ❖

Seek the welfare of the city to which I have exiled you;
pray for it to the Lord, for upon its welfare
your own depends.

- *JEREMIAH 29:7*

I T IS HARD enough to forgive one person. Sometimes our task
is multiplied and we need to forgive a group of people. People
have a sad tendency to gang up, and the unthinking mob mental-
ity takes over. Rightly or wrongly, groups of people often create
a scapegoat on whom to vent their frustrations. If you have ever
been on the receiving end of the madness of a crowd, you know
how daunting it can be. You may have experienced this with a
group of people in your family, school, workplace, or your church.
Perhaps you were bullied, misjudged or rejected. Your reputation
and self-esteem may have suffered. Gossip and the court of public
opinion are harsh and unforgiving. Remember what the crowds
did to Jesus? They crucified him. Just as Jesus prayed, you are
called upon to pray for those who persecute you. Others may have
caused you to feel like an outcast in your own home or an exile in
your own city, but God wants you to pray for others. Your welfare
depends upon it. Why? Because God is love, and love always seeks
the best for others, and God wants you to be like him!

⌐

Pray: O Lord, help me to pray for the group of people
who persecuted me. Help me sincerely to forgive them.

SHAKE THE DUST FROM YOUR FEET

❖ ❖ ❖

Whoever will not receive you or listen to your words
go outside that house or town and
shake the dust from your feet.

- *MATTHEW 10:14*

IS IT OKAY to give up on a difficult person or group? We are called to forgive others an unlimited number of times, because that is how often God forgives us, but that does not mean we cannot walk away from them in certain circumstances. St. Paul says you must try to reach all people in your life, but if they refuse to receive you or listen to you, at some point you may be justified in leaving. The decision to leave is not to be taken lightly, but only after careful consideration and good counsel. If you ever decide to depart from others, you are obliged to continue to pray for them. More to it, you should always remain open to the possibility that they may someday repent and return to you. Nevertheless, when you leave, you may disengage so completely that you carry no trace of lingering sadness or residual sorrow. *Shake the dust from your feet.* You may disconnect in every way to keep a clean heart. God wants you to be free to minister to new people in your life. *If the house is worthy, let your peace come upon it; if not, let your peace return to you.*

⌒

Pray: O Lord, I want to forgive others so completely
that it feels like shaking the dust from my feet.

I WILL HEAR YOU

❖ ❖ ❖

*You will call upon me and come and pray to me,
and I will hear you.*

- JEREMIAH 29:12

D O YOU FRET and fume that God does not answer your prayers? Perhaps you have been asking him to help you with forgiveness or reconciliation. When you pray to God day after day with no result, it is tempting to think that he is absent. Yet we are reminded throughout the Bible that God cares about us deeply. He is always near, lending an ear. Our prayers to him are crystal clear. He wants to banish all our fear. Whenever we pray, day or night, God promises that he hears. What a comforting thought! Just knowing that the Creator of the Universe hears us and knows exactly what we need is enough to bring us comforting relief and catapult us into a state of pure gratitude. When we place our lives in God's care, we know we are in good hands. God may answer us immediately or he may remain silent, but he is always at work behind the scenes. Imagine God smiling at you and saying, "I hear you. I'll take it from here. Now go out and play."

⌐

Pray: O Lord, just knowing that you hear me when I pray is enough to make me rejoice. I trust your plan for my life!

WITHOUT COST YOU ARE TO GIVE

❖ ❖ ❖

Without cost you have received,
without cost you are to give.

- MATTHEW 10:8

IMAGINE WINNING A huge lottery and receiving far more money than you can possibly spend. But it comes with one requirement: you must give away a small portion of it, one million dollars a day, for the rest of your life. That will certainly be an exciting challenge! While you remain rich beyond measure, you can happily go forth every day seeking to provide money to needy people and being generous to worthy causes. Think of all the happy faces you will see and all the new friends you will make! You will fall asleep every night with a contented smile. This dreamy scenario can be yours today. You need only ask God's forgiveness, and he will shower you with his mercy in superabundance. Thus assured of your place in heaven, what other riches do you need? Your newfound wealth is unlimited, enriching you more than all the gold and silver in the world. *His divine power has granted to us everything.* Your enrichment comes with only one requirement: you must give to others as you have received. What you have received freely from God without cost, you must now give freely to others.

⌐

Pray: O Lord, I know you give me all the mercy I need for eternal life. Now I want to share your mercy with others.

I Was Their Healer

❖ ❖ ❖

The more I called them, the farther they went from me.

- HOSEA 11:2

F EW EXPERIENCES ARE as heartbreaking as reaching out to loved ones and being rejected. Often, the more you try to reach out in love, the farther they run away. You may have tried in vain to reconcile with a spouse, a parent, a child, or a friend. If you take one loving step forward, the other person jumps two rebellious steps away. When nothing seems to work, you know the anguish of unrequited love. Have you considered that God feels the same way when you neglect him? *I drew them with human cords, with bands of love.* Perhaps God is allowing this distress in your life to help you understand his passionate love for you. God has been reaching out to you with open arms your entire life. Those times in the past when you ran away from him caused him the same sadness you are feeling now. It may feel overwhelming, but your sadness is limited by your humanity, while God's sadness is perfect and divine. Yet he patiently calls out to us all the days of our lives to return to him. His only desire is to forgive us and show us his mercy. *They did not know that I was their healer.*

⌒

O Lord, I know your heart aches when I reject or neglect you. I want to turn to you for your healing embrace.

BLESS THOSE WHO PERSECUTE YOU

❖ ❖ ❖

Bless those who persecute you; bless and do not curse.

- ROMANS 12:14

CAN YOU REMEMBER a mean statement said to you by someone when you were very young? The hurt can last a lifetime and be difficult to forgive and forget. Sadly, many of us have sharp tongues and we are quick to slash people when we are angry or upset. We can spit venomous curses like snakes to inflict harm or punishment on others. Saint Paul begs us to stop cursing. For God's sake, he counsels us to bless those who persecute us and not to curse. Instead of using our tongues to cast aspersions against others and damn them to hellfire, we can train our tongues to bless them and pray for their eternal salvation. *Do not repay anyone evil for evil; be concerned for what is noble in the sight of all.* What a difference we will make! With Jesus as our example, we can practice patience in the face of tribulation. We can be living examples of true love. *If possible, on your part, live at peace with all.*

⁓

Pray: O Jesus, I want to be like you, blessing others and praying for them. I wish to live at peace with everyone.

In Him We Live And Move

❖ ❖ ❖

In him we live and move and have our being.

- Acts 17:28

How often do you stop to marvel at the miracle of your life? The fact that you are alive at this very moment, living and breathing, cannot be explained by natural or scientific laws. How can you explain that you are alive and not dead? Of course the only explanation is that you are the heavenly handiwork of God. He breathed his divine breath of life into you. Remove God's holy breath that you inspire and you instantly expire. Withdraw his loving hands that sustain your beating heart and you drop dead on the spot. You are alive, moment by moment, only because he wills your existence, he sustains your life. Because God created everyone, that means we all share our Creator in common — we are all connected! This is one of the most profound truths in life. When we recognize our common humanity we see others in a new light, not as strangers and enemies to be eliminated, but as brothers and sisters to be embraced. Since God created you, your life is not your own — you owe your life to God. Meditate upon this truth and let it fill you with gratitude! What is God asking of you today? Is he asking you to be more sensitive, loving, or forgiving? You know he wants you to become more like him.

Pray: O Lord, I know I owe you everything. Help me to understand clearly what you are asking me to do today!

You Have Mercy On All

❖ ❖ ❖

*You have mercy on all, because you can do all things,
and you overlook sins for the sake of repentance.*

- Wisdom 11:23

W HY DOES GOD have mercy on evildoers? Would it not
show greater justice and fairness if God condemned
evildoers and punished them? He will indeed judge everyone
in good time, in his perfect time. In the meantime, he can do
anything he wishes because he is the Creator and he can do all
things. It is not for us to judge but rather for God to judge others. Like a patient father, he overlooks a multitude of sins committed by his children. With the benefit of his perfect wisdom,
God forbears to chastise us for our pride and disobedience. Is
he not spoiling his wayward children by letting them break his
rules? No. The reason God overlooks our sins is that he wants
to give us sufficient time and space to come to our senses and
turn to him with repentance. Our Creator will not force us to
love him, yet he loves us unconditionally. *Before you the whole
universe is like a grain from a balance, or a drop of morning dew
come down upon the earth.*

Pray: O Lord, I thank you for having mercy on us. I trust
your loving plan to give everyone time for repentance.

YOU LOVE ALL THINGS

❖ ❖ ❖

For you love all things that are and loathe nothing
that you have made.

- WISDOM 11:24

I F SOMEONE HAS injured us grievously, in a life-changing way, it can be difficult to contain a sense of outrage. The very thought of that person or the mention of his or her name can provoke our anger anew. How can we not loathe that person? The only way to get past your resentment is to release that person to God in prayer. Picture yourself physically lifting the person up and releasing him or her into God's hands. Then walk away free. You will begin to notice a surprising change. Gradually, you will begin to see the other person as God does. As a parent who cannot help but love a child, God loves all things he has made. As a child's misbehavior cannot cancel a parent's love, so our sinfulness cannot eclipse God's love. At first reluctantly, we begin to see that God loathes nothing in his creation except sin. Slowly, we grow to love all sinners in spite of their sins that disconnect them from us and separate them from God. At last we can praise God for his fundamentally lovable creation. *For you would not fashion what you hate.*

⌐

Pray: O Lord, I thank you for showing me how to love others
as you love them, in spite of their sins.

CALLED FORTH BY YOU

❖　❖　❖

How could a thing remain, unless you willed it;
or be preserved, had it not been called forth by you?

- WISDOM 11:25

WE ALL WISH at times that we could change certain people and circumstance in our lives. If only that person were different or we had never suffered that hurtful experience, we think, everything would be different. If we could just close our eyes and wave a magic wand, we know just what we would change in our lives to make everything better. Yet we open our eyes and realize that nothing has changed. To our dismay, the people and circumstances of our lives are still the same. How can we cope with life when it does not conform to our desires? We may take heart by knowing that all things are part of God's divine plan. God wills only good things, yet he allows bad things to happen for mysterious reasons, and he promises to transform the bad into good. Whatever people and circumstances exist today in your life, both good and bad, they are part of God's active or permissive will for your life. You may trust God with total confidence that you can embrace and enjoy the good while enduring and overcoming the bad.

⤳

Pray: O Lord, I trust that everything is
within the providence of your perfect will.
I believe you work all things for good!

YOUR IMPERISHABLE SPIRIT

❖ ❖ ❖

But you spare all things, because they are yours,
O ruler and lover of souls, for your imperishable spirit
is in all things!

- WISDOM 11:26

WHAT IS THE reason God so passionately longs to forgive us our sins? We certainly do not deserve it! God ardently desires to spare us because we are his. He creates us, not because he needed to, but because he wishes to share his love with us. That is the nature and essence of love. Into each one of us God breathes his imperishable spirit, his Holy Spirit. Since God created each one of us with an eternal soul, is it any wonder that he loves us with an everlasting love? We are living, breathing temples of the Holy Spirit, destined to eternal life. This is why God loves us with divine love, for he loves us as he loves himself. God is love and each member of the Holy Trinity shares perfect love infinitely. God wants you to share his life and his love. God loves us for our own sake and because he loves himself in us. We may glimpse the love of God for us in the love of a parent for a child. Do you want to be part of God's family?

⌐

Pray: O Lord, lover of my soul, lover of all souls, take me
into your embrace and make me part of your family.

HE WILL GIVE US EVERYTHING

❖ ❖ ❖

If God is for us, who can be against us? He who did not spare his own Son but handed him over for us all, how will he not also give us everything else along with him?

- ROMANS 8:31

I F YOU CANNOT forgive because you think someone has ruined your life, think again. The truth is that your life is in God's hands and he will make it better than ever. Whatever the circumstances of your life at this moment, accept them as God's active or permissive will. That means God actively creates the good and allows the bad. Do not trouble yourself about what might have been or what you would prefer for your life. God meets us where we are. He is working in your life at this very moment to bring about whatever is best for you. All you need to do is to conform your will to his, and you may rest assured that the outcome will be to your advantage. God will see to it that your circumstances are tailor-made to make you holy. It may not be the life you imagined or the life you wished, yet you may still rejoice day by day because you are completely in God's hands. By abandoning yourself in faith to God's divine providence, you will find yourself liberated to experience and enjoy God's life in you, in all circumstances, every day of your life.

⌐

Pray: O Lord, help me to let go of the past and enjoy my present life. I release everything into your loving hands.

WE ARE MORE THAN CONQUERORS

❖ ❖ ❖

What will separate us from the love of Christ?
Will anguish, or distress, or persecution, or famine,
or nakedness, or peril, or the sword?

- *ROMANS 8:35*

HAVE THE OFFENSES of others made you feel anguished and alone? Sometimes the hurtfulness of others can make us feel separated from the love of God. In our distress we may fear a future filled with ill health or poverty. We may worry that we will not be able to provide the basics like food and clothing for ourselves and our families. The early Christians faced the same anxieties with life-threatening persecution, famine, and perilous warfare. They lived in daily fear that their enemies would attack them and ruin their lives. They wondered if their enemies would separate them from the love of Christ. To banish their fears, St. Paul proclaimed the answer. *No, in all these things we are more than conquerors through him who loved us.* Because Christ loves us and he has conquered the world, we too are conquerors, indeed we are more than conquerors, through Christ. The victory is ours, we have already won.

∽

Pray: O Lord, I rest assured in trusting that nothing in my life can separate me from your eternal victorious love.

NOTHING CAN SEPARATE US

❖　❖　❖

I am convinced that neither death, nor life, nor angels,
nor principalities, nor present things, nor future things,
nor powers, nor height, nor depth, nor any other creature will be
able to separate us from the love of God
in Christ Jesus our Lord.

- ROMANS 8:38

IT IS TRUE: you have nothing to fear because God is near. Can this really be true? There is no power in heaven, and no person on earth, who can change that reality. As long as you want God to be active in your life, he promises to remain inseparably at your side. You may have suffered hurtful experiences in the past, or you may be faced with painful challenges today, or you may be worried about an uncertain future. Fear not, fear nothing, fear no one. Nothing that has happened in your past, nothing that is happening at the present moment, and nothing that will happen in the future can separate you from the love of God. Everything that has ever happened to you in the past, everything that is happening to you in the present, and everything that will happen to you in the future is made good in God's hands. Be free to live your life fearlessly and forgive others heroically.

⁓

Pray:　O Lord, I believe no evil can separate me from your perfect love, so I praise you with joy and gratitude.

WITH ALL YOUR HEART

❖ ❖ ❖

When you search for me, you will find me;
if you seek me with all your heart.

- JEREMIAH 29:13

I F YOU HAVE come to the end of this book and still struggle to forgive others, yourself, or God, do not despair! You know by now that you cannot do it by yourself, you need God's help. You also know that God is seeking you and wants to find you. He wants to save you with all his being, for he is love, and love seeks the best for the beloved. But our God is jealous for you, in a good way; he wants you to love him as wholeheartedly as he loves you. Here we discover a wonderful pearl of wisdom, one of the great secrets to finding God and being found by him. *When you search for me, you will find me; if you seek me with all your heart.* If you seek God half-heartedly, you will not find him. More to it, if you want to be found by God, but only in a lukewarm way, he will not reveal himself to you. Only when you seek God wholeheartedly, and with joyful abandon, will he will reveal himself to you. Do you desire with complete commitment and sincerity for God to find you? Do you seek God with all your heart? This interior journey is the greatest adventure of your life. Rejoice in this quest that will lead you to a surprise rendezvous, a divine destination beyond your wildest imagination: into the heart of God.

Pray: O Lord, help me love you wholeheartedly. I want
to be found by you more than anything else in my life.

SPIRIT AND LIFE

❖ ❖ ❖

*The words that I have spoken to you
are spirit and life.*

- JOHN 6:63

I F YOU ARE in distress and someone tries to encourage you with a Bible verse, the words may sound empty. You think the words of God seem useless and meaningless, while the help you need right now must be real and tangible! On a natural level, you may be right. God works through others to provide for our physical needs. Hunger demands food, thirst insists on water, and hurt requires healing. Yet Jesus reminds us that there is a much larger supernatural reality. *One does not live by bread alone, but by every word that comes from the mouth of God.* Calm yourself and contemplate the words of God. You will gradually discover God speaking to you always and everywhere, not just in the Bible or in Church but equally in friends and loved ones, sometimes even in strangers. Soon you will find yourself comforted and healed by the life-giving words of God speaking to you in all creation. Can you hear God humming with the birds in the trees and whispering with the wind in the leaves? The words of God are *spirit and life.*

⌐

Pray: O Lord, open my ears and let me hear your voice
speaking more clearly to me in my daily life.

BE MERCIFUL TO ME

❖ ❖ ❖

But the tax collector stood off at a distance and would
not even raise his eyes to heaven but beat his breast and prayed,
'O God, be merciful to me a sinner.'

- LUKE 18:13

WE COME TO a great turning point in our spiritual lives
when we recognize our own sinfulness. At first we are
understandably reluctant to look at ourselves in the mirror.
Deep down we are afraid at what we might see. However, as we
mature, we slowly turn our gaze inward. Gradually our outrage
at the sins of others subsides and is replaced by a profound sadness in the face of our own weakness. Like the tax collector
who stood off at a distance and would not even raise his eyes
to heaven, we beat our breast and ask God to forgive our sins.
This is the time and place for God, now is the ever-present
moment he can do his healing work. In this instant, and without reserve, he will engulf us in the ocean of his forgiveness.
Swept away in his loving embrace, we are cleansed at last by his
powerful grace.

Pray: O Lord, be merciful to me a sinner.

I WILL FORGIVE THEIR INIQUITY

❖ ❖ ❖

I will forgive their iniquity and
no longer remember their sin.

- JEREMIAH 31:34

ARE YOU TROUBLED by recurring memories of your sins? Remember that God calls us to forgive ourselves as completely as we forgive others. Once we have confessed our sins, God forgives us and wants us to live in peace. God does not want us to be troubled by our past. He does not want us to wallow in self-pity or self-condemnation. God does not want us to be sad; he wants us to be free. If you find yourself still tormented by memories of your past sinfulness, it helps to remember that God forgives your sins so completely that he does not remember a single one! God is perfect, so he can forget perfectly. But we are imperfect human beings, so we may struggle to forget our painful memories. While we may never completely forget the past, God's forgiveness will completely heal us of the pain associated with our troubling memories. We find freedom in knowing that we are a new creation in Christ. So be liberated from your past, be healed of the pain of your memories, forget your sins as God has forgotten them, and be free to enjoy your life as God desires.

⁓

Pray: O Lord, I thank you for forgiving me and no longer remembering my sins. Heal my memories and set me free!

STOP CONDEMNING YOURSELF

❖ ❖ ❖

Stop condemning and you will not be condemned.

- LUKE 6:37

You may say, 'I can forgive others, and I know God forgives me, but I can never forgive myself.' Forgiving yourself is a lifelong commitment. In precisely the same way that you must forgive others daily, you must also forgive yourself. If you cannot forgive yourself, how can you truly forgive others? Until you have fully accepted and experienced the complete healing power of God's mercy, you cannot fully extend that mercy to others. You cannot give what you do not possess! If you have not experienced complete forgiveness for your own sins, you cannot offer complete forgiveness to others. You must accept God's mercy before you can give it to others. Unless you have compassion toward yourself, you cannot give total compassion to others. Jesus commands us to love our neighbors as much as we love ourselves. This implies that we must love ourselves enough to accept God's forgiveness. If you want to love others as God loves you, you must first accept God's invitation to be forgiven and allow yourself to be transformed.

Pray: O Lord, I gladly accept your invitation to forgive all my sins. Forgive me so I may truly forgive others.

THINK ABOUT THESE THINGS

❖ ❖ ❖

Whatever is true, whatever is honorable, whatever is just, whatever is pure, whatever is lovely, whatever is gracious, if there is any excellence and if there is anything worthy of praise, think about these things.

- *PHILIPPIANS 4:8*

INSTEAD OF BEING troubled by memories of our sins or the sins of others against us, we can change the channel and think about good things. God wants to replace our negative thoughts with positive thoughts. All we have to do is ask him for help, and then he will spring into action. We have to do our part by avoiding the temptation to dwell on thoughts of condemnation. Instead we can fill our minds with whatever is true, honorable, just, pure, lovely, gracious, excellent, and praiseworthy. As we think about these things, our minds are being renewed and transformed daily by God. We start to see past the masks that people wear and we perceive their potential. We begin to see the world and all the people around us in a new light, the way they could be, the way God meant them to be. We are becoming that light to others who live in darkness, illuminating their lives with the love of God.

⌒

Pray: O Lord, I am so relieved and excited to think only good thoughts worthy of truth, love and praise!

GOD IS LOVE

❖ ❖ ❖

Whoever is without love does not know God,
for God is love.

- I JOHN 4:8

HERE IS THE heart of our Christian faith: God is love. If someone has acted in an unloving way toward you, feel compassion because he or she does not know God. What kind of a person would you be if you did not know God? When we think back with humility to the days when we did not know God, we cringe in shame to remember our vain behavior. What sorry souls we were when we did not know God! But now everything has changed. Now that we know God, and the closer we draw to God's side day by day, the more we recognize that God is indeed love, pure love, seeking whatever is best for all souls, both lost and found. Now it makes sense to us that God is three persons in one, the Father, Son, and Holy Spirit, existing for all time in a dynamic relationship, for love exists only in relationship to the beloved. God reaches out in all times and all places with kindness and forgiveness, gathering his beloved souls to his side. This is a profound truth. When we accept God's love for us, we realize that those who act in an unloving way towards us do not know God, *for God is love.*

⌒

Pray: O Lord, I thank you for revealing yourself to me. Now I understand your forgiving, gathering, abundant love.

THE LOVE OF GOD

❖ ❖ ❖

In this way the love of God was revealed to us:
God sent his only Son into the world so that
we might have life through him.

- 1 JOHN 4:9

A S LONG AS someone hides from us, we can never get to know that person. In the same way, if God had not revealed himself to us, we would never have experienced his love. God is love, and love reveals; love never conceals. God has not hidden his love for us; he has put it on full display for all the world to see. The way we know this awesome love of God is because he revealed it to us by sending his only Son into the world as a living sacrifice for our sins *so that we might have life through him.* We discover God's passionate love for us in the life and death of Jesus, the ultimate gift! God shows us the nature of his love: seeking, gathering, forgiving, comforting, and uniting. God seeks us to deliver us from our sins and to share his divine life with him eternally.

Pray: O Lord, thank you for revealing your love for me
by sending your Son so that I might enjoy new life.

This Is Love

❖ ❖ ❖

In this is love: not that we have loved God, but that
he loved us and sent his Son as expiation for our sins.

- 1 John 4:10

ONE OF THE most important things we learn on our faith journey is that we are incapable of loving others unconditionally. Similarly, we are unable to forgive others completely. Because of our fallen nature, we cannot offer wholehearted love or forgiveness to others, ourselves, or God. We need assistance from outside ourselves; we need God's help. Not one of us is capable of love by ourselves; God must love us first. We are candles of his desire; God is the flame of love. Once God lights us on fire with the spark of his Holy Spirit, we become enflamed with his sacred compassion and we shine brightly for all to see.

Pray: O Lord, I know I am only able to love because you loved me first. Thank you for lighting my heart on fire.

LOVE ONE ANOTHER

❖ ❖ ❖

Beloved, if God so loved us, we also must love one another.

- 1 JOHN 4:11

B ECAUSE GOD HAS loved us, he expects us to love one another. This simple verse contains the wisdom of the ages. God has filled up your cup; now go and fill up the cup of another person. This can be as simple as smiling at someone who is sad, visiting the sick, or comforting the lonely. But it has much more far-reaching consequences. Consider the nature of God's love. By it you are forgiven, redeemed, and given a new life in Christ. More profoundly, you are empowered by God's love to help him transform others in the same way, if they wish. As you have received forgiveness and a new life from God, you are enabled to go forth, freely forgive others, and lead them to new life in Christ. Now that you can do all things through Christ, reach out to others and show them the love of Christ. Having received the power of the Holy Spirit into your heart, open your heart to others to share with them this healing power. You are an adopted child of God, sharing in the divine life of the Holy Trinity. Go forth and share this love with others. When you love others, you invite them into the life of God.

⁓

Pray: O Lord, I thank you for loving and healing me.
I want to overflow your divine love to help heal others.

IF WE LOVE ONE ANOTHER

❖ ❖ ❖

*No one has ever seen God. Yet, if we love
one another, God remains in us, and his love
is brought to perfection in us.*

- 1 JOHN 4:12

MANY PEOPLE DOUBT the existence of God because they cannot see him. But is he really invisible? God is readily apparent in the love we show to one another. God is love, and his love is reflected in the words and deeds of those who love him. When we are filled with the love of God, it shows in the way we live and love and act towards others. We especially demonstrate the existence of God and the power of his love when we love our enemies and forgive those who have offended us. When we love those who are sinful and unlovable, we shine the light of God's love into their lives. For many people who live in darkness, we help them glimpse the light of the Son of God. In our generosity we may provide them with food, water, medicine, or mercy that gives sinners the only tangible evidence they will ever experience of the reality of God's love. Be the face of God to someone today by forgiving him or her with a smile.

⁓

Pray: O Lord, thank you for loving me. Help me
to show your love to others today in new small ways.

There Is No Fear In Love

❖ ❖ ❖

*There is no fear in love, but perfect love drives out fear because
fear has to do with punishment, and so
one who fears is not yet perfect in love.*

- 1 John 4:18

ARE YOU AFRAID of someone who has offended you, or afraid of admitting your own sins, or fearful of an unknown future? Fear is like the poison of a snakebite, inflicted upon you by the evil one, meant to distress you and do you harm. It requires an antidote that is even stronger than fear. You need the medicine of truth to counteract the toxin of a lie! Listen to the wisdom of Saint John as he gives you the remedy. *There is no fear in love, but perfect love drives out fear.* Let love wipe away all your tears and banish all your fears. That is what God wants to do for you if you will accept his perfect love. God wants you to live fearlessly in the face of all bullies, adversaries, enemies, and obstacles. In whatever situation you need courage and serenity, ask God for his perfect love. He will immerse you in his perfect love to let you face all your fears today as if you were going for a pleasant walk in the park. Let God drive out your fears today.

⌐

Pray: O Lord, I know your perfect love is the answer to all
my fears. Shower me with your love all day and always!

HE FIRST LOVED US

❖ ❖ ❖

We love because he first loved us.

- 1 JOHN 4:19

THIS IS THE beginning of wisdom and the starting point of faith. We are able to love only because God loved us first. We were nothing before God conceived us in his eternal mind. We were dust before God made us from the earth. We were formless until God formed us in the womb and lifeless until God gave us the spark of life. Because God created us, we owe him everything. *In him we live and move and have our being.* Our abilities to taste, see, touch, hear, think and act come from him. As we live day by day, moment by moment, we thank God. We were empty vessels before God filled us to the brim with his divine love. As God pours his love into us, it overflows and we can share it with others. God delights in pouring his love into us abundantly, not sparingly. He loves and forgives us generously, not meagerly. We can feel great affection toward others with our natural sentiments, but we can only love others with an unselfish love when we allow God to love others through us.

Pray: O Lord, I know I can truly love others because you first loved me. Thank you for loving me first!

I LOVE GOD

❖ ❖ ❖

*If anyone says, "I love God," but hates his brother, he is
a liar; for whoever does not love a brother whom he has
seen cannot love God whom he has not seen.*

- 1 JOHN 4:20

I F YOU PROFESS your love of God but secretly hate someone
in your heart, you are a liar. You may attend church or pray
every day but if you harbor resentment toward your neighbor,
you are a hypocrite. God calls us to love our enemies and to
pray for them. In practicing this selfless love for others, we
come to know more deeply the love of God for us. God loved
us while we were yet sinners, so he calls us to love others while
they are yet sinners. When we allow God to liberate us from
our hidden resentments, we discover the freedom to love others
as God loves us. Our bitterness is miraculously transformed by
God into compassion. *This is the commandment we have from
him: whoever loves God must also love his brother.* We display our
gratitude toward God, whom we have not seen, with forgiveness toward our brethren, whom who have seen. When others
witness our compassion, they are seeing God's love in action.

Pray: O Lord, help me to show my love for you
by showing your love to other people.

Generous Persons Will Prosper

❖　❖　❖

Generous persons will prosper; those who refresh others
will themselves be refreshed.

- Proverbs 11:25

H AVE YOU EVER made a mistake and felt an overwhelming sense of dread that the consequences would be disastrous, only to find out that everything was okay after all? Or perhaps you once offended someone and you worried it would ruin the relationship, but that person forgave you generously and you breathed a big sigh of relief? Like a summer storm that rumbles in and blots out the sun, our mistakes make the world seem dark and thundery until we are forgiven; then the skies clear, the sun comes out again and everything returns to normal. Being forgiven by another person is one of the most refreshing experiences in life. In the same way, when you generously forgive others, you refresh them and give them new life. You blow the away the dark clouds of condemnation hanging over their heads. When you pardon others with generosity, they are renewed and you are too.

Pray: O Lord, I want to be as generous in forgiving others as you have been with me. Help me to refresh others!

No Testing Has Overtaken You

❖ ❖ ❖

No testing has overtaken you that is not common to every-one. God is faithful, and he will not let you be tested beyond your strength, but with the testing he will also provide the way out so that you may be able to endure it.

- 1 Corinthians 10:13

SOMETIMES WE WORRY that our difficulties are overwhelming. Whether they concern relationships, health, finances or legal issues, we protest against God for placing us in situations that seem impossible to handle. We know we are being tempted to the point of desperation when we say, 'I cannot take this anymore!' But this statement is a lie from the evil one who desires nothing more than to make us hopeless. The truth is that God promises he will absolutely not allow us to be tempted beyond our strength. At times God allows trial and tribulations in our lives, but only for our good and never beyond our ability to handle. Knowledge of this truth should fill us with courage and hope! Because God is with us, no obstacle in our lives is insurmountable, no testing will break us, no fear will overcome us. Mysteriously hidden within the test itself, God has provided the way out so that we may be able to endure the test. With God we will win; the victory is ours.

⌒

Pray: O Lord, I thank you for promising me that you will never allow me to be tested beyond my strength!

WE BOAST OF OUR AFFLICTIONS

❖ ❖ ❖

*We boast in hope of the glory of God. Not only that,
but we even boast of our afflictions, knowing that affliction
produces endurance, and endurance, proven character,
and proven character, hope.*

- *ROMANS 5:2*

IN THE MIDST of our difficulties, when life seems dark and hopeless from a worldly perspective, we are able to smile and boast of our hope in God's promises that all will be well. What a gift we have as believers! We even boast of our afflictions! How is such behavior possible? Because we know we are in good hands. We can say with confidence that if God wishes it or allows it, we gladly trust in him. This is exactly what Jesus said, that he came not to do his own will but the will of his Father. We may suffer for a time, but we know that our temporary affliction, far from ruining us, is actually renewing us. Our hardship is changing us deep in our souls, infusing us with divine endurance, proven character, and heavenly hope. When we have hope that God is completely in control, we have all we need in all circumstances because *hope does not disappoint.*

⌒

Pray: O Lord, thank you for giving me hope that you will
never disappoint me. Today I smile at my afflictions!

CHRIST DIED FOR US

❖ ❖ ❖

*Only with difficulty does one die for a just person,
though perhaps for a good person one might even find courage
to die. But God proves his love for us in that while we were
still sinners Christ died for us.*

- ROMANS 5:7

M OST OF US would volunteer to die for a loved one. If you
have ever had a friend or family member who faced a
life-threatening illness, you know the sentiment. If we knew
our death would save the person whom we love, we would con-
sent to sacrifice our life. This would certainly prove our love
for that person beyond the shadow of a doubt. On the other
hand, who among us would give up our life to save a person
who is a grave sinner, for example, someone who is guilty of
murder? Yet this is exactly what Jesus did for us. He sacrificed
himself on the cross *while we were still sinners.* He died for us
while we were still dead in our sins. He suffered death in order
to give us new life. This is what we are called to do for others.
As Jesus died for our sake to give us new life, we are called to
die to ourselves to give others new life. You may resent another
person who has injured you in a life-changing way. Offer your
injury to God. Let your self-sacrifice be a loving gift to God.
He will make good come out of it.

Pray: O God, just as you proved your love by sending
your Son to die for me, I want to prove my love for others.

WHILE WE WERE ENEMIES

❖　❖　❖

*If while we were enemies, we were reconciled to God through
the death of his Son, how much more, once reconciled,
will we be saved by his life.*

- ROMANS 5:10

H OW WOULD YOU like to be best friends with God? Few of
us think of ourselves as enemies of God. But we are God's
adversaries when we fall into sin or unforgiveness. Whenever
we do something opposed to God's will, we are indeed his
enemies. To make us his friends, God in his infinite mercy
offers us forgiveness and reconciliation through the death of
his Son. If we accept this great gift of reconciliation with God,
we become his friends. Our renewed relationship came at great
cost to God, so to speak, because it required the death of his
Son. But if we are now reconciled with God through the death
of Jesus, how much more will we be reconciled by the life of
Jesus? Since God raised Jesus from death to new life, he will
also raise us to new life. We have new life in Christ, and Christ
has been raised to eternal life. Our forgiveness in Christ is
absolute, so our reconciliation with God is secure. Knowing
this makes it easier to forgive others.

⌒

Pray: O Lord, thank you for forgiving me and changing me
from an enemy into a friend through the death of your Son.

THE STONE REJECTED

❖ ❖ ❖

*The stone the builders rejected has become
the cornerstone.*

- PSALM 118:22

DESPITE OUR BEST intentions, we are frequently rejected by others. Their reasons may be valid, invalid, or nonexistent. Whether we are young or old, rich or poor, it hurts all the same. As children we may be ridiculed for something beyond our control, or not chosen by our schoolmates in the playground. As adults we may be rejected by a parent, spouse, or child. We may be passed over for a promotion at work or fired from our job. We never quite get used to it. Like the stone rejected by the builders, we are overlooked in the quarry of life. Jesus was that stone rejected by the builders. He was unfairly rejected, mocked and scorned by both powerful and ordinary people. Then when he was crucified, all his disciples deserted him except one. They did not know who he was. But God knew who he was: Jesus was his only Son, his chosen One. God chose Jesus to become the cornerstone. On his foundation God builds his holy Church. If you are feeling rejected today, put yourself in God's hands. Let God use you as a cornerstone to build something marvelous today. *By the Lord has this been done; it is wonderful in our eyes.*

Pray: O Lord, no matter who has rejected me in
life, even if I am broken, I know you can use me
as a cornerstone.

Light Came Into The World

❖ ❖ ❖

The light came into the world, but people
preferred darkness to light, because their works were evil.

- John 3:19

WHEN PEOPLE COMMIT grievous offenses and violate the normal standards of human conduct, we are left in confusion about their motives. We question how anyone can be so cruel, so careless, so selfish. We wonder why, why, why would anyone do something so bad? It is especially perplexing when someone we love responds by rejecting or persecuting us. Here we confront the mystery of evil. Jesus came into a darkened world to light our way to eternal life but most people rejected him. Why? *Everyone who does wicked things hates the light and does not come toward the light, so that their works might not be exposed.* People who reject us are rejecting the light. Those who hide from us are hiding from Jesus. Speak the truth to lost souls, as far as possible, and pray that they see the light. *Whoever lives the truth comes to the light, so that their works may be clearly seen as done in God.*

⌒

Pray: O Lord, let me be a light to others in a darkened
world. I want to live in the light of your truth!

WHOEVER SINS BELONGS TO THE DEVIL

❖ ❖ ❖

*Whoever sins belongs to the devil, because the devil
has sinned from the beginning.*

- 1 JOHN 3:8

I N OUR MODERN way of thinking we do not believe in the
existence of the devil. We casually dismiss any mention of
the devil as medieval, archaic, and superstitious. Instead we
try to explain the misbehavior of others by using psychologi-
cal terms such as pathological, antisocial, or narcissistic. While
modern psychology is useful, we must recognize that Jesus
often referred to the existence of the devil as a real being. Our
faith teaches us that Satan, the brightest of angels, suffered the
fatal sin of pride. In his envy he turned against God for all
time and took one third of the angels with him. Satan's greatest
accomplishment is convincing us that he does not exist because
this leaves us more vulnerable to his stratagems. The truth is
that Satan and his legion of demons want nothing more than
to thwart us, accuse us, and drag us into the abyss. He is the
tempter, the deceiver, and the father of lies. We need to know
who is our enemy and who is on our side. *The Son of God was
revealed to destroy the works of the devil.*

⌒

Pray: O Lord, I thank you for revealing that Jesus your Son
destroys all the works and wounds of the devil in our lives!

THIS IS THE DAY

❖ ❖ ❖

This is the day the Lord has made; let us rejoice in it and be glad.

- PSALM 118:24

WHEN THINGS ARE not going our way, it can be difficult to face a new day. We might prefer to leave the curtains closed and pull the blankets up over our heads. At times like this we need to remember that God has created this day. As hard as it is to believe, the truth is that everything in our lives is either ordained by God or allowed for our good. He watches over us and holds us in the palm of his hand. Everything good comes to us from God, and no evil can touch us unless God allows it to pass through his fingers. God may permit suffering for a time, but only for a greater good. He is the author of every aspect of our lives and wants to make us the hero in our life story. Behind the scenes he is writing and re-writing our story every day as it unfolds, catapulting us over deep chasms, dropping us lifelines at the last moment, and rescuing us from the most impossible predicaments. We need only run headlong up the path that he draws before us to find our way to a happy ending. *Every day is created by our Heavenly Author, let us rejoice in it and be glad.*

Pray: O Lord, you are the author of my life. I rejoice knowing that you invite me to be your hero and co-author!

LOVE ONE ANOTHER

❖ ❖ ❖

*We know that we have passed from death
to life because we love one another.
Whoever does not love abides in death.*

- 1 JOHN 3:14

How can we know when we have successfully forgiven someone? It is difficult to hate another person yet it seems impossible to forgive. It feels like dying when we strive to forgive someone day after day, year after year. The reason it feels like dying is that we actually are dying — to our strongly held feelings of pride, egotism, and arrogance. Then one day, in God's good time, we awaken with new sensations of humility, self-giving, and compassion. Tingling with joy, we can feel that something is changing profoundly, almost imperceptibly, deep within the cathedrals of our souls. It dawns upon us that we are passing from death to new life. We are successfully dying to ourselves and God is giving us new life. God is giving us the exhilarating ability to forgive others. The world looks new to us, multi-colored and covered with dew, sparkling in the sunlight.

Pray: O Lord, I thank you for helping me pass from death to new life. How marvelous it is to love one another!

WE KNOW LOVE

❖ ❖ ❖

We know love by this, that he laid down his life for us –
and we ought to lay down our lives for one another.

- 1 JOHN 3:16

HOW CAN WE know love unless someone shows it to us first? How can we know anything until someone else helps us to understand it? We are empty clay pots that must be filled with the water of love before we can pour out that living water to others. We only know love because it has been given to us by Jesus. He has demonstrated true love to us in the most selfless, spectacular, and wholehearted way possible: by laying down his life for us. There is no greater way to show love for anyone than by sacrificing one's own life for the good of another. Now that Jesus has willingly laid down his life for you, are you willing to lay down your life for a friend or stranger? You may do so in small ways, such as smiling or being polite, or you may do so in life-changing ways, such as forgiving and forgetting. If you are willing to let go of your pride and self-importance in order to forgive another, you are loving that person. If you lay down your life selflessly, in any way, for the sake of another, you are showing that person the highest form of love, the sacrificial love of Christ.

Pray: O Lord, thank you for sacrificing your life so I can live eternally. Help me to love others as you love me!

TRUTH AND ACTION

❖ ❖ ❖

Let us love, not in word or speech,
but in truth and action.

- 1 JOHN 3:18

IT IS EASY for us to say we love someone. Likewise, it is a breeze to declare that we forgive a person. The proof is in our actions. While our words are essential, our deeds are necessary to demonstrate our wholehearted commitment. Announcing that we are going to bake bread is only an idea, the first step before actually baking the bread. If we say we love someone but fail to make it real with action, we have not spoken the truth. In the same way, if we say we have forgiven someone but we harbor a grudge or nurture resentment, we have not truly forgiven that person. True love is not passive; it actively seeks to provide the best for the beloved. True forgiveness is not indifferent; it earnestly finds expression in praying for the offender. We who have received God's life-saving love will thrive only by extending that same love to others. *How does God's love abide in anyone who has the world's goods and sees a brother or sister in need and yet refuses help?*

⸺

Pray: O Lord, as you have loved me in life-changing ways,
help me to actively love others and pray for them.

I Must Decrease

❖ ❖ ❖

He must increase; I must decrease.

- John 3:29

O UR NATURAL DESIRE is to increase; we reject anything or anyone that causes us to decrease. While we instinctively push to grow, expand, and prosper, we fear to decline, contract, or diminish. In this verse John the Baptist expresses a humble attitude by saying that he must decrease so that Jesus may increase. Like the best man at a wedding who thinks not of himself, we must stand back in a diminished, supporting role. The best man rejoices with the bridegroom because he has found his bride, so he is increasing. In the same way, Jesus has found his bride, the church, so he is increasing. Our role is secondary, to rejoice because Jesus has found his church – Jesus is increasing in the lives of all true believers! God calls us to decrease because he wants us to make room within ourselves for him. As we empty ourselves, there is more space for God to enter our hearts and dramatically increase his presence in our lives. God does not seek to diminish us but rather to pour his love into us and magnify us with his life. *I will increase them, they will not decrease, I will glorify them.*

⌒

Pray: O Lord, I rejoice to see you burst forth your presence in my life — I must decrease so that you may increase!

LOVE COVERS A MULTITUDE OF SINS

❖ ❖ ❖

Above all, let your love for one another be intense,
because love covers a multitude of sins.

- 1 PETER 4:8

HAVE YOU EVER wished you could start your life over with a clean slate? Like an artist with a fresh white canvas, you could paint an entirely new and beautiful scene. In earlier times, when canvas was expensive, starving artists frequently retrieved paintings they had rejected to re-use them. By painting over the unsatisfactory pieces, artists created entirely new and beautiful works of art. The underlying image was forgotten for all time, covered forever by the new landscape or portrait for all the world to see. Can you hear God calling you to be a great artist? Can you hear him encouraging you? Put on your smock. Pick up your brush and palette. Face the offensive canvas in front of you. Choose and mix your colors of mercy. Now paint with a flourish! With broad strokes of forgiveness here and pleasing colors of mercy there, repaint the canvas. See your unique design come to life! Let your love for others be so intense that it covers a multitude of sins. Your audience will gasp with delight and applaud with gratitude. Create a new and joyful masterpiece in your life for God.

⁓

Pray: O Lord, I want my love for others to be so intense
that my forgiveness covers a multitude of their sins!

THE STRENGTH THAT GOD SUPPLIES

❖ ❖ ❖

*Whoever serves, let it be with the strength
that God supplies.*

- 1 PETER 4:11

AT THE END of your rope, if you cannot cope, when your strength is spent, and you're malcontent, do not despair, God hears your prayer. We are only human, so we are born with certain limitations. We may wish to be of service to others, but our strength can only take us so far. At some point we reach the limits of our natural strength. That can be discouraging, frustrating, even frightening. In your exhaustion you may be tempted to give up. You may cry out to God in desperation, 'Why do you give me this task without giving me the strength to accomplish it?' This is the moment for which God has been waiting. Now when you acknowledge your weakness and your need for him, God rushes to your side. If you depend on him, God will supply you with his strength to supplement your weakness and perfect your faith. Where you are weak, God is strong. With his strength you can accomplish everything he wants you to. Why does God make us weak and dependent upon him to accomplish our journey? *So that in all things God may be glorified through Jesus Christ, to whom belong glory and dominion forever and ever.*

⌒

Pray: O Lord, I praise you for supplying your strength when
I am weak. I can do all things with your help!

HAND YOUR SOUL OVER

❖ ❖ ❖

*Those who suffer in accord with God's will hand
their souls over to a faithful creator.*

- *1 PETER 4:19*

WHATEVER IS CAUSING you pain or suffering today, hand it over to God. If you question whether you are suffering in accord with God's will, you needlessly burden yourself. God does not want us to suffer, he does not will us to suffer, but on occasion he may allow us to suffer. If we entrust our difficulties to God without reservation or restraint, he is faithful to comfort us in our distress, encourage us in our weakness, and heal us in our infirmity. Because we are part of the Body of Christ, we may confidently join our sufferings with those of Jesus on the cross. Collect all your worries and hand them over to God. In fact, hand your entire life over to God. Freely give to God your body, mind, and soul. Surely you can trust the Creator of the universe! As God refreshed, restored, and redeemed his Son, so will he do the same for you. In fact, the moment you offer your troubles up to God, he starts working behind the scenes to renew you, reconcile your relationships, and redeem lost souls.

⌒

Pray: O Lord, I accept all my sufferings today. I gladly hand
my soul over to you, knowing you are my Creator.

A Thorn In The Flesh

❖ ❖ ❖

To keep me from being too elated, a thorn was given me
in the flesh, a messenger of Satan to torment me,
to keep me from being too elated.

- 2 Corinthians 12:7

D O YOU HAVE a thorn in your flesh? It may be a person who betrayed you, or an injury that hurts every day, or a painful memory that will not go away. Like a splinter in your finger, its piercing pain robs you of peace and prevents you from feeling healthy. Perhaps you have prayed to God to remove your thorn but still it remains. Paul had such a thorn. He called it a messenger of Satan, a tormenting pain allowed by God to keep him from being too elated by the life-transforming revelations God was giving to him. *Three times I appealed to the Lord about this, that it would leave me, but he said to me, "My grace is sufficient for you, for power is made perfect in weakness."* If you have a thorn in your flesh that will not go away, perhaps God is allowing it as a painful reminder to trust him more completely to heal you in his good time. If you were freed from your thorn too soon, you might not be fully prepared to receive his miraculous healing presence in your life.

⌒

Pray: O Lord, please remove the thorn from my flesh or let it prepare me to be more completely healed by your love!

I Will Boast Of My Weaknesses

❖ ❖ ❖

I will boast all the more gladly of my weaknesses, so that the power of Christ may dwell in me.

- 2 Corinthians 12:9

WHAT IS THIS? I am supposed to boast of my weakness? I prefer to brag about my strength! Why am I supposed to proclaim my weakness? In this verse Paul *gladly* boasts of his weakness! What is this all about? When we are strong, we have a tendency to push God away and do things our way. Paul has come to the realization that when we are weak, we fall to our knees and place ourselves in God's hands. When we depend utterly on God to help us, we are in a blessed state, for then God can fill us with his divine power. God delights in coming to our assistance but only when we ask for his help. Paul wants to help us discover one of the great secrets of life. When we are strong and insist on doing things our way, God steps aside. But if we hail God in prayer and allow him to help us, he works through us. We become a channel for the overflowing power of his love for others. To our amazement, we discover that if we gladly boast of our weaknesses, the power of Christ dwells in us.

⌒

Pray: O Lord, help me discover how to be grateful for my weaknesses so that you may dwell powerfully in my soul.

When I Am Weak

❖ ❖ ❖

I am content with weaknesses, insults, hardships, persecutions,
and calamities for the sake of Christ;
for whenever I am weak, then I am strong.

- 2 Corinthians 12:10

THE INESCAPABLE FACT is that when other people offend us, they weaken us. Whether we are injured in body, mind, heart or soul, we are diminished. It would be easier to forgive others if we were not adversely affected! If a thief steals a coin from you but drops two coins as he runs away, it is easy to forgive him. It is harder to forgive a thief who steals your coin and leaves you penniless. So what are we to do with the injuries, insults, and calamities we have suffered at the hands of others? Without question we are weakened, reduced, or diminished. Paul reminds us in this verse above how we can accept our wounds. We can be content with our troubles *for the sake of Christ*. We know Jesus is watching over us and walking beside us. He has promised to revive, restore, and renew us. We rest in his reassurance that he is filling all our cracks with the mortar of his love. Jesus is pouring his healing power into all our hurting places. Wherever I am weak and broken, there Christ is supernaturally strong and alive.

Pray: O Jesus, help me to be content with my weaknesses. I trust you completely to fill me with your healing power!

MAKE CROOKED WAYS STRAIGHT

❖ ❖ ❖

I will lead the blind on a way they do not know; by paths they do not know I will guide them. I will turn darkness into light before them, and make crooked ways straight.

- ISAIAH 42:16

THE HARDEST PEOPLE to forgive are those who have caused us a permanent injury. One day we are merrily walking along the path of life without a care in the world, when suddenly someone rejects or hurts us. Our injuries may be severe in body, mind, heart, or soul. As if struck by lightning, we lie dazed and broken in a ditch, our lives forever changed. The path is now crooked, and we do not know which way to go. Darkness envelops us, we are blind, we cannot see the way ahead. How shall we live? God reminds us that we do not need our sight; he will lead us by the hand. We need not worry if we do not see a way out of our troubles; he will guide us surely on secret paths known only to him. God will restore our sight, and will turn our darkness into light. Though every path in front of us seems crooked and blocked, he will make the crooked ways straight. God assures us he created us for a good purpose and will guide us every step of the way. *These are my promises: I made them, I will not forsake them.*

Pray: O Lord, I trust you completely to guide me, through the darkness into light, along pathways known only to you!

THE RACE THAT IS SET BEFORE US

❖ ❖ ❖

*Let us run with perseverance the race that is set before us, looking
to Jesus the pioneer and perfecter of our faith,
who for the sake of the joy that was set before him
endured the cross.*

- HEBREWS 12:1

HAVE YOU EVER run a race in which you grew weary?
Perhaps you ran out of breath or another runner made
you stumble and fall. We all share similar experiences in the
race of life. We get bruised and exhausted. The finish line is
nowhere in sight. This is the time to pray. Ask the Holy Spirit
to breathe his divine inspiration into you to give you a second
wind. Call for God to revive you and feel the power of his love
coursing through your veins. Ask Jesus to give you the same
perseverance he showed on the cross. How did Jesus endure the
cross? For the sake of the joy that was set before him. What was
this joy exactly? His faith in God's loving presence and promise
of eternal life. If your trust in God is fading, look to Jesus who
has pioneered the way and who will perfect your faith. Recall
how Jesus endured his painful cross joyfully, *disregarding its
shame, and has taken his seat at the right hand of the throne of
God.*

⌐

Pray: O Lord, though I stumble and fall, I will run the race
you have set before me. Give me your endurance and joy!

TRIALS FOR THE SAKE OF HOLINESS

❖ ❖ ❖

We had human parents to discipline us, and we respected them.
Should we not be even more willing to be subject
to the Father of spirits and live?

- HEBREWS 12:9

REMEMBER WHEN YOU were young and your father or mother disciplined you in a good way? You probably resented it at the time. But years later you look back and realize it was for your own good. Your parent knew best after all. God's discipline is the same. He permits us to endure trials, disappointments, and difficulties caused by others in order to teach us how to forgive. *God is treating you as children; for what child is there whom a parent does not discipline?* If you see someone who is misbehaving without consequences, remember that he or she may not be a child of God like you. Why does God discipline us? *In order that we may share in his holiness.* Do you unconditionally trust God to know what is best to make you holy? *Discipline always seems painful rather than pleasant at the time, but later it yields the peaceful fruit of righteousness to those who have been trained by it.*

⌒

Pray: O Lord, I trust you completely to know exactly what I need every day of my life. I want you to make me holy!

STRIVE FOR PEACE

❖ ❖ ❖

Strive for peace with everyone, and for that holiness without which no one will see the Lord.

- HEBREWS 12:14

YOU MAY HAVE noticed that peace does not just happen; you have to work for it. You have to strive for it. That means reaching out to your family members, neighbors, and strangers around you. It means taking the initiative to start conversations and listening to other points of view. It involves your time, your heart, and your mind. When peace is lacking, we may wish we could just go away and live alone in the woods, but that does not solve anything. God wants us to be connected to others and strive for peace with everyone. Just by working and praying for peace we get a reward, even if we cannot achieve perfect peace. What is our reward? *That holiness without which no one will see the Lord.* God rewards our peacemaking by making us holy, as he is holy, for God is love, and God loves peacemakers. An extra reward is that God allows us to see him more clearly. We see him in other peacemakers, we see him reflected in the love we share with others, and we see him hidden and wounded in those people who disturb the peace. Remember that the most important thing we can do to create peace with others is to forgive them.

⤳

Pray: O Lord, help me to seek peace with all people in my life. I want to show them your love so they see you clearly!

I Have Washed Your Feet

❖ ❖ ❖

*If I then, your Lord and Teacher, have washed your feet,
you also ought to wash one another's feet.*

- John 13:14

IN ANCIENT TIMES the lowest servant was given the job of washing the feet of guests. This was a dirty job because people walked in sandals through village streets covered with dust and littered with human waste, garbage, and animal manure. So imagine the disciples' surprise when Jesus began washing their feet during supper! They protested but their Lord and Teacher insisted on bowing down before them with a bowl of water, saying *what I am doing, you do not understand now, but you will understand later.* Jesus was doing the will of his Father by demonstrating the cleansing power of forgiveness. Then Jesus instructed them to do the same for others. We are called by God to act as servants to others, even if they offend us. Why do we have to serve others and forgive them, especially when they do not deserve it? It may seem mortifying, humiliating, and degrading. We may not understand it now, but we will understand it later in God's perfect timing. *I have given you an example, that you also should do as I have done to you.*

⤴

Pray: O Lord, you have washed my feet and forgiven my sins.
Help me learn humility by washing the feet of others!

ONE OF YOU WILL BETRAY ME

❖ ❖ ❖

When Jesus had thus spoken, he was troubled in spirit,
and testified, "Truly, truly, I say to you, one of you
will betray me."

- JOHN 13:21

HAVE YOU BEEN betrayed by someone you love? While it is difficult to be offended by a stranger, it is immeasurably more hurtful to be betrayed by someone we trust. A stranger may wound us, but a loved one can break our heart. No experience on earth is more woeful, excruciating, and desolating. How can we forgive someone who has betrayed us? At the last supper, Jesus knew he was going to be betrayed by Judas, one of his beloved disciples. It filled Jesus with profound sorrow and caused him to be *troubled in spirit*. Yet Jesus did not reject Judas; instead he offered Judas broken bread to eat! Jesus allowed Judas the freedom to betray his trust. Can we do the same with our loved ones? Judas betrayed Jesus to the Roman guards with an intimate gesture of friendship -- *with a kiss*. Imagine Judas, clutching his bag of silver coins, kissing Jesus on the cheek. Picture the sorrow and disappointment on Jesus' face. Judas could have repented and received forgiveness. Yet Jesus allowed Judas to choose his course. God lovingly allows us to be free. Can we allow others this same freedom?

Pray: O Lord, I know it pains you when we betray your trust.
Help me to forgive others when they betray me.

LOVE ONE ANOTHER

❖ ❖ ❖

I give you a new commandment: love one another.
As I have loved you, so you also should love one another.

- JOHN 13:34

AFTER JESUS HAD washed the feet of his disciples during the last supper, he gave them this new commandment to love one another. We know we are supposed to love one another, and we try to love each other, but do we really love each other? Deep down in the secret recesses of our hearts, do we really and truly love others? If we harbor hidden grudges, resentments and bitterness for the pain caused by others long ago, we need to ask Jesus to help us forgive. Jesus will empower us with his mercy to forgive others. He frees us to live, laugh, and love again. There is a deeper mystery here. Jesus commands us to love not merely for the sake of peace, but rather because God is love. God created the entire universe out of love! God's love infuses everything and everyone, except where there is sin, which is the absence of love. Jesus calls us to love one another as God loves each one of us. Jesus calls us imitate his love for us. Are we willing to suffer and perhaps even to die for the sake of others? *This is how all will know that you are my disciples, if you have love for one another.*

⁓

Pray: O Jesus, teach me to show others the same self-giving, life-giving, sacrificial love you have given to me.

CAST ALL YOUR ANXIETY ON HIM

❖ ❖ ❖

Humble yourselves therefore under the mighty hand of
God, so that he may exalt you in due time. Cast all your
anxiety on him, because he cares for you.

- 1 PETER 5:6

ARE YOU TROUBLED by anxiety or fear? Worries and concerns about ourselves, our families, or our circumstances
have a tendency to drain our energies. When we are worn down,
we find it more difficult to forgive others, and this perpetuates
a self-defeating cycle. Do you know you can live a worry-free
life? It's true — God wants to give you the peace that passes
all understanding. You may be feeling hopeless, depressed, and
alone, like a castaway who is marooned on a desert island. You
may see no outward sign of a ship on the horizon to rescue you
or a Savior to save you. Do not be downcast. Soon you will see
sails billowing toward you and all will be well. If you humble
yourself under the mighty protective hand of God, he will exalt
you in his perfect time. God is lifting you even now, at this
very moment. Can you feel the fresh breath of the Holy Spirit
on your face? Soon he will fill your sails and you will be on
your way. Cast all your troubles and anxiety on God, trusting
that he is holding you in the palm of his mighty hand.

⌐

Pray: O Lord, today I cast all my anxieties on you, every last
one! Thank you for freeing me to sail on my way!

LIKE A ROARING LION

❖ ❖ ❖

Keep alert. Like a roaring lion your adversary the devil prowls around, looking for someone to devour.

- 1 PETER 5:8

YOUR REAL ADVERSARY is not the person who offended you. Believe it or not, your real adversary is the devil. He is the one who deceives people, tempting them and leading them astray. He is the father of lies, the prince of darkness, the accuser of souls. He is the law-breaker, the trouble-maker, and the heart-forsaker. The devil is like a roaring lion who prowls around the forest day and night, never sleeping, restlessly looking for someone to devour. Stealthy and surreptitious, he is a wolf in sheep's clothing. He seeks to take advantage of any weakness such as sloth, doubt, envy, or unforgiveness. But we have no fear of our adversary the devil because Jesus already fought him and won! The battle is not yet over, but victory is assured. Our job is to keep alert and resist the devil; then he will flee. *Resist him, steadfast in your faith, for you know that your brothers and sisters in all the world are undergoing the same kinds of suffering.* We take comfort in knowing that we are part of a vast faithful army of followers of Christ who march forward to certain victory!

Pray: O Lord, thank you for allowing me to see my enemy clearly. Help me to enlist other souls to enjoy your victory!

GOD WILL RESTORE YOU

❖ ❖ ❖

After you have suffered for a little while, the God of all
grace, who has called you to his eternal glory in Christ,
will himself restore, support, strengthen, and
establish you.

- 1 PETER 5:10

YOU MAY BE tempted to think your suffering will never end. It may seem that your losses are irreparable. From a natural point of view, it often appears as if you can never regain what you have lost. Someone may have wrongly caused you to lose a spouse, a child, your health, your job, or your peace of mind. As a result, when you are experiencing a time of desolation and deprivation, remember this is only a temporary time. In his perfect time, God himself promises you that he will restore what you have lost. It may not look the same as what you lost or be what you expected, but God will provide; he is faithful to his promises. Whatever you have lost, even though it was as precious to you as life itself, God will restore it to you tenfold, sixtyfold, a hundredfold. God gave you all good things in your life, so offer what you have lost to him as a sacrifice. Trust him to give you good things again. Wait upon the Lord with joyful anticipation. Give thanks for his blessings now, before you even receive them.

⌒

Pray: O Lord, I freely offer to you all that I have lost. I believe you will restore me to wholeness and much more!

I Thought I Had Toiled In Vain

❖ ❖ ❖

*Though I thought I had toiled in vain, for nothing and for
naught spent my strength, yet my right is with the Lord,
my recompense is with my God.*

- Isaiah 49:4

HAVE YOU EVER thought all your labors were in vain, all
your work was for nothing, and all your plans were for
naught? Sometimes it seems all our hopes and dreams have
gone up in flames. Everything seems hopelessly burned into
smoking ash. It is difficult to forgive others when our lives
seem ruined. We may take heart from the prophet Isaiah, who
encourages us with his faith. In the midst of his discourage-
ment, when he is convinced that he toiled in vain, he falls to
his knees and raises his eyes to heaven. Rather than becoming
bitter or melancholy, he chooses instead to believe in God's
loving presence. Despite all evidence to the contrary, Isaiah
believes God will restore all that he has lost. His faith is not
doubtful, quiet, or passive. He writes it down, he proclaims it
for all to hear, and then he lives it. He lives his life by the light
of his faith in God. Like Isaiah, we can believe that we have not
toiled in vain. We can live today in the fullness of God's love,
as if our Creator has already restored everything we have lost.
My recompense is with my God.

⌒

Pray: O Lord, I know I have not labored in vain. I believe
you will restore me. You make all things fruitful and ripe.

A Light To The Nations

❖ ❖ ❖

*It is too little... for you to be my servant... I will make you
a light to the nations, that my salvation may reach to
the ends of the earth.*

- *Isaiah 49:6*

I F SOMEONE HAS walked all over your feelings, you may feel downtrodden. It is hard to act like a welcome mat when others only use us as a doormat. To make matters worse, when other people are careless towards us, we begin to question whether God cares about us. When we serve others and get nothing in return, we tend to think that God only wants us to be useless servants too. Nothing could be further from the truth. If you listen to God attentively today, you will hear him say that he has bigger plans for your life. By serving others, you are demonstrating your faith. While you may be experiencing a season in which you are serving others who do not appreciate you, rest assured that your future is very bright indeed, above and beyond your imagination. *I will make you a light to the nations.* If you serve God with humility, he will ignite your heart with the passionate fire of his love. With his light illuminating your life, you will be a beacon of his brilliant mercy to a darkened world.

Pray: O Lord, make me content to be your humble servant.
Use me to reflect the light of your love to others in need!

BEFORE I FORMED YOU

❖ ❖ ❖

Before I formed you in the womb I knew you, and
before you were born I consecrated you.

- JEREMIAH 1:5

IN SOME UNFATHOMABLE way we existed in the mind of God before we were conceived in the womb. All we can say in the face of such a profound mystery is that we are each the manifestation of God's divine Love, eternally planned for all time and joyfully welcomed into existence by our all-knowing Father. None of us is an accident for God does not make mistakes. We are individually wanted and passionately loved for all time by the great Life-Giver. Knowing this makes our lives infinitely more precious, beautiful and meaningful. While we are merely pilgrims traveling this earth for a short time, we have an infinite radiance to our being. Human life is indeed full of miraculous love and sensational wonder. Knowing this makes us more loving and forgiving toward others. One vision of heaven describes unborn children as little floating sparks of light that appear to be inhaled and exhaled by God. Can you imagine that?

Pray: O Lord, I thank you for giving me the gift of life!

WILL YOU LAY DOWN YOUR LIFE?

❖ ❖ ❖

Peter said to him, "Lord... I will lay down my life for you."
Jesus answered, "Will you lay down your life for me?

- JOHN 13:37

WHAT IS JESUS asking you to lay down today? Think about it right now. Is he asking you to let go of your anger, bitterness, pride, or regret? Perhaps you hear him calling you to give up resentfulness or unforgiveness? Whatever it is, release it with gratitude. Picture yourself offering it up to Jesus and placing it in his hands. Tell him you want him to take it away permanently so you can be free. As you unburden yourself, feel the sensation of lightness and relief flood your soul. Now hear Jesus tenderly asking you to give him more. He asks you to give him everything. *Will you lay down your life for me?* You want to say yes but you may be afraid. He is not asking without a reason, and he is not asking you to waste your life. Jesus is inviting you to lay down your life for his sake, as he laid down his life for your sake, so that he can raise you to new life, an abundant life, eternal life with him. You can trust him, he is faithful, he is the son of God. When you lay down your life for him, you will not lose your life, but find it. This is a great mystery. There is no loss in Jesus, only gain.

⌐

Pray: O Jesus, I want to lay down my life for you. I trust you to give me new life whenever and however you please!

MY LIFE'S REFUGE

❖   ❖   ❖

The Lord is my life's refuge; of whom should I be afraid?

- PSALM 27:1

I F SOMEONE OR some life circumstance is striking fear into your heart today, fear not. God is with you, rest assured. He is your light in the midst of darkness. He is your protector from all harm, your provider in time of need, your salvation for eternal life. Close your eyes and think for a moment of the one special place in your life where you always felt the safest, a place of peace and happiness and refuge from the turmoil of the world. Can you picture it? Is it a childhood playground, a familiar place near the beach or mountains, a quiet chapel or a lakeside cabin? This is the place of refuge God is building in your soul. This is actually God's living presence within you, available to you now and always. You can find peace in God's presence no matter who is disturbing you. God is your shelter, your hideaway, your sanctuary. With God as your refuge, you need not fear anyone or anything. *God will hide me in his shelter in time of trouble.*

⌐

Pray: O Lord, I know that your loving presence in my life
gives me a special place of security, serenity and peace!

ONE THING I ASK

❖ ❖ ❖

One thing I ask of the Lord; this I seek:
to dwell in the Lord's house all the days of my life,
to gaze on the Lord's beauty.

- PSALM 27:4

IN THE MIDST of trials and tribulations, do you know how to rest in the ultimate safe place? If you ask him, God will deliver you to dwell in his house in heaven forever. In the meantime, all the days of your earthly life, he sends the Holy Spirit to dwell in you. So you get the best of both worlds! In this life the Holy Spirit dwells within you, giving you all strength you need to face life's problems with wisdom, courage, and confidence. In the next life you will dwell in the house of the Lord in perfect peace forever. But your blessings can begin immediately. Starting today, you can gaze on the Lord's beauty as he works to heal you and others in body, mind, and spirit. You can begin to praise God now as you forgive others and help him recreate and redeem their broken lives. *I will offer in his tent sacrifices with shouts of joy; I will sing and chant praise to the Lord.*

⌐

Pray: O Lord, I ask this one thing; to dwell in your house all the days of my life, now and forever. Today I will gaze on your beauty and seek to enhance it in myself and others.

I Believe I Shall See

❖ ❖ ❖

I believe I shall see the Lord's goodness
in the land of the living.

- Psalm 27:13

I
F YOU WANT to enrich your life today, spread joy to others, and give glory to God always, believe in God before you see him. Believe that you will see his goodness in the land of the living, before you get to heaven. Live your life every day with complete faith and hope that you will receive all the blessings God has promised. In other words, live your life now to the fullest with total trust in God. Praise him in advance of actually seeing his blessings; live as if you have already received them. Do not count your sorrows; count your blessings and share them with others. Do not withhold forgiveness from others until they repent; give it to them unconditionally today. You are like a poor tattered beggar who has inherited a vast estate but must wait until the funds are deposited in your bank account. As you wait, are you rich or poor? Are you happy or sad? Of course you rejoice in your new wealth today, even before you receive it. You live in happy expectation that you will soon enjoy spending your wealth thoroughly on good causes to make the world a better place. *Wait for the Lord, take courage; be stouthearted, wait for the Lord!*

Pray: O Lord, I wait in joyful anticipation to receive
all your promises of healing, consolation, and restoration!

THE TOSSING SEA

❖ ❖ ❖

The wicked are like the tossing sea that cannot keep still,
its waters toss up mire and mud.

- ISAIAH 57:20

HAVE YOU EVER tried ocean surfing with a surfboard? First
you paddle out with a lot of effort into the ocean. Next
you swim and kick furiously to get ahead of a chosen wave. The
real excitement starts when you find yourself perfectly poised
in front of the wave and you ride it effortlessly to shore. What
fun! Forgiving others is a lot like surfing. It requires effort to
paddle in front of the wave of an offense, but once you position yourself above it and balance on your surfboard of faith,
you can enjoy the ride of your life. All your cares are washed
away as you glide above the rocks of resentment. The wind is in
your hair and you know God is there. *You will cast all their sins
into the depths of the sea.* Once you get the hang of it, you can
forgive anyone for anything. You can ride on top of any wave,
large or small. People will look at you with astonishment and
wonder how you can be so well-balanced and compassionate.
If they ask, tell them your secret. *More than the sounds of many
waters, than the mighty breakers of the sea, the Lord on high is
mighty.*

⌒

Pray: O Lord, I thank you for teaching me the exhilarating gift
of forgiveness. Help me show others how to do it too!

EVERY PROMISE IS TRUE

❖　❖　❖

*Not one of all the promises the Lord, your God,
made concerning you has failed. Every one has come
true for you; not one has failed.*

- JOSHUA 23:14

HAVE YOU EVER experienced the heartache of a broken promise? You know that imperfect human beings have trouble keeping promises. Broken promises cause division, discord, and disunity. They make it hard to trust others. Nevertheless, we forgive others and move forward. Realistically we must recognize that only God's promises are perfectly trustworthy. God is perfect, so you can always trust his promises to come true; he is the ultimate Promise Keeper. Whatever the Creator promises always becomes reality. Since God lives outside of time, his promise to you today is already true for eternity. You can enjoy a promise from God as if it has already been fulfilled. Which one of God's promises do you need to hear today? He promises protection, guidance, forgiveness, healing, peace of mind, companionship, fearlessness, deliverance, consolation, and eternal life.

Pray: O Lord, thank you for all your promises. I know
I can trust you because your promises always come true.

I WILL TEACH THE WICKED

❖ ❖ ❖

I will teach the wicked your ways,
that sinners may return to you.

- PSALM 51:15

D O YOU KNOW you can teach people who offend you about God? You might relish the idea or find it repulsive, but you have an opportunity to teach others about God by the way you respond to them. If you respond like Jesus, others will experience Jesus! Think of the different ways Jesus responded to transgressors. Depending on the circumstances, Jesus rebuked the wicked, instructed the ignorant, called for repentance, prayed for healing, turned the other cheek, or suffered in silence. Practicing tough love with firmness and fairness, Jesus offered forgiveness and freedom to everyone he met. His goal was always to lead sinners back to God. How do you know the best way to respond to others in your circumstances? Pray to Jesus and ask for his wisdom to know the right answer. He will show you how to teach others, using your words and actions. *Lord, you will open my lips; and my mouth will proclaim your praise.*

⌐

Pray: O Jesus, show me the best way to respond to others so they get to know you better. Help them return to you!

HE HEARS US

❖ ❖ ❖

We have this confidence in him, that if we ask anything according to his will, he hears us.

- 1 JOHN 5:14

IF GOD APPEARED at your side right now and promised to give you anything, what would you ask for? What a wonderful, thrilling prospect to contemplate! The good news is we have this confidence in God today, that if we ask him anything, anything at all, he hears us. No matter where we are or what we are doing, we can talk to God and he listens to every word. Pray with the certain knowledge that you have his undivided attention. You may get distracted but he remains attentive. You may grow weary of praying but he never tires of listening. More amazingly, if you ask anything according to his will, he will supply it to you. What does it mean to pray according to God's will? It means you may pray for your desire but then tell God that you accept his will. As a perfectly loving parent, God wants to give you everything you desire - if it is good for you. When you conform your will to God's will, then you may rest assured that he hears you and he will provide. *We know that he hears us in regard to whatever we ask, we know that what we have asked him for is ours.*

⌐

Pray: O Lord, I have complete confidence that you listen when I pray and will provide everything that is best for me!

I Am Doing Something New

❖ ❖ ❖

Remember not the events of the past, the things of long ago consider not; see, I am doing something new! Now it springs forth, do you not perceive it?

- Isaiah 43:18

IT IS IMPOSSIBLE to forgive someone as long as we persist in recalling and rehashing the injury. Like a dog with an old bone, some people will not let go of a past grievance. Occasionally a poor soul will chew on a dusty old memory and insist on clenching it right down into the grave. Give God the dry bones of your broken past for a proper burial. God wants to heal you of your painful past, hurtful memories, and bitter emotions. He wants you to stop looking backward so you can enjoy the view ahead! Do you want to be healed? Step under the waterfall of his mercy. Let the cascading waters of his love wash away all your memories of past events. Step forward now and begin to walk upstream. Can you hear the gurgling of the crystal blue springs? Can you see that God is doing something new? *I put water in the wilderness and rivers in the wasteland for my chosen people to drink, the people whom I formed for myself.*

⌐

Pray: O Lord, I gladly give you all the painful events and bad memories of my past. Now show me something new!

ALL THINGS NEW

❖ ❖ ❖

Behold, I make all things new.

- REVELATION 21:5

WE BECOME LIBERATED to be more forgiving by contemplating God's promise to make all things new. This wonderful truth unlocks the chains that bind us to our present circumstances. Free from the bondage of thinking that our current problems will never end, we find it easier to forgive others for their sins that trouble us only temporarily. Our burdens seem lighter when we glimpse a view of eternal life. At the end of time, God will right all wrongs, restore all losses, and redeem the world. A more immediate consolation comes when we realize that God is also making things new here and now, in this world. When we forgive others, God is instantly working through us to enlighten darkened minds, rebuild broken relationships, reconcile families, and redeem lost souls. God is making his kingdom here on earth, just as it is in heaven! Look carefully and see how God is making all things new.

⌒

Pray: O Lord, I can see how you are making all things new with your mighty hand. Show me how I can help!

WIPE EVERY TEAR

❖ ❖ ❖

He will wipe every tear from their eyes, and there
shall be no more death or mourning, wailing or pain,
for the old order has passed away.

- REVELATION 21:4

INJURIES AND DISAPPOINTMENTS always lead us to discover hidden blessings. For example, when we are disillusioned by others and disenchanted with the sinfulness in the world around us, we discover to our surprise that we start turning our attention away from this temporary life and more towards heaven. What is heaven like? God promises that he will wipe every tear from our eyes. There will be no more sorrow or pain. Death and mourning will be no more. We will have perfect bodies and enjoy perfect health forevermore. Best of all, we will share fully in the life of the God forevermore. Talk about living happily ever after! Everything will be beautiful beyond your wildest dreams. You will not have to search for heaven. The Holy Spirit will guide you, Jesus will take you by the hand, and the Father will be waiting for you with open arms. *I saw a new heaven and a new earth.*

Pray: O Lord, since you have a heavenly life in store for me,
help me be a blessing to others here on earth!

MORE BLESSED TO GIVE

❖ ❖ ❖

It is more blessed to give than to receive.

- ACTS 20:35

IN THESE WORDS, Jesus gives us a life-changing truth. We cannot learn this truth merely by reading or hearing it, we must experience it. Until we experience this truth we remain spiritually immature. When we are young and self-centered, we delight in receiving gifts for our birthdays. As we grow older we gradually discover that giving is more fun. All good parents know the sheer joy in giving good gifts to children! The same joy is unwrapped in the gift of forgiveness. As wonderful as it is to receive forgiveness from someone else, it is immeasurably more delightful to give it to someone else. When you forgive someone else, watch that person's eyes light up with gratitude and the weight disappear from his or her shoulders. Even if we give the gift of forgiveness to someone who refuses it or carelessly discards it, we still experience the freedom, joy and liberation of having given it anyway. Life in the spirit is like that: the more we give to others, the more God gives to us. The more generous we are to others, the more generous God is to us. This is a great spiritual truth. Try it today.

Pray: O Lord, I want to experience how much more blessed it is to give than to receive. Help me give to others!

Your Body Is A Temple

❖ ❖ ❖

*Do you not know that your body is a temple of
the Holy Spirit within you, whom you have from God,
and that you are not your own?*

- 1 Corinthians 6:19

Do you know that your body is a temple of the Holy Spirit? On the day of your baptism, the Holy Spirit came to dwell deep within your heart and soul. Thank God! Like a familiar house guest, the third member of the Trinity quietly resides deep within you to guide, defend, and befriend you. Think about it: you are a house of God! That means you should treat yourself well. You should love and cherish your body in the same way that you love and cherish God. It also means that anyone who hurts you also hurts God. That person injured your body, which is finite, but more grievously that person injured God, who is infinite. Going deeper, since your body is redeemed by the presence of the Holy Spirit, you are no longer your own. You have been purchased, as it were, and now you belong to God. That means listening when he asks you to forgive the person who offended you. God desires that you forgive that person on his behalf. Forgive that person for God's sake, not your own. The Holy Spirit will empower you to do it.

⌐

Pray: O Holy Spirit, my dear friend, give me your grace to completely forgive those who have offended me and you!

WE RESPOND GENTLY

❖ ❖ ❖

When ridiculed, we bless; when persecuted, we endure;
when slandered, we respond gently.

- 1 CORINTHIANS 4:12

T HE NEXT TIME someone ridicules you, respond with 'God bless you.' If you are persecuted today, endure it in the peaceful fortress of your soul. Whenever you are slandered, respond gently with a kind word. These loving responses will not only defuse the situation and quiet your soul, they will also open the doors to dialogue, understanding, and perhaps reconciliation. You may convert an enemy into a friend. Even better, you will show that person the face of Christ. Instead of responding in anger - our natural impulse - you can be a channel for the love of Christ to flow through you. Keep in mind that you may be the first person that individual has ever met who demonstrates the love of Christ. Just as Christ used his love in the past to change your heart, he may be using you now to lead your adversary to come home to God. What a priceless opportunity for you! Imagine your enemy rushing to embrace you in heaven while exclaiming, 'You led me here!'

Pray: O Jesus, give me the grace to respond to others with firm and gentle kindness, the same way you respond to me.

TREASURE IN EARTHEN VESSELS

❖ ❖ ❖

We hold this treasure in earthen vessels,
that the surpassing power may be of God and not from us.

- 2 CORINTHIANS 4:7

IN THE OLD days, farmers used to hide their gold coins in clay jars and bury them in the earth for safekeeping. The only trouble was when they forgot where they buried the clay jars. They would have to dig hole after hole in the field until they found the clay jars. Like those farmers we sometimes forget where we have buried our greatest treasure. What is this treasure? It is the life of Christ within us. Though we are only humble earthen vessels, created like clay jars from the dust of the earth, God in his infinite humility has seen fit to dwell in us! This is a great mystery, that the Creator of the universe would condescend to live in such humble abode. Like a king who chooses to dwell in a dirty adobe hut with a thatched roof, Christ makes his home in you. We must take care to welcome him with humility and serve him faithfully. We can joyfully proclaim that all our accomplishments are due not to our own efforts but rather to his surpassing power.

Pray: O Lord, I cherish the divine life you live within me and through me. Renew me with your loving power!

WE ARE AFFLICTED

❖ ❖ ❖

We are afflicted in every way, but not constrained; perplexed,
but not driven to despair; persecuted,
but not abandoned; struck down, but not destroyed.

- 2 CORINTHIANS 4:8

N O MATTER HOW bad things get, we are never defeated because God is with us. If you do not believe this, ask God to help you believe it. He wants you to believe it. God sent his son Jesus to help you believe it. Your life is a lot like the life of Jesus, did you know that? Like you, Jesus was afflicted in every way, perplexed by his friends, persecuted by his adversaries, and struck down by his enemies. Yet he was not prevented from accomplishing his mission, he did not despair, God never abandoned him, and he rose to new life after his death. We suffer in our earthly life the same way. We may fear at times that we will be overwhelmed but we always manage to survive and prosper with the help of Jesus. We understand that in the midst of our suffering we are *always carrying about in the body the dying of Jesus, so that the life of Jesus may also be manifested in our body.*

Pray: O Lord, I thank you for reassuring me that all my suffering is worthwhile to help bring about the life of Jesus!

LIFE IN OUR MORTAL FLESH

❖ ❖ ❖

*We who live are constantly being given up to death
for the sake of Jesus, so that the life of Jesus may be
manifested in our mortal flesh.*

- 2 CORINTHIANS 4:11

WHY DO WE have to suffer and die? If God is good, why
would he create a world that contains suffering? If God
is merciful, why does he allow bad things to happen to good
people? These questions about suffering have been cried out
by all people since the beginning of time. Though this question has been pondered by philosophers, priests, princes, and
paupers throughout the course of human history, one answer
is sufficient. God originally created the universe to be perfect
and without suffering. Human disobedience introduced suffering into the world, so God in his infinite mercy sent his
son Jesus to forgive sins and re-create the world. Now we live
in that time of re-creation in which suffering is still permitted
by God according to his mysterious plan for our salvation. Far
from being meaningless, our suffering in this life is infinitely
meaningful, if we offer ourselves as a living sacrifice to God,
because God uses our suffering to manifest the life of Jesus in
our mortal flesh. Just as God brought new life to the world
through the death of his Son, he brings new life in Jesus to us
through our suffering.

Pray: O Lord, I do not understand the mystery of suffering, but
I trust your promise that it brings healing to the world!

OUR INNER SELF IS BEING RENEWED

❖ ❖ ❖

*Although our outer self is wasting away, our inner self
is being renewed day by day.*

- 2 CORINTHIANS 4:16

HAVE YOU EVER worried you were just wasting away? When things get difficult you may feel as if you are simply falling apart physically, mentally or emotionally. Every day seems to bring a backache, headache or heartbreak. You fear you are wasting your time, wasting your life, wasting away into nothingness. This may be true for your outer self, for we are all destined to experience a season of decay, decline, and ultimately death. But you need to remember that your inner self is being renewed every day. God is at work within you, if you allow him entry, creating everything anew in the cathedral of your soul. You may look in the mirror at your outer self with dismay, but God looks with delight beneath the surface of your appearance into the depths of the growing beauty of your unfathomable soul. Despite life's temporary afflictions, contradictions and rejections that cause your body to wilt like a flower, God is busy growing your soul with his supernatural power. *For this momentary light affliction is producing for us an eternal weight of glory beyond all comparison.*

Pray: O Lord, help me to see past my outer self and see what you see: my inner self being renewed day by day!

WHAT IS UNSEEN IS ETERNAL

❖ ❖ ❖

We look not to what is seen but to what is unseen;
for what is seen is transitory, but what is unseen is eternal.

- 2 CORINTHIANS 4:18

DO YOU REMEMBER when it first dawned on you that life is far greater than the visible world? Perhaps you were sitting on a beach looking at the blue ocean melting into the horizon, or maybe you were gazing at the night sky filled with twinkling stars and galaxies, or possibly you were praying in a small quiet chapel. Most of us remember the marvelous feeling of glimpsing the infinite, the thrilling realization that what is unseen is vastly more immense and real than what is seen. While the visible universe is stupendous and beautiful, the invisible reality of God's creation is indescribably more real, exquisite, and infinite. While we cannot comprehend this wondrous mystery that originated in the mind of God, he has created us sufficiently in his image to allow us to be astonished by understanding a glimmer of it. When we face transitory problems in this life, the best solution is to look not to what is seen but what is unseen. The solution to most of our problems begins when we glimpse the face of God.

Pray: O Lord my God, Creator of the universe, open my eyes today to see another glimpse of your unseen reality!

LET THERE BE LIGHT

❖ ❖ ❖

God said: Let there be light, and there was light.

I F YOU FEEL as if you are living in darkness because someone trespassed against you, lift your eyes and see the light of the words of God. God's words contain all the light you need for comfort, healing, and illuminating the path ahead. Remember that God's divine words are more resourceful and fruitful than ours. Our words are dim and descriptive while God's words are radiant and creative. The words that God speaks are so potent, passionate, and productive that they change the world. How did God create the universe, light, and human beings? He *spoke* them into existence. Such is the mighty power of God that when he speaks, his words do not just affect reality, they create a new reality. God's words are light, life and love. Meditate on this. Gods words are alive and at work in you and throughout the universe in utterly mysterious, surprising and exuberant ways. Gods wants you to hear his words in order to fill you with his light, his truth, and his new life. Will you listen to God today and let his words change your life? *By the word of the Lord the heavens were made, and all their host by the breath of his mouth.*

⌒

Pray: O Lord, thank you for your holy words.
Your words bring me forgiveness, healing, and new life!

WHEN I FOUND YOUR WORDS

❖ ❖ ❖

*When I found your words, I devoured them; they became
my joy and the happiness of my heart.*

- JEREMIAH 15:16

ONCE YOU DISCOVER the power of the words of God, your
life is transformed every time you read them. When God
opens our eyes to the truth of his words, we realize they are
not dead letters or ancient superstitions. As you read God's
words, they come alive and dance in front of your eyes, then
jump off the page into your heart and become a fountain of joy
and happiness in your life. They are life itself, emanating from
the mind of God, breathed from his mouth into your nostrils,
infusing you with divine vitality. Devour them with delight as
one who is famished enjoys a sumptuous feast of succulent fruit.
*One does not live by bread alone, but by every word that comes
forth from the mouth of God.* His words provide all the nourishment you need because he lives in his words and his words live
in you. When you understand God's words and absorb them
into your life, you are welcoming God himself into your soul.
Gods words are mysteriously renewing the entire universe and
everything in it. Hear God's words forgiving you today and use
them to forgive others. *Pleasing words are a honeycomb, sweet to
the taste and invigorating to the bones.*

⌒

Pray: O Lord, your words are light and life, better than the best
wine or corn. Teach me to speak your words to others!

IN THE BEGINNING WAS THE WORD

❖ ❖ ❖

*In the beginning was the Word, and the Word was
with God, and the Word was God.*

- JOHN 1:1

IF YOU STILL struggle to receive divine forgiveness and genuine healing from God, contemplate the fact that God and his Word existed before time began. God the Great Lover exists eternally, outside of time, with his beloved Son. Jesus is the eternal expression of his Father's loving, living, breathing Word, through whom God created the universe. *He was in the beginning with God. All things came to be through him, and without him nothing came to be. What came to be through him was life, and this life was the light of the human race.* Thus we know that the words of God are not hollow sounds that echo in our ears or scrawls of ink that fade before our eyes; rather they are the living, loving, laughing source of all life and light in the universe. When God says he loves you, you may be certain that you are infused with an everlasting love. When God says he forgives you, you are truly cleansed and healed eternally. When God asks you to forgive others, he empowers you to do it and illuminates your path forward with joy. *The light shines in the darkness, and the darkness has not overcome it.*

⤳

Pray: O Lord, awaken me to the astonishing power of your divine Word. Heal me and help me to heal others too!

THE WORD OF THE CROSS IS FOLLY

❖ ❖ ❖

The word of the cross is folly to those who are perishing,
but to us who are being saved it is the power of God.

- 1 CORINTHIANS 1:18

WHEN WE HEAR Jesus asking us to forgive our enemies it can sound like pure folly. What is the use in forgiving someone who has not apologized; what is the point in showing mercy to an individual who does not deserve it; where is the justice in releasing a person who is guilty? We are aggrieved when we are left behind to nurse our injuries and sad memories. All this talk of loving our enemies and turning the other cheek seems stupid and foolish. The answer is that the words of Jesus appear weak and laughable to those who do not know God. To those who are perishing without faith, the wisdom of God sounds like utter nonsense, no better than the ravings of a lunatic. Typically they mock, jeer, and ridicule his way of living. Who wants to die to oneself, pick up a cross and carry it daily? Yet for those of us who hear the words of Jesus inviting us to pick up our crosses and follow him, his words are the power of God. To us happy few, the word of the cross resides in the deepest recesses of our hearts, calling us to forgiveness and leading us along the path to salvation.

Pray: O Lord, your way of life seems foolish to others. Help me show them how your way leads to new life!

SEEK FIRST THE KINGDOM

❖ ❖ ❖

*Seek first the kingdom of God and his righteousness, and
all these things will be given you besides.*

- MATTHEW 6:33

WHAT DO YOU desire in your life today? Most of us spend most of our time lamenting what we have lost in the past, grasping what we desire in the present, or craving what we seek in the future. Our appetites make us lustful, self-seeking and unforgiving. If only we had a better job or a bigger house, better health or a new spouse, we imagine our lives would be perfect. We fret that we will never get to where we want to be or that God is holding us back. The truth is that our natural desires can never be satisfied by worldly things because we were made by God and only he can satisfy us with his holy presence. God made us in his image with eternal souls, so we have an inborn desire for his infinite love. Thus no finite person or possession on earth can ever fully satisfy us. Only when we seek God above all in our lives will we find him. Then his inexhaustible love will meet our insatiable desire for him, and he will engulf us with grace. Jesus tells us not to worry about mere food, clothes, health or long life. He invites us to seek a relationship with his Father. Then he promises to give us all the other things we desire.

Pray: O Lord, I want to seek you above everything and everyone else in my life. Fill me with your graceful love!

NEW THINGS HAVE COME

❖ ❖ ❖

*The old things have passed away; behold,
new things have come.*

- 2 CORINTHIANS 5:17

I F YOU ARE haunted by old memories that make you sad, let them go and let God heal your mind. God wants to heal you in every way, including hurtful memories of the past, so you can enjoy the new things, experiences and relationships he wants to give you. Memories are like old photos: most of them are good but you have to throw away the bad ones. This is what God does: he throws away all the bad memories in our lives that make us sad. If we feel them being dredged up again, tempting us to feel accused or mortified or condemned, that is a temptation from the evil one. So we also need to throw the devil out of our lives like a moldy, sticky, faded old photo. God sent us his son not to condemn us, but rather to save us, to heal us, and to give us new life abundantly. How do we know this? Jesus said it himself. *I came not to judge the world but to save it.*

⌒

Pray: O Lord, today I give you all my sad memories of the past. Heal me so I can enjoy my new future with you!

LIFE IS LIKE A MOVIE

❖ ❖ ❖

I am confident of this, that the one who began
a good work in you will continue to complete it
until the day of Christ Jesus.

- PHILIPPIANS 1:6

SOMETIMES WE CANNOT forgive people because we have frozen their offense like a photo in time. Especially when someone offers no apology or shows no signs of remorse, we mistakenly think that person will never change. We make it harder to forgive that individual because we have given up on the wrongdoer. But life is not a still photo; life is a movie. People do change because life is constantly changing. People do not always change for the better, but they do change. We are all actors in this epic movie called life and we are making it up as we go. Some people say whatever they please, while others seek to memorize and proclaim the words of God. Some people act however they wish, while others seek to be a blessing to the audience. God is sitting quietly in the audience, watching intently, smiling at some actors and frowning at others. He does not judge us based upon one flawed performance. Instead he allows us to appear in a second and third act, as needed, hoping each time we will get it right. God began a good work in us, and he wants us to help him complete it.

⌒

Pray: O Lord, help me forgive others even before they change. Like you, I will never give up hoping they repent!

He Will Change Our Lowly Body

❖ ❖ ❖

*He will change our lowly body
to conform with his glorified body.*

- Philippians 3:21

O FTEN WE STRUGGLE to forgive others because they have caused permanent injuries to our bodies. By the same token, we can find it hard to forgive ourselves if we have caused permanent harm to others. We discover freedom from this heavy burden by remembering that God promises to heal us completely, renew us in every way, and give us perfect bodies in heaven. In other words, if God has not healed you yet, he will heal you soon. *I will restore you, and you shall be rebuilt.* If you are eagerly waiting to be healed, let God use this time to turn your attention heavenward. You will soon have the body you always wanted! What will it look like? We know that God will transform our broken bodies and make them radiant like his glorified body, perfect in every way. *We know that when He appears we shall be like him.* No aches or pains, no disease or missing limbs. We will exult forever in heavenly health, immaculate complexion, and pristine perfection. *Just as we have borne the image of the earthly one, we shall also bear the image of the heavenly one.*

⌒

Pray: O Lord, help me to keep in mind your promise to give me a glorified body with perfect health in heaven!

My Ways Are Higher

❖ ❖ ❖

As the heavens are higher than the earth, so are my ways higher than your ways and my thoughts than your thoughts.

- *Isaiah 55:8*

THE MORE LIFE hurts, the more we think God is not fair. How could he allow this to happen? We cry out in pain as people have done throughout history. *The Lord's way is not fair!* In our misery we are tempted to think we could do a better job than God. If only we were in charge of the universe, we imagine we could do it the right way. For starters, we would certainly eliminate all suffering, conflict, and distress. But that would mean depriving people of their free will. God has given us each free will to choose whether to follow him or not. This is the essence of God's love for us: he does not force us to love him in return. But what about all the suffering in the world? It is a profound mystery. We can only rest with God's promise that he is actively at work in ways that are often hidden to our eyes, making everything beautiful beyond our imagining. He is weaving a stupendous multicolored tapestry on the top side, yet we see only the bottom side with its confusing web of knots and tangled thread. *My thoughts are not your thoughts, nor are your ways my ways, says the Lord.*

⌐

Pray: O Lord, I understand you are re-creating the world in ways that I will only know in heaven. For now, I trust you!

WHATEVER WE ASK

❖ ❖ ❖

We receive from him whatever we ask, because we keep his commandments and do what pleases him.

- 1 JOHN 3:22

CAN WE REALLY get whatever we ask from God? This is a very frustrating verse because we ask God for many things without result. How can we explain this promise that we will receive from God whatever we ask? Let us look deeper. God's gifts depend upon our keeping his commandments — what parent rewards a child for disobedience? Like a loving parent, God knows what we want, what we need, and what is best for us. But first he wants us to be obedient! He wants us to obey his commandments because he knows they will lead us to happiness. We know God's greatest commandment: loving him, loving our neighbors, and loving ourselves. This means forgiving others as we forgive ourselves. Have you forgiven others today? Have you forgiven yourself? As you learn to forgive, you are pleasing God. But do not expect God to grant all your childish desires. Like a good parent, God gives us only what is best — what parent gives a child candy before dinner? *If you then, who are wicked, know how to give good gifts to your children, how much more will your heavenly Father give good things to those who ask him!*

⌒

Pray: O Lord, I wish today to please you in every way!

SEEK AND YOU WILL FIND

❖ ❖ ❖

Ask and it will be given to you; seek and you will find;
knock and the door will be opened to you.

- MATTHEW 7:7

THERE HE GOES again. Jesus is always promising to give us whatever we want! How can we believe this when he does not answer our prayers? God may be withholding good things from you until you conform your life more fully to him. You must lose your selfish desires. *You ask but do not receive, because you ask wrongly, to spend it on your passions.* Another reason God may be withholding good things from you is to lead you more deeply into prayer and more intimately into holy communion. He wants to enlarge your heart so that you may more fully receive the superabundance he intends to pour into you. God knows what you need and he wants to give it to you. Your Father wants to provide you his abundance more than you want to receive it! He has more in store for you than you can possibly imagine. Pray without ceasing and soon the day will come when you receive everything that God has stored up for you. Like a pile of carefully wrapped and brightly colored birthday gifts, God's blessings are waiting for you. *For everyone who asks, receives; and the one who seeks, finds; and to the one who knocks, the door will be opened.*

⤍

Pray: O Lord, I ask to receive, I seek to find, and I knock knowing that in your perfect time the door will be opened!

PEARLS BEFORE SWINE

❖ ❖ ❖

*Do not give what is holy to dogs, or throw your pearls before
swine, lest they trample them underfoot,
and turn and tear you to pieces.*

- *MATTHEW 7:6*

D O WE REALLY have to turn the other cheek to those who
offend us, walk the extra mile with those who mistreat
us, and offer our cloak to those who would be happy for us
to freeze? Jesus provides the answer with the words he spoke
and the life he lived. He sought out the lost sheep but rejected
the wolves. He healed the sick but admonished those who
thought they needed no physician. He comforted the lonely
but departed from the proud. He loved and prayed for everyone but ultimately released his persecutors to pursue their own
selfish desires. Jesus cautions us to do likewise. *Behold, I am
sending you like sheep in the midst of wolves; so be shrewd as serpents and simple as doves.* We must not be naive; we need to recognize the deceptive ways of the world. We need not give our
holy presence to dogs or throw our pearls of wisdom to pigs.
We can be shrewd as serpents when we possess God's wisdom.
We may be simple as doves when we rely on the Holy Spirit for
guidance. We must be loving and trusting as sheep with Jesus
as our watchful shepherd.

⌐

Pray: O Lord, give me the wisdom to know when to depart
from others, as you did, while continuing to pray for them.

PUT OUT INTO DEEP WATER

❖ ❖ ❖

Put out into deep water and lower your nets for a catch.

- LUKE 5:4

I F YOU ARE in despair today, you are like Peter and his fishermen friends. They had *toiled all night and caught nothing*, so they were exhausted. They had no fish to sell and no food to eat. Here comes a stranger named Jesus who walks, uninvited, into Peter's boat, and invites him to sail into deeper water and try again. This action is typical of Jesus: he enters into our lives in surprising ways when we need him most. Peter protests that they have tried and failed, but they relent and sail out again to deeper water. This time the caught so many fish their nets were tearing and their boats were in danger of sinking. *When Peter saw this, he fell at the knees of Jesus and said, "Depart from me, Lord, for I am a sinful man."* Peter was so astonished by this unexpected abundance, so sorrowful for his previous doubts, and so grateful for his good fortune that he dropped his net and fell to his knees right there in the boat. Can we live like this? Can we expect Jesus to change our lives when we need him most? Can we trust him and sail into deeper waters even when we are exhausted? Can we be grateful for God's blessings even before we receive them?

Pray: O Jesus, lead me into deeper waters today where I can joyfully cast my net again to catch all your blessings!

THEY LEFT EVERYTHING

❖ ❖ ❖

When they brought their boats to the shore,
they left everything and followed him.

- LUKE 5:11

WHEN JESUS JOINED the poor fishermen and they hauled in the biggest catch of their lives, they were astonished. Who was this stranger in their midst? What would you do if Jesus appeared to you today and granted all your desires? Suppose he answers all your prayers, heals your wounds, reconciles your relationships, and gives you unlimited wealth? What will you do? Surely you will thank him enthusiastically. Then you might share your newfound wealth with family, friends, and perhaps strangers. But will you change your attitudes, beliefs, or habits? Will you surrender some oppressive sin or practice a holy virtue? Will you be more forgiving, loving, or grateful? Will you tell people about the abundance that Jesus can provide? Will you be like the hungry fishermen who bring their boats to the shore, drop their nets, leave everything behind and follow Jesus? Perhaps you are not called to leave your ordinary life behind, yet you can still leave your sinful life behind and follow Jesus with all your strength and mind. You can become a fearless follower of Jesus with a higher purpose; to fish for people's hearts and souls.

Pray: O Lord, show me today how I can joyfully leave
my past behind, follow you eagerly, and lead others to you.

Do Not Fear Bad News

❖ ❖ ❖

They are not afraid of evil tidings;
their hearts are firm, secure in the Lord.

- Psalm 112:7

WHEN A WRONGDOER offends us, that offense sometimes sets off a chain reaction of negative events. Like an earthquake that shakes the earth, an adversary can devastate our lives and cause multiple aftershocks that last for days or years. A divorce may cause ongoing arguments and legal problems. An injury may require extensive medical treatment. A financial loss can cause bills to pile up and collection agencies to demand payment. In the midst of our trials and tribulations, how can we possibly find peace? By turning to God and placing our hope and trust in him, we receive his intimate peace. *My peace I give you,* says the Lord. This is not the peace of the world; it is his divine presence. It is the heavenly peace of God in our hearts that he gives to those who love him. God makes our hearts firm by setting us on a rock high above the pounding surf. From our high perch we are not afraid of any evil tidings. No evil report surprises or capsizes us. With serenity we observe the churning ocean below and cast our gaze to the horizon as it glows with the brilliant colors of each new day that greets us with the rising Son. *Their hearts are steady, they will not be afraid.*

Pray: O Lord, I give myself to you today fearlessly and wholeheartedly. Thank you for your security and serenity!

SPEAKING THE TRUTH IN LOVE

❖   ❖   ❖

Speaking the truth in love, we are to grow up in every way into him who is the head, into Christ.

- EPHESIANS 4:15

ONE OF THE temptations we face when we have been hurt is to withdraw. Just as we snatch our sensitive fingers away from a hot fire, so too we recoil when our feelings are hurt. We dislike getting burned physically or emotionally so our natural inclination is to nurse our hurt feelings in isolation while resenting the other person. But God wants us to speak the truth to others. And he gives us the response-ability to do it with love. We need to speak words of kindness, correction, and forgiveness. We need to reach out to wayward souls with gloves of courage and words of love, past the flames of resentment, over the hot coals of anger, and through the sparks of misunderstanding. Our goal is to quench the flaming bonfires of conflict by dousing them with words of wisdom from the clouds of heaven. When the fires of discord are quelled, God willing, the dampened earth will show fresh signs of life and rebirth. By speaking the truth in love, you may have softened a heart, made a new friend, and saved a lost soul.

Pray: O Lord, thank you for giving me the courage and wisdom to reach out to others and speak the truth in love!

WHAT TO SAY TO AN OFFENDER

❖ ❖ ❖

*Do not worry about how you are to speak
or what you are to say. You will be given at that
moment what you are to say.*

- MATTHEW 10:19

WHEN YOU HAVE decided to speak the truth in love to someone who has offended you, do not worry about what you are going to say. You may write down your thoughts but you need not rewrite and rehearse endlessly. Simply pray for God's grace, wisdom, and peace. He will give you the right words at the right time! This is possible because God has sent the Holy Spirit to dwell within you. If you relax and get out of the way, the Holy Spirit will actually speak through you. At that moment you will become a channel through which the Holy Spirit can speak. You will be God's spokesperson, a messenger of the Holy Spirit! What you speak will not be your words alone; you will speak God's message. Remember that God's words do more than describe and persuade; they are supernaturally powerful to create, forgive, and redeem lost souls. Your offenders may choose to turn a deaf ear to you, but your words will contain the healing power of God. *For it will not be you who speak but the Spirit of your Father speaking through you.*

⌐

Pray: Come Holy Spirit, help me to say the right words at the right time. I want to speak your truth in love to others!

GOD LOVES A CHEERFUL GIVER

❖ ❖ ❖

Whoever sows sparingly will also reap sparingly,
and whoever sows bountifully will also reap bountifully.

- 2 CORINTHIANS 9:6

WHEN IT COMES to forgiveness, be like a farmer and sow bountifully. All farmers know that if they sow only a few seeds in the ground they can expect to reap a meager harvest, but if they sow bountifully they will also reap bountifully. They know generous sowing is repaid sixtyfold or a hundredfold in their harvest. This applies to forgiveness too. If we offer forgiveness to others sparingly, we will receive meager forgiveness from God, but if we give forgiveness to others freely, we will receive an abundance of forgiveness from God. Furthermore, when we spread seeds of mercy on the dry soil of hardened hearts we may transform barren lives into a bountiful harvest of faith, gratitude and love. This is one of the great mysteries of life: the more you give, the more you receive. The more you give the gift of forgiveness, the more you receive God's abundant grace. Do you want to be rich in spirit? Sow the seeds of forgiveness generously, then you will reap a bountiful harvest, *for God loves a cheerful giver.*

Pray: O Lord, I want to be a farmer in your field of love,
sowing forgiveness bountifully and reaping abundantly!

Always Having All You Need

❖　❖　❖

*God is able to make every grace abundant for you, so that
in all things, always having all you need, you may have
an abundance for every good work.*

- 2 Corinthians 9:8

OFTEN ONE OBSTACLE that prevents us from forgiving others is the fear that we will appear weak and vulnerable.
We fear that others will take advantage of us. Yet God assures
us that he will make every grace abundant for us, so that in
every situation he will provide all we need. If we trust him to
guide us, he promises to resupply all our necessities. God calls
us to do his good work, and that includes offering mercy and
forgiveness to wrongdoers. He outfits us with his armor, equips
us with hearty supplies, and empowers us to accomplish his
will. It is as if he points across a trackless desert toward the
horizon and invites us to journey forth with the assurance that
he walks beside us laden with food, water, and medicine. God
knows what we need and he knows the way ahead. We travel
with confidence, courage and gratitude. We enjoy an abiding
sense that God will provide for all our needs along the way. *The
one who supplies seed to the sower and bread for food will supply
and multiply your seed.*

Pray: O Lord, I know that as long as I walk with you by my
side, you will supply everything I need to proceed!

WHY HAVE YOU FORSAKEN ME?

❖ ❖ ❖

My God, my God, why have you forsaken me?

- MARK 15:34

AFTER ALL IS said and done, the person we may need to forgive the most is God. We assume he has forsaken us in our time of need. After all, is it not obvious that God deserted his son as he hung on the cross? In his most desperate hour Jesus cried out, *My God, why have you forsaken me?* We too cry out to God and ask why he allows us to suffer. Yet we must look deeper now and farther than our earthly eyes can see. We must listen more keenly than our human ears can hear. We must reach out past our worldly perception, past the point where our feeble senses fail, past our problems covered by a heavenly veil. God's absence is only a delusion, a temptation by our adversary to despair. We must learn to see with eyes of faith, hear with ears of hope, and touch the face of God. We realize with surprising gratitude that God is within us, giving us life, courage and supernatural intimacy. He has never been far, he is always near, cradling us in the palm of his hand. *I will never leave you, I will never forsake you, I will be with you until the end of the age.*

Pray: O Lord, now that I know you are with me
all the days of my life, I cry out to you with joyful praise!

They Do Not Know

❖ ❖ ❖

Father, forgive them; for they do not know
what they are doing.

- Luke 23:34

AFTER ALL OUR reading about forgiveness, hearing about it, avoiding it, and anguishing about it, we have no better example than Jesus forgiving his enemies on the cross. Here he hung in agony, condemned by his own people, deserted by all but two of his beloved friends, and crucified by the powers of the government. Yet in his final hour Jesus calls out to heaven and asks his Father to forgive them *for they know not what they do.* But wait, we protest, they knew exactly what they were doing, they were killing him! But Jesus knew that in truth they knew nothing of the love of God. Their eyes were blind, their ears were deaf, and their hearts were made of stone. Jesus' persecutors promoted pride, craved condemnation, and loved death. Such were some of us at one time, adding to Jesus' wounds. While Jesus is unable to forgive those who scoff at mercy, yet he is our faithful advocate who cries out to our Father to have mercy upon us all. We can do likewise for our persecutors. We can imitate Jesus by praying to our Father and asking him to forgive the lost souls who know not what they do.

Pray: O Lord, today I ask you to forgive my persecutors because they do not know what they are doing.

FATHER KNOWS BEST

❖ ❖ ❖

Father, into your hands I commend my spirit.

- LUKE 23:46

ANYTIME YOU FIND yourself suffering for any reason, you may freely put yourself in God's hands. Any heartache will do, any reason is sufficient, any sadness is welcome. God wants you to bring him all your troubles: he wants to help you carry your heavy burdens: he wants to lift you off your painful cross. You do not need to wait until you are on your deathbed to rush into his loving arms. God is always waiting to embrace you, willing to console you, wanting to save you. Such a comforting thought: the Great Physician wants to hold you in the palm of his hand and heal you. To show us the way, Jesus commended his spirit into his Father's hands as he hung on his cross. This was not the first time Jesus put himself in God's hands; he lived his entire life this way, daily declaring his compete surrender, total dependence and absolute trust in his Father's loving care. We can live the same way by trusting that our Father knows best. We can discover the freedom to live, laugh, and love again.

⌐

Pray: O Jesus, thank you for showing me how to trust you completely and place my entire life in your loving hands!

ALL HAVE SINNED

❖　❖　❖

All have sinned and fall short of the glory of God.

- 1 JOHN 1:8

WHY IS IT so tempting to focus on the sins of others? Because this allows us to feel superior by comparison. It also diverts our attention away from our own sins. Yet while the offenses of others may be more grievous than ours, we need to acknowledge that we are sinners too. We need to look in the mirror and recognize that we have all fallen short of the glory of God. This is due to the fact that we were born into a fallen world in a state of original sin. It is also a result of our own selfish choices. Our stiff-necked pride prevents us from seeing the truth, and we lock ourselves in a dark prison of self-deception. *If we say, 'We are without sin,' we deceive ourselves, and the truth is not in us.* The truth sets us free; when we confess our sins to God with a contrite heart, he breaks the chains and shackles that bind us. Liberated from our own sins and grateful for God's mercy, we see clearly that the sins of others are not so different from our own, and we find it easier to forgive them.

⁓

Pray: O Lord, help me acknowledge and confess my sins. I want to be free to forgive others as you forgive me!

GREATEST IN THE KINGDOM

❖ ❖ ❖

Whoever breaks one of the least of these commandments and teaches others to do so will be called least in the kingdom of heaven.

- *MATTHEW 5:19*

WE TEND TO excuse our own sins because they are less grievous than the sins of other people. For example, we may think our gossip, envy or unforgiveness is trivial and insignificant when compared to other people stealing, lying or murdering. But we must not excuse ourselves so lightly. Jesus cautions us by saying those who commit even the least sins and teach others to do so will be called the *least in the kingdom*. Little sins are not equal to big ones, but all sins require repentance. Even our littlest sins are contrary to God's perfect will and require us to seek his forgiveness! *Whoever keeps the whole law, but falls short in one particular, has become guilty in respect to all of it.* Even our smallest sins separate us from God's love to some degree, so we must repent of all sin. Jesus wants us to be perfect, even as our heavenly Father is perfect, so he empowers us to hear and obey God's will in our lives. *Whoever obeys and teaches these commandments will be called greatest in the kingdom of heaven.*

⌐

Pray: O Lord, help me to gratefully hear, willingly obey, and joyfully teach others your loving commandments!

CLEANSE US FROM EVERY WRONGDOING

❖ ❖ ❖

*If we acknowledge our sins, he is faithful and just
and will forgive our sins and cleanse us from
every wrongdoing.*

- 1 JOHN 1:9

YOU MAY HAVE forgiven others, and you may have forgiven God, but you may find it hardest to forgive yourself. If you have hurt someone else, apologize and make amends, of course. Then acknowledge your offense with courage to God, a priest, or a pastor. Believe God when he promises to forgive our sins and cleanse us from every wrongdoing. If the trauma of your offense still prevents you from accepting God's mercy, ask for the grace of deeper humility and wholehearted faith. Place your offense and the injured person at the foot of the cross and ask Jesus to heal you both. Surrender to God's promise that he will take care of that person and bring a greater good out of the injury. *We know that in everything God works for good with those who love him.* This is your time to trust God completely. While you may not see the good that God is working in you or the other person, trust that he is indeed recreating all things for good. God delights in supernaturally bringing about something better than before — just as he used the occasion of Jesus' death to bring about his resurrection to new life!

⌐

Pray: O Lord, I abandon myself to your divine mercy. Help me believe that you work out everything for good!

ALL THINGS ARE POSSIBLE

❖ ❖ ❖

For human beings this is impossible,
but for God all things are possible.

- MATTHEW 19:26

DO YOUR CIRCUMSTANCES seem hopeless today? Perhaps you have lost your health, wealth, or a relationship. You see no way out of your predicament, no possibility of change on the horizon, no hope for the future. You may be correct from a natural point of view, but remember that the Creator of the Universe is on your side. It may be impossible for you or any other human being to improve your condition, but for God all things are possible. He operates daily in a supernatural way. Take your problems and offer them up to God. Release yourself to him. He is reaching out right now to receive you. Just as he created everything out of nothing by speaking it all into existence, God can change your life with one holy word. With one gentle wave of his hand or a soft snap of his fingers, God can radically renew your life. So ask God to change your life today. He is waiting for you to ask, willing for you to receive him, and wanting to answer your prayer. You may see his results instantly or you may have to wait until you get to heaven, but he is working on your case right now. Give yourself wholeheartedly to the one for whom all things are possible.

Pray: O Lord, I know I cannot solve my problems alone, but
I trust that with you all things are possible,
and I thank you in advance for your mercy!

OFFER YOUR LOSSES TO GOD

❖ ❖ ❖

I lay down my life in order to take it up again.

- JOHN 10:17

ONE OF THE most difficult obstacles to forgiving others is the grief we experience from genuine loss. We resent being deprived of our health, wealth or relationships. We cannot forgive others because we cannot forget what they have taken. When we are lamenting whatever we have lost, forgiveness seems like an unbearable additional cost. But Jesus shows us how to transform a loss by freely giving up that which is taken. *This is why the Father loves me, because I lay down my life in order to take it up again.* Give up your loss, lay it down, and let God take it up again. Some losses are irretrievable in this life and must be accepted in faith. God does not will our misfortune, but sometimes he allows it. The fact that God has allowed a loss in your life makes it your new reality. You can accept your wound in faith as his permissive will for your life and offer it up to God. No one can take anything from you if you freely give it up. As Jesus willingly laid down his life, you can too with his promise that he will renew everything. *No one takes it from me, but I lay it down on my own. I have power to lay it down, and power to take it up again.*

Pray: O Jesus, help me today to offer all my losses to you in faith. I trust that you will wonderfully restore my life!

No Greater Love

❖ ❖ ❖

*No one has greater love than this, to lay down
one's life for one's friends.*

- John 15:13

WE FIND IT much easier to forgive others when we freely give up what we have lost. This is the greatest love — offering to others that which we would prefer to keep for ourselves. You may not be called upon to lay down your life for others as Jesus did, but you will undoubtedly find small ways to die to yourself today. In what way is your life burdened with a cross that hinders and handicaps you in body, mind, or soul? Imagine God gently handing you this cross and asking you to carry it for him. Hear him whisper reassuringly that he will help you and that it will strengthen your love of others, yourself, and him. Lay down your preferences, comforts, and fears by the roadside. Embrace your cross, shoulder it with confidence, and step forward with courage. It scrapes your neck, hurts your back, and bows your head. But look now, Jesus is helping you, carrying most of the weight. Feel yourself inspired by his presence, fortified by your faith, and strengthened by his love. With every painful step, you are being liberated to forgive more truly, live more fully, and rejoice with the realization that *no one has greater love than this.*

Pray: O Jesus, I want to lay down my life for you, as you did for me, to show your greatest love to others in need!

GAINS AND LOSSES WITH CHRIST

❖   ❖   ❖

*Whatever gains I had, these I have come to consider
a loss because of Christ.*

- *PHILIPPIANS 3:7*

WOULD IT BE easier to forgive others if you learned that everything you thought you had lost in the world is actually a gain and everything you have gained is actually a loss? This is the astonishing truth Paul discovered after God opened his eyes; he saw clearly that all his earthly gains were as nothing compared to Christ, from whom all good things come. With his radical new vision, he considered his gains as a loss because they had prevented him from seeing Christ and experiencing his love. He also recognized that his losses and resentments blinded him as well. *I even consider everything as a loss because of the supreme good of knowing Christ.* Like Paul we may come to understand this mystery of how our gains and losses are equally blinding. If we have all the riches in the world without knowing Christ, we have nothing, but if we have Christ and nothing else, we have everything. For the same reason, if we lose all our worldly treasures but we have Christ, we possess everything for through him all things were made. *For his sake I have accepted the loss of all things and I consider them so much rubbish, that I may gain Christ.*

⌣

Pray: O Jesus, help me to see past my earthly gains and losses
to experience a personal relationship with you!

GOD SO LOVED THE WORLD

❖ ❖ ❖

For God so loved the world that he gave his only Son,
so that everyone who believes in him might not perish
but might have eternal life.

- *JOHN 3:16*

WHEN WE TAKE this truth to heart, we discover to our delight that we can truly forgive anyone for anything. What are the offenses of others in light of the fact that we have a loving, caring, redeeming Father who holds us in the palm of his hand? What sins of others, or mistakes of our own, do not vanish in the unfathomable mercy of his Son, whom he sent into the world as a demonstration of pure love and a living sacrifice for the forgiveness of sins? What are our temporary pains, losses, and sufferings in comparison to the good news that we who believe in him will not perish but instead will enjoy eternal life? When we humble ourselves in prayer before God, we quickly discover the heavenly light that illuminates all darkness, the divine mercy that forgives all sins, and the sacred love that raises us up to eternal life. In all circumstances we know that God gives us our light, our life, and our love. With God we have everything we need and we lack nothing. Every moment of every day of our lives we may rest and rejoice in the absolute assurance that God provides us with all faith, hope, and love.

Pray: O Lord, I praise your holy name!

He Gave Himself

❖ ❖ ❖

He gave himself to rescue us from everything that is
evil and to make our hearts pure.

- Titus 2:14

I MAGINE WALKING BY a frozen lake and seeing a child walking on the icy surface. Suddenly he breaks through the ice, plunges into the frigid water and starts to drown. Would you would attempt to rescue him, even at the risk to your own life and safety? This is exactly what Jesus did: he gave his own life to rescue us from sin and everything that is evil in this world. By offering himself as a perfect living sacrifice, he atoned for our sins, released the reservoir of his Father's mercy, vanquished death for all who believe in him, and opened the gates of heaven to those who call upon his holy name. Most certainly Jesus does not leave us helpless in our natural state; he also makes our hearts pure. He takes our frozen, ice-cold hearts and warms them gently with his passionate love. He changes our hearts of stone into living hearts of flesh and then purifies us with his mercy. Can you feel your heart beating faithfully in your chest, pumping the blood of forgiveness through your veins?

Pray: O Jesus, thank you for rescuing me from my sins and giving me a new heart filled with your passionate love!

THE ABUNDANT LIFE

❖ ❖ ❖

I came so that they might have life
and have it more abundantly.

- JOHN 10:10

ARE YOU LIVING an abundant life or are you in despair? If you are feeling weighed down and depressed by the cares and anxieties of everyday life, listen carefully to what Jesus has to say. He reveals the reason he came to earth was so that you might have life and have it more abundantly! So if you are not living a joyful life, simply invite Jesus to come into your life. Try it right now, this very moment. Ask Jesus to enter into your mind and heart. Explain your troubles and ask him to set things right. Tell him your sins that have been holding you back and complicating your life. Ask him to be your Shepherd, Guide, Brother or Father. Tell him you need him to give you a sign to prove that he really cares about you. He may work a miracle in your life by changing your circumstances, healing your hurts, or restoring a lost relationship. But his greatest miracle is giving you his divine presence and vibrant love that progressively transforms your life. You know you have received Jesus when you can begin to accept your heartaches and pains, forgive others freely, and experience the abundance of his love in all circumstances.

Pray: O Jesus, come into my life today and show me your love in a real way. I want to have a new life abundantly!

DO NOT COMPLAIN

❖ ❖ ❖

Beloved, do not grumble against one another,
so that you may not be judged.

- JAMES 5:9

ONE OF THE surest signs we have not yet forgiven others is that we complain about them. When we persist in rehashing their offenses, railing against their faults, and grumbling about our grievances, we display our unforgiving spirit. Like a woodsman who spends all day proudly grinding his ax, we never get around to chopping down the trees of our discontent. Until we swing our ax at the roots of anger and revenge we cannot plow the field of forgiveness. By constantly complaining about the injuries we have suffered, the misfortunes that have befallen us, and the burdens of injustice, we upset ourselves unnecessarily, grieve those around us, and set ourselves up for greater calamities when we are judged by God. The day is coming when God will surely judge us with the same severity that we presume to judge the faults of others, and that day may come soon and suddenly. *See, the Judge is standing at the doors!*

⌒

Pray: O Lord, help me to hear my complaining clearly, repent of it completely, and replace it with a spirit of love.

CHOOSE LIFE OR DEATH

❖ ❖ ❖

*I have set before you life and death, blessings
and curses. Choose life.*

- *DEUTERONOMY 30:19*

WHEN LIFE SEEMS overwhelmingly complicated, we need to slow down and gather our thoughts in prayer. We need to center ourselves in prayer, reach out to those we trust, and ask God to remind us that life is pretty simple. Every day we have set before us good things and evil, blessings and curses, prosperity and adversity. We can freely choose among all these things. If our choices seem confusing, we discover simplicity by remembering that every choice makes us either more loving or hateful, selfless or selfish, forgiving or unforgiving. Every decision in life either brings us closer to God or farther away. God wants us to choose wisely, he helps us to choose wisely, and he even tells us how to choose wisely with two simple words: *Choose life.* Whatever fills us with life, exercises our faith, and enlarges our hope is the right decision. We choose wisely when we choose whatever is best for others to lead them to the light of Christ. When we choose to be forgiving, life-giving, and thanks-giving, that choice may appear to diminish us but God assures us that he is giving us new life.

⌐

Pray: O Lord, in every decision I face today, help me choose
your loving way — I choose life!

FORGIVENESS IS A DAILY DEVOTION

❖ ❖ ❖

*If any want to become my followers, let them deny
themselves and take up their cross daily and follow me.*

- *LUKE 9:23*

S OMETIMES FORGIVENESS IS like a cross; we need to deny
ourselves, take up our cross daily and follow Jesus' example
of forgiving others. When someone offends us day after day,
we know we need to forgive that person seventy times seven,
meaning an unlimited number of times. But the same is true
for a single offense that keeps haunting our mind; as often as
we remember an offense from the past, we must address it and
forgive it all over again, as often as necessary. Our forgiveness
must go deeper than the hurt. God's perfect will is to heal us
completely, but in his permissive will we may need to forgive
the same offense many times over a span of weeks, months or
years. Each time the nagging memory returns, we must pause
for a moment to deliberately forgive again, release the other
person once more into God's loving hands, and ask for God's
renewed blessings on the whole world. One fine day, in God's
perfect time, we will awaken to discover that he has indeed
healed us so that we can live, laugh, and love again.

⌒

Pray: O Jesus, help me to take up my cross of forgiveness,
carry it daily as long as you wish, and follow you always!

You Will Find Rest

❖ ❖ ❖

Come to me, all you who labor and are burdened,
and I will give you rest.

- Matthew 11:28

I F YOU ARE tired and weary from carrying heavy burdens, here is the way to find comfort and rest. Jesus invites you right this moment, and every day of your life, to come to him and he will personally give you rest. Listen to his helpful suggestion. *Take my yoke upon you and learn from me, for I am meek and humble of heart; and you will find rest for yourselves.* Rest sounds good, does it not? You need not carry your burden alone or plow your field by yourself; Jesus wants help you. He offers you his sturdy yoke, known to farmers as a wood-hewn crosspiece that is harnessed over the necks of two oxen to draw a plow or load. Take his yoke on your shoulders. Feel how he has crafted it to fit you perfectly. Now yoked beside Jesus, start forward and feel his strength as you pull the plow through the fertile soil. Learn to move forward easily and confidently in coordination with Jesus, placing your steps alongside his. Listen with humility and wonder as Jesus teaches you how to find it easy, gentle and restful to plow the fields of forgiveness that surround you. *For my yoke is easy, and my burden light.*

Pray: O Jesus, I am grateful to share your yoke. It fits me perfectly, makes my burden light, and gives me rest!

LOOK DEEPER THAN APPEARANCES

❖ ❖ ❖

*People judge others by what they look like, but
I judge people by what is in their hearts.*

- 1 Samuel 16:7

THERE IS A special feeling of exasperation when someone wrongs us but no one else seems to understand. Especially when the wrongdoer is someone of high position, power or prosperity, other people tend to overlook or dismiss their transgressions. Our friends, acquaintances, and even family members may be oblivious to our injury. Their blindness, gullibility, and ignorance magnifies our hurt and makes us feel as if we suffer alone. By judging a book by its cover, people can be very naive, beguiled and deceived by superficial appearances. As a result, wrongdoers may continue to prosper as if nothing has happened. *They grow powerful and rich, fat and sleek. They pass over wicked deeds.* We may take comfort in knowing that while people see only outward appearances and judge others by what they look like, our Lord looks deeper beneath the surface. *I judge people by what is in their hearts.* Woe to those who appear as angels of light on the outside but whose hearts are darkened by sin. They will be judged not by what is seen but by what is unseen, not by their outward appearance but by the kindness of their inner hearts.

⌐

Pray: O Lord, I forgive my offenders and release them into your hands, for only you can see deep into their hearts.

I Will Seek The Lost

❖ ❖ ❖

I will seek the lost, bring back the scattered, bind up
the broken and strengthen the sick.

- JEREMIAH 5:27

ARE YOU FEELING lost and scattered, broken or weak? What you are feeling is the typical result of abuse or neglect. You are experiencing the consequences of sin that cry out for the healing love of God. You need not fear, for God is near; he is right by your side, as always. When you begin to see the world through God's eyes, you can spot the destructive aftermath of sin a mile away, and more delightfully you can recognize the healing presence of God's love everywhere. Sin breaks and scatters, while love binds up and gathers. Sin weakens and sickens, while love strengthens and quickens. Sin divides and derides, while love guides and provides. God is seeking you, not to weaken you but to give you strength. He is reaching out to you, not to put you down but to build you up and raise you to new heights of wisdom, forgiveness, and compassion. Pity those poor souls who resist God's love, for they are lost but do not know it. *Do not envy the wicked for you do not know when their day will come.*

⌐

Pray: O Lord, I want to be found by you. Gather me, heal me, and strengthen me so that I may reach out to others!

A Light Has Dawned

❖ ❖ ❖

The people walking in darkness have seen a great light;
on those living in the land of deep darkness
a light has dawned.

- Isaiah 9:1

It helps to forgive others when we remember that we too were once like them. Perhaps not as bad, nevertheless lacking in love. Even in the best earthly circumstances we are all born into spiritual darkness in this fallen world. We begin life with naturally selfish desires, and we fumble around for a familiar light. Having never seen the light of God's love, how can any of us know what we are seeking unless a kind soul shows us the way? So we stumble and grumble through the gloom and frequently knock into each other, causing and receiving many bumps and skinned knees. Then happy are we who see a great light, for on us a new light has dawned! To us is given the greatest of all blessings; God himself has shown us the light of his love shining brilliantly in the person of his Son. Now at last we who were blind can see; our eyes and minds and hearts are illuminated by the greatest vision of all. *For to us a child is born, to us a son is given… and he will be called Wonderful Counselor, Mighty God, Everlasting Father, Prince of Peace.*

Pray: O Lord, thank you for showing me the light of your love and mercy. Help me show your great light to others!

PREPARE HIS WAYS

❖ ❖ ❖

You will go before the Lord to prepare his ways,
to give his people knowledge of salvation
through the forgiveness of their sins.

- LUKE 1:76

WHEN WE LEARN to forgive others as God forgives us, we unlock the doors of heaven and find our way to salvation. As children need to learn smaller things before they can understand greater things, we need to learn how to give and receive forgiveness. While learning how to forgive others may seem impossible, once we learn how to do it with God's help, he opens the doors of our minds to glimpse the indescribable beauty of his kingdom and the fathomless mystery of eternal life. Once we are given this priceless gift of faith, in which we realize our need for forgiveness, ask for God's mercy, and allow him to transform our lives with his loving presence, then we are inspired and empowered to go forth like John the Baptist to prepare the ways of the Lord. By forgiving others and showing them the love of God, as Jesus did for us, we are doing God's most delightful work. If they receive our forgiveness and recognize it as gift from God, it may serve to open their eyes, soften their hearts, and lead them to knowledge of their eternal salvation.

Pray: O Lord, send me forth to forgive others, as you sent Jesus to me, to give them knowledge of their salvation!

NO LONGER I WHO LIVE

❖ ❖ ❖

I have been crucified with Christ; it is no longer
I who live, but Christ who lives in me.

- GALATIANS 2:20

WHEN WE EMBRACE the cross God has given us, allow our thoughts to become attuned to God's thoughts, and imitate the actions of his Son, we cannot fail to become like Jesus. Now our painful, prideful, sin-stained past dissolves in God's mercy. Then suddenly it reappears in a new recreation with an astonishing beauty and crystal clarity we never knew possible. As we adjust to our rapidly expanding vision of heaven and earth, of things seen and unseen, we experience the life-changing moment of an ecstatic encounter with God. Falling to our knees with an overwhelming sense of gratitude, we gradually understand the most profound transformation in our life. *It is no longer I who live, but Christ lives in me.* When we begin to think as God thinks, and will as he wills, we discover the ability to love as he loves and forgive as he forgives. Nothing will ever be the same. Now we are the hands and feet of Christ, his eyes and ears and lips, proclaiming with exultation that the Kingdom of Heaven is near. Behold now, we proclaim, it is already here in our hearts.

⌐

Pray: O Lord, now that I live in you and you live in me,
I am able to love as you love and forgive everyone!

SEEK WHAT IS ABOVE

❖ ❖ ❖

*Seek what is above, where Christ is seated
at the right hand of God.*

- COLOSSIANS 3:1

I F YOU ARE weighed down today by the difficulty of forgiving your own sins or the sins of others, look up. Do not look down, behind, within, or outside yourself for worldly answers. Instead seek what is above, in the spiritual realm, and allow your Creator to lift you up. Turn your attention to the One who knows what is best for you. *Think of what is above, not of what is on earth.* You cannot find the sunshine beneath the clouds; you must fly above the clouds to see the light. You will never find true happiness by vainly searching within yourself or in worldly pursuits; you must rise above yourself and seek the Son. This is not a physical journey but a journey of the heart. When you find the Son, you will find him seated at the right hand of the Father. They have been seeking you all along, using the power of the Holy Spirit to draw you near. God wants to give you everything that you hold dear. *All good giving and every perfect gift is from above, coming down from the Father of lights, with whom there is no alteration or shadow caused by change.*

Pray: O Lord, I know that you want to give me every good and perfect gift. Today I turn my attention up towards you!

CLOTHE YOURSELF WITH COMPASSION

❖ ❖ ❖

As God's chosen ones, holy and beloved,
clothe yourselves with compassion, kindness,
humility, meekness, and patience.

- COLOSSIANS 3:12

EVERY MORNING YOU get up and put on clothes that are appropriate for the day. As followers of Christ, you can just as easily clothe yourself with his colorful virtues. You may choose to put on the rags of resentment, but as God's chosen one you are given a closetful of his perfectly tailored garments such as *compassion, kindness, humility, meekness and patience.* God is your personal tailor, his favorite fashion is forgiveness, and he wants you to be well-dressed for any occasion. So wrap yourself with his righteousness, dress yourself in his mercy, and make a fashion statement for all the world to see. *Above all, clothe yourselves with love, which binds everything together in perfect harmony.*

⌣

Pray: O Lord, I want to clothe myself daily with perfect love
and show your mercy to an unforgiving world!

BEAR WITH ONE ANOTHER

❖ ❖ ❖

Bear with one another and, if anyone has a complaint against another, forgive each other; just as the Lord has forgiven you, so you also must forgive.

- COLOSSIANS 3:13

Y OU KNOW YOU are unforgiving if you complain. If you continually nag someone about certain faults or if you frequently criticize someone behind his or her back, you may as well shout in the public square that you have an unforgiving heart. Today Paul reminds us that since we each possess faults, we must bear with the faults of others. Since our imperfections are often a burden to others, they must bear your burdens while you must bear theirs. *Love bears all things.* We must remember that Jesus bore all of our sins as he carried his cross. He willingly took up his cross because he knew it was the will of his Father to show us the extent of his love, the radical nature of his sacrifice, and the redeeming power of his forgiveness. Rather than complain like a drenching rain, we do better to forgive each other, as God has forgiven us, and let the sun shine again. *Let the peace of Christ rule in your hearts, to which indeed you were called in the one body.*

Pray: O Lord, help me to forgive the sins of others as you have forgiven me. I want your peace to rule in my heart!

WHATEVER YOU DO

❖ ❖ ❖

Whatever you do, in word or deed, do everything in the name of the Lord Jesus, giving thanks to God the Father through him.

- COLOSSIANS 3:17

ONE OF THE nicest benefits of forgiveness is that it liberates us to live the abundant life God wants us to live. While we may yet lack worldly wealth or bodily health, the gift of forgiveness engulfs us with surprising spiritual wealth and supernatural prosperity. When we release others from our prideful expectations, selfish denunciations, and blinding condemnations, we find ourselves relieved from resentment, absolved of our own sinfulness, and reborn to new life. When we forgive others, God frees us to live, laugh, and love again. We have not so much freed our offenders as we have liberated ourselves. We have kicked off our shackles and unlocked our fetters. Like a bird that has learned how to fly, we have discovered how to soar above all the clouds in the sky. Mercy has given us wings like eagles. We know we are mastering the art of forgiveness when gratitude becomes our daily song and in everything we delight to sing along. Whatever we do now, and whatever we say, we do everything with thanksgiving to our Lord Jesus today.

⌣

Pray: O Jesus, today I want to say and do everything in your name with gratitude. Thank you for giving me wings!

I Rejoice In My Sufferings

❖ ❖ ❖

Now I rejoice in my sufferings
for your sake.

- Colossians 1:24

WAIT A MINUTE, this sounds crazy. How is it possible to rejoice in suffering? Doesn't every sane person think suffering is an evil to be avoided? How can anyone enjoy suffering? Let us dive deeper into what Paul is saying. It is not so much that suffering is pleasant and enjoyable as that it may be willingly embraced when we understand that it is necessary and effective for the healing and salvation of souls. Certainly suffering is to be avoided or remedied whenever possible; we do not prefer to suffer. But when it is unavoidable, we accept it as God's permissive will in our lives. Indeed, we can do more than that; we can welcome it and embrace it as Jesus did with his cross. For the love of God and all souls, Jesus rejoiced in his suffering because he knew that his temporary pain was for the sake of others' permanent gain. Likewise, we can accept, endure, and rejoice in our suffering with Jesus' assurance that we are uniting ourselves with his agony on the cross to help redeem lost souls. This is truly agape love, the selfless love that sacrifices for the sake of others, the highest form of love.

⌒

Pray: O Jesus, I want to rejoice in my sufferings and my love for others. Help me to live with a sense of wonder!

IN MY FLESH

❖ ❖ ❖

*In my flesh I am filling up what is lacking in the afflictions
of Christ on behalf of his body, which is the church.*

- *COLOSSIANS 1:24*

SOMETIMES WE SUPPOSE we could forgive others more easily
if only our injuries did not hurt so much. We may be still be
suffering from injuries today that someone caused us years ago.
If God has not yet chosen to heal us, the passage of time may
not have eased our pain. Far from being at ease after all these
years, we may be increasingly ill at ease. Paul tells us that our
pain is not meaningless and our suffering is not wasted. On
the contrary, we are *filling up what is lacking in the affliction
of Christ.* In some mysterious way we are sharing in Jesus' suffering on behalf of all souls. While his suffering was sufficient
once and for all, it pleases Jesus to offer us the chance to suffer
with him for the sake of the world. We supplement, enhance,
and redeem the ongoing suffering of all people for the redemp-
tion of his body which is the church. Jesus suffers within us;
he makes us his companions in suffering so we may share in
his resurrection. In this way we *bring to completion... the word
of God, the mystery hidden from ages and from generations past.*

⁓

Pray: O Lord, I thank you for allowing me to share in your
afflictions. I suffer with you and I know you suffer too!

BE OF GOOD COURAGE

❖ ❖ ❖

Be strong and of good courage, do not fear or be in dread
of them: for it is the Lord your God who goes with you;
he will not fail you or forsake you.

- DEUTERONOMY 31:6

FORGIVENESS MEANS SPEAKING the truth in love. If you are reluctant to speak the truth to someone because he or she is intimidating or hard-hearted, listen to this message from Moses; do not fear or be in dread. This is the same message he delivered to his people who were afraid to confront their adversaries. Like the Israelites, you need not fear anyone because the Lord goes with you. Imagine God marching before you, clearing the way! Take courage as you picture multitudes of angels sounding trumpets and carrying the banners of heaven. God will lead your way, helping you do what needs to be done so you can take possession of the land that is rightfully yours, the promised land of peace and tranquility. Have no fear of forgiving your enemies, overpowering them with God's mercy, and vanquishing them with his love. The battle is won; the victory is God's; let him lead you into the land of your inheritance where all are reconciled and praise his holy name.

Pray: O Lord, I go forth carrying your banners of mercy and love. You lead the way and I will march behind you!

BECOME LIKE CHILDREN

❖ ❖ ❖

*Unless you change and become like children, you
will never enter the kingdom of heaven.*

- MATTHEW 18:3

IF WE REALLY want learn how to forgive, we need to become like a child sleeping in the arms of his mother or father. Observe the child breathing softly, nestled comfortably, resting peacefully. The child is a picture of absolute trust and total contentment. We need to allow ourselves to trust our Father if we are to forgive. If we are filled with grown-up feelings of worldly anger, confusion, or resentment, we need to change and become like children. We need to reach out to God for help and allow him to pick us up and enfold us in his loving arms. We can ask him to help us forgive, we can even ask him to do the forgiving for us. God does not want us to remain immature and childish in our faith; instead he wants us grow up by rediscovering the trusting faith of a child. Ironically, we are most mature when we hearken back to the eager innocence and trusting faith of our youth. Once we are blessed with this wisdom, we will forgive completely, nestle into our Father's arms peacefully, and sleep sweetly. *Whoever becomes humble like this child is the greatest in the kingdom of heaven.*

Pray: O Jesus, help me change and become like a child,
youthful in faith and joyful with innocent trust in you!

GO IN SEARCH OF THE STRAY

❖ ❖ ❖

*If a man has a hundred sheep and one of them
goes astray, will he not leave the ninety-nine
in the hills and go in search of the stray?*

- *MATTHEW 18:12*

ONE OF THE most vexing side-effects of offenses is that the wrongdoer can become the center of our daily attention. To our dismay, we may find ourselves fretting about that individual, stressing about what to say or do in response to their wrongdoings, and resenting the offender for robbing us of our peace of mind. Yet Jesus counsels us that our precious time is well-spent. He compares us to a shepherd who leaves his flock of sheep in the hills in order to search for one gone astray. The stray causes the shepherd to depart from his comfortable campsite and neglect all his other sheep in order to seek the one that is lost. *If he finds it, amen, I say to you, he rejoices more over it than over the ninety-nine that did not stray.* So must we accept that we will be disturbed sometimes in our comfortable lives by lost souls. We must welcome the opportunity to seek the lost and return them to God. The best way to retrieve a lost soul is to help untangle it from the thorny brambles of sin and hoist it on our shoulders of forgiveness. *In just the same way, it is not the will of your heavenly Father that one of these little ones be lost.*

Pray: O Jesus, I want to be a good shepherd. Help me to seek
and find lost souls just as you sought and found me!

FAR MORE THAN WE ASK

❖ ❖ ❖

*Now to him who is able to accomplish far more
than all we ask or imagine, by the power at work
within us, to him be glory.*

- *EPHESIANS 3:20*

WE COME TO a great turning point in our lives when finally, after exhausting our own efforts to forgive others, we humble ourselves and admit that we cannot do it alone. At long last we realize that we need God to come to our assistance. He has been waiting for this moment when we turn to him and now he makes haste to help us. Not only will he meet our expectations but he delights in surprising us by exceeding our hopes and dreams. He is able to accomplish far more than we can ever ask or imagine. So open your heart and let God in. Unlock your mind and invite God to sweep out your dusty old thoughts and bring in new wisdom. Ask him to work his mighty power within you and channel his healing love through you. Let God transform you into the person he wants you to be. One fine day you will awaken and realize that you have successfully forgiven everyone for everything. Now you are free. *For human beings this is impossible, but for God all things are possible.*

⸺

Pray: O Lord, I wait with joyful anticipation for you
to give me far more than I ask or imagine!

THE GREATEST COMMANDMENT

❖ ❖ ❖

You shall love the Lord your God with all your heart,
and with all your soul, and with all your mind. This is
the greatest and first commandment.

- MATTHEW 22:36

HERE WE STAND on holy ground because Jesus is telling us the greatest commandment. Here is the key that unlocks our happiness and leads us to eternal life. Amidst the seeming chaos and confusion in life, amongst all the people and circumstances that divide our attention, Jesus points us to God. *You shall love the Lord your God with all your heart, and with all your soul, and with all your mind.* When we seek to love God wholeheartedly, single-mindedly, and soul-powerfully, he engulfs us with real love. In the beginning and in the end, our lives are all about love because *God is love.* God is love because he is three persons in one, existing eternally in a perfectly loving, mutually giving, harmonious relationship. When we put God first, all our other relationships fall into order according to his perfect love. He supernaturally infuses all our relationships with his passionate, sacrificial love and puts our lives in order. Suddenly we begin to see things clearly, as if a veil has been lifted for the first time, and we experience a glimmer of his heavenly peace of mind.

Pray: O Lord, infuse me with your love, help me to love you
with all my heart, all my soul, and with all my mind!

LOVE YOUR NEIGHBOR

❖   ❖   ❖

You shall love your neighbor as yourself.

- MATTHEW 22:39

A s WE LOVE God with all our hearts, Jesus emphasizes that it is equally important to love our neighbors and ourselves. Here again the greatest commandment from Jesus is about love, because *God is love.* You must love your neighbor because God loves your neighbor, and you must love yourself because God loves you. Do you love God, all other people, and yourself? If you do not love God, you cannot truly love others or yourself. Likewise, if you do not love your neighbor, or if you do not love yourself, then you do not yet know the love of God. If you love your neighbor and you love yourself, the love of God is in you. To understand divine love and how to give it freely in all circumstances, say this to yourself: God first, others second, me third. In other words, love God first, others second, and yourself third. This will put your life in order. You will experience God's love as liberating, sacrificial, and life-giving. His love connects us all together in a paradise of passion, a rhapsody of forgiveness, and an ecstasy of harmony. God is indeed our Great Lover; he is always entreating, enchanting and empowering us to love him, our neighbors and ourselves as he loves us eternally.

⌒

Pray: O Lord, please give me your divine love so I can love you, all my neighbors, and myself wholeheartedly!

OWE NOTHING TO ANYONE

❖ ❖ ❖

Owe nothing to anyone, except to love one another;
for the one who loves another has fulfilled the law.

- ROMANS 13:8

D O YOU KNOW how to get rich by forgiving debts? We can indeed grow wealthy in grace by forgiving everyone who owes us an outstanding debt of sin. When someone trespasses against us and deprives us of our health, wealth, or peace of mind, we naturally feel that he or she owes us an apology and some kind of repayment. Our natural sense of justice demands some kind of compensation for such behavior! Yet in God's court of law, we owe forgiveness to others in the same way that he forgives us for our sins. When we forgive others, we tear up the memory of the debt they owe us. This may be difficult because the size of their debt may be huge. But even if they have not apologized, we still forgive their debts as God has forgiven us our debts. Then we are set free to love them as God loves us: unconditionally, selflessly and compassionately. Our love of God empowers us to love those whom God loves — and loving others magnifies our experience God's love for us. By forgiving others their sins, we make a secret and sacrificial investment deep in their souls that will pay priceless dividends if it gives them a glimpse of the love of God.

Pray: O Lord, help me realize that forgiveness gives me the greatest wealth — the ability to love others as you do!

LIKE THE DAWN

❖ ❖ ❖

Then your light shall break forth like the dawn,
and your wound shall quickly be healed.

- ISAIAH 58:8

IF YOUR LIFE is filled with confusion and God seems like just an illusion, now is precisely the time to test your faith and rest in your faith. When your path is dark and you cannot see the way, you must walk in the darkness of faith. Faith looks to God for light, strength and guidance. Yet the more we look toward God, the more we are blinded by the brilliant light of his love. The closer we get to God, the source of all light, the more we may expect to be dazzled and unable to see. Just as looking at the sun blinds us, so does turning toward the Son overcome our feeble sight; we think we are in darkness when really we are bathed in God's pure light. When we allow God to infuse us with the light of his love, it heals our wounds like a laser and illuminates our souls. Then it breaks forth from us like the dawn, emanating from our eyes, lips, fingers and toes, and we delight to realize that we are born anew. Now God lives within us and shines forth to all those around us who live in darkness, showing them the way forward. *You are the light of the world.*

Pray: O Lord, I look to you in my present darkness, for I know that you are pure light and someday I will be too.

HERE I AM

❖ ❖ ❖

You shall call, and the Lord will answer, you shall
cry for help, and he will say: "Here I am!"

- ISAIAH 58:9

GOD IS NEAR you. Do you believe this? Believe it or not, it is true. Do you long to see his face, feel his comforting presence and know that he is close at hand? Rest assured that your Creator watches over you day and night as a mother gazes at her nursing child. God holds you in the palm of his hand and cradles you in his arms. As you breathe softly, listen for his gentle words of wisdom. Inhale his words and make them your own. Open your eyes now and see God in the faces of the people around you, especially your loved ones who love you and forgive you unconditionally. He created us all in his image, so you can see a reflection of his image in everyone, more clearly in some while hidden in others. Feel God's presence in loving people, his touch in their touch, his spark in their glistening eyes. Ask God to come into your life; he wants to reveal himself to you more than you want to find him. Gradually you will begin to see God everywhere, in all of his creation, except where there is sin. The closer you allow God to draw you near, the more easily you will call and he will answer. *You shall cry for help, and he will say: "Here I am!"*

Pray: O Lord, help me believe that you are close to me, living inside me, loving me more than I love myself!

SATISFY YOUR THIRST

❖　❖　❖

The Lord will guide you always and
satisfy your thirst in parched places.

- ISAIAH 58:11

D O YOU FEEL lost in a desert today, parched and confused? Rejected by others and squinting under a blazing sun, you may see nothing but dry sand stretching to the horizon. Surely God is not in this place, you think, or he must be a mirage because he would not lead someone he loves into such desolation. Or would he? God allowed the Holy Spirit to lead Jesus into the desert for forty days in order to test his faith. Jesus was sorely tempted by the devil to give up, but he held fast to the promises of his Father. Then God sent his angels to minister to Jesus and revive him. You too will find beauty and triumph in your desert experience. Crawl on your hands and knees, if you must, but pray to God and praise him always. God will surely lead you through the desert, satisfy your thirst in unexpected places, *and you shall be like a watered garden, like a flowing spring whose waters never fail.*

Pray: O Lord, guide me in the desert, fortify my faith, then satisfy my thirst with the living water of your love!

REBUILD THE RUINS

❖ ❖ ❖

*Rebuild the ancient ruins; the foundations
from ages past you shall raise up.*

- ISAIAH 58:12

S IN SHATTERS OUR relationships, but forgiveness rebuilds them stronger than before. One careless offense can destroy a beautiful relationship that required years to build. Like an earthquake that reduces a house to rubble, a selfish act can cause massive damage. If the wreckage is abandoned in fear or deserted in bitterness, everything crumbles and turns into ruins. God calls us to rebuild these ruins with the humility of forgiveness. He wants us to raise up these foundations, even from ages past, with the power of reconciliation. Like the humble Saint Francis who set himself the task of rebuilding the old chapel at Assisi, stone by stone, God smiles as we forgive others and ourselves, sin by sin. We may rebuild and renew our relationships quickly or over many painstaking years, but others will notice and be glad to see our labor of love, for it brings joy to the hearts of all when someone builds people up and does not tear them down. *"Repairer of the breach,"* they shall call you, *"Restorer of ruined dwellings."*

⌐

Pray: O Lord, I want to repair and restore my relationships
with forgiveness and reconciliation. Help me start today!

LET THEM GROW TOGETHER

❖　❖　❖

Let them grow together until harvest.

- *MATTHEW 13:30*

As a farmer does not uproot every weed in his field, we need not fret about every sinner in our life. Our natural desire is to pull up all the weeds in our garden and eliminate every sinner in our life. We want to be rid of weeds that choke our nice plants and we want to be free of wrongdoers that disturb our peace of mind. But Jesus counsels patience. *If you pull up the weeds you might uproot the wheat along with them.* Jesus wisely suggests forbearance for weeds and forgiveness for sinners. He knows that we are not capable of rightly judging the hearts of sinners, so he suggests that we allow them to live in our midst, cultivate our gardens in peace and simply enjoy the loving people in our lives. *Let them grow together until harvest.* We may rest assured, Jesus says, that at the harvest time he will instruct the angels, who cannot make mistakes, to separate everything and everyone properly. *First collect the weeds and tie them in bundles for burning; but gather the wheat into my barn.*

Pray: O Jesus, I tend the garden of my life in peaceful joy. I forgive the weeds, knowing the harvest will soon be here!

There Is Nothing Hidden

❖   ❖   ❖

For there is nothing hidden that will not become visible,
and nothing secret that will not be known
and come to light.

- Luke 8:17

D O NOT FRET about the hidden sins of other people. Certainly
you must try to bring wrongdoers to justice for this is loving
your neighbor as yourself. In the same way you bring your own sins
into the healing light of Christ, you must love others enough to
bring them to justice. Having tried, however, and failed, you may
forgive them and release them into God's hands. Do not trouble
yourself about the secret sins of others for their day of reckoning
is coming soon. *There is nothing covered, that shall not be revealed;*
and hid, that shall not be known. During the final judgement there
will be no secrets as there are in this life. On that fearful day in
which the divine light of God illuminates all things, all people in
the entire world will know every detail of every wrong they have
done, except for their repented sins, for those sins are forgiven and
forgotten by God and he remembers them no more.

⟿

Pray: O Lord, forgive those who have committed
hidden sins; I pray that you have mercy on them!

YOU OF LITTLE FAITH

❖ ❖ ❖

Why are you terrified, you of little faith?

- MATTHEW 6:26

BE CALM AND fearless about the storms in your life. Do not worry when thunder crashes and lightning flashes all around you. You are like the disciples who went out in a boat when suddenly a violent storm arose and the waves threatened to capsize them. Yet Jesus was sleeping peacefully in the boat. Surely they thought he did not care about their dangerous predicament! Fearing for their lives, they awakened Jesus and shouted at him to save them! Jesus quietly arose and reproached them for being unnecessarily afraid and lacking in faith. *Why are you terrified, O you of little faith?* Then Jesus rebuked the winds and sea, *and there was great calm.* If you are sailing through stormy seas, you may think that Jesus is absent and does not care. Call out to Jesus, and you will discover that he is near. Wait patiently and call his holy name. As you wait, breathe easily and sleep peacefully alongside Jesus. Rest with complete faith that Jesus will rebuke the storm at the appropriate time and that your life will be calm again. Then, like the disciples, you can marvel at his holy power. *What sort of man is this, whom even the winds and the sea obey?*

Pray: O Jesus, as I wait with confident faith for you to calm the storms in my life, I rest peacefully at your side!

GATHERING OR SCATTERING

❖ ❖ ❖

Whoever is not with me is against me, and whoever
does not gather with me scatters.

- MATTHEW 12:30

THE WAY TO distinguish good vs. evil in people's actions is easy. Good gathers while evil scatters. Virtuous behavior draws people together and builds them up, while sinful actions separate people and tear them apart. Jesus makes this distinction when teaching how to recognize evil and the devil. Jesus says that his Father seeks to gather while the devil schemes to scatter. Jesus gives us a simple choice; we can be with him or against him — there is no middle ground. We can either follow Jesus or the devil. Wherever we see the division and destruction of individuals, families, businesses, communities, churches or countries, that is a sign of the dark powers. In contrast, God is a great gathering force. Whenever things come together in a good way and a family or community forms to unify and build up its members, that is the unmistakable sign of the Holy Spirit at work. When we follow Jesus by forgiving others, we immediately become part of God's divine gathering force that is healing and uniting the world. *I will gather my people, my sheep on the last day.*

Pray: O Jesus, I want to be with you, not against you. Help
me to gather people together under God as you do!

GOD IS TRUTH

❖ ❖ ❖

I am the way, and the truth, and the life.

- JOHN 14:6

HAVE YOU BEEN hurt deeply by an untruth that someone has said about you? Even though it was a lie, it can still hurt years later. Consider the fact that God is truth. God is the creator of the universe, so he embodies absolute truth. He cannot lie because it is contrary to his essence. Jesus reveals this when he says, *I am the way, and the truth, and the life.* When we follow Jesus, he shows us the way to truth and new life. In contrast, the devil is referred to in the Bible as 'the father of lies' and 'the accuser'. Whenever someone seeks to accuse us, gossip about us, or deceive us, we know the dark powers of evil are at work. Wherever there is untruth, there is darkness. Happily, we need not stumble in darkness; we can walk confidently toward the light. We know we are walking on the right path when we choose forgiveness at every turn. We know we are going the right way when we are truthful about ourselves, our families and our relationships. This is what it means to follow Jesus on the way of truth that leads to love, harmony, and eternal life.

Pray: O Lord, light my path. I want your way to be my way, your truth to be my truth, and your life to be my life!

GOD DOES NOT CONDEMN US

❖ ❖ ❖

God did not send his Son into the world to condemn
the world, but that the world might be saved through him.

- JOHN 3:17

I F YOU THINK God is angry at you, judging you or condemning you, you are mistaken. God is not your enemy and adversary; truly he is your advocate and friend. If your earthly father was absent or unloving, you must look higher to see your Father in Heaven more clearly. God is always loving, ever-present, and all-forgiving. He hates sin but he loves sinners. He never mocks, taunts, or ridicules. He does not want to pull the rug out from under you, torment you with misfortune, or toy with you as a cat does with a mouse. God sent his Son to save you, not condemn you, to raise you up and give you wings like an eagle. Believe this and it will change your life. If you allow God's love to transform your mind and heart, he will melt away your anger, bitterness, and unforgiveness. He will revive your soul and give you an entirely new outlook on life. You will see others and yourself with his eyes, think with his mind, forgive with his mercy, and love with his heart. To your everlasting delight, you will discover that you are now filled to overflowing with faith, hope, love, and gratitude.

Pray: O Lord, I believe you do not want to condemn me.
Instead you want to save me and give me eternal life!

THE UNFORGIVABLE SIN

❖　❖　❖

Whoever blasphemes against the Holy Spirit will never have forgiveness, but is guilty of an everlasting sin.

- MARK 3:29

Do YOU THINK some sins are unforgivable? Are you convinced that certain sins are so terrible they are beyond forgiving? Jesus says there is one unforgivable sin: blasphemy against the Holy Spirit. What does this mean? It is not necessarily offending against the Holy Spirit with words — it refers to our refusal to repent and accept God's forgiveness. Specifically, it means our refusal to accept the mercy that God offers through the Holy Spirit, working through the power of Jesus' sacrifice on the Cross. In other words, if we refuse to repent and accept God's forgiveness that heals all sins, we commit the only unforgivable sin. God cannot heal us if we do not want to be healed. God wants to forgive all our sins, but he cannot forgive us if we refuse to be forgiven. While God does not damn us, we are free to refuse his salvation — this is the only unforgivable sin. If we accept his forgiveness, *this is good and pleasing to God our savior, who wills everyone to be saved and to come to knowledge of the truth.*

⌐

Pray:　O Lord, I repent of all my sins and I accept your divine mercy. Help me forgive others as you forgive me!

YOU CAN MAKE ME CLEAN

❖ ❖ ❖

Lord, if you wish, you can make me clean.

- MATTHEW 8:2

D O NOT LET your ills, afflictions or injuries prevent you from forgiving others, yourself or God. Do not resent the fact that God can heal you completely but has not yet chosen to do so. Instead, accept your condition with the gratitude that comes from knowing that he has the power to heal you with a wave of his hand today, tomorrow, or next year. He who searches your inmost heart knows best the perfect time and place to take you by the hand and raise you up to new life. In the meantime, glory in the knowledge that he is sovereign over all his creation, and let your faith prompt you to praise his holy name. God heals our souls instantly of our worst sins the moment we confess them with the assurance of his forgiveness. But often he allows us to continue to suffer the consequences of sin in our bodies, minds and hearts. This is a great mystery, and the reasons are known only to him. For our part, we forgive those whose trespasses have injured us, accept our crosses in humility, and believe with complete faith that God is using our suffering to bring about a greater good.

Pray: O Jesus, I do not resent my injuries. I know you have the power to heal me and make me clean anytime!

WE SHALL BE LIKE HIM

❖ ❖ ❖

What we shall be has not yet been revealed.
We do know that when it is revealed we shall be like
him, for we shall see him as he is.

- 1 JOHN 3:2

D O NOT BE discouraged by your lack of health, wealth, or beauty. If you have lost a limb or a loved one, your youth or health, think nothing of it. You will receive all these things and more in God's good time. For the time being, rest in the loving hands of God. He knows what you need and will supply it to you in abundance beyond your imagining. As you wait, ask God for patience. Do not look in the mirror and dwell on your imperfections. Neither should you turn your attention excessively inward at your conflicting desires and unrequited loves. Instead, turn your gaze outward and upward toward your heavenly Father from whom all good things come. As he reveals himself to you, gradually your heart will rest and your eyes will shine. When he reveals himself to you fully, you will see him as he is. On that day the brilliance of his Son will illuminate your mind, glorify your body, forgive all your sins, and transform your soul. You will be like God.

⤳

Pray: O Lord, I wait in prayerful patience and joyful hope as
you reveal yourself to me more and more each day!

A Hundred Times More

❖   ❖   ❖

*Everyone who has given up houses or brothers or sisters
or father or mother or children or lands for the sake of
my name will receive a hundred times more,
and will inherit eternal life.*

- *Matthew 19:29*

I F YOU OFFER up your losses to God with gratitude, he will return
them to you a hundredfold. But if you cling to your losses with
bitterness, you will lose them forever. Offer to God what you have
lost and cannot reclaim, whether it is your health, wealth, a loved
one, or your dreams. Do not be angry at the thief who stole it from
you or resentful against God for allowing your deprivations. God
permits everything to happen for a reason, so open your clenched
fists and offer your cherished losses to him. Offer them now willingly, and with confidence that he will restore them to you. Offer
everything as a personal sacrifice to God with supernatural joy
and gratitude that springs from your deepening faith in his promise that nothing is lost, misplaced, or forgotten. God is storing all
your losses, and magnifying them, in order to give them back to
you multiplied. Your special deliveries from God will arrive soon,
in this present age. Later, when you least expect it, you will receive
a white gift box stamped "Eternal Life".

⌒

Pray: O Lord, I willingly offer you everything I have lost. I
know it is all safe and multiplying in your hands!

BLESSINGS WITHOUT MEASURE

❖ ❖ ❖

Put me to the test, says the Lord of hosts, and see if I do not open the floodgates of heaven for you, and pour down upon you blessing without measure!

- *MALACHI 3:10*

PUT GOD TO the test! Do not doubt him, but rather expect him to fulfill all his promises. God does not want us to wallow in pitiful, passive, lukewarm hope. He wants our hope to be filled with excitement, anticipation, and expectation! He wants us to be vibrant in our faith, confident in his goodness, and trusting in his love. In other words, he wants us to live courageously, as if we have already received our reward. Faith is not just believing the truth; it is living according to the truth every day. God wants our faith to be alive, flowing through every cell of our bodies, pumping life-giving love into everything we do and everyone we meet. Our faith does not consist of dead letters on a page, but rather it is the living Word of God who is Christ Jesus, the Word made Flesh. *The Word became flesh and made his dwelling among us, and we saw his glory.* So move beyond your passive hope today, put God to the test, and live in joyful expectation that he will *open the floodgates of heaven for you, and pour down upon you blessing without measure!*

Pray: O Lord, I want to live each day with faith, hope and love. I fully expect you to pour your blessings upon me!

SET YOUR HAND TO THE PLOW

❖ ❖ ❖

*No one who sets a hand to the plow and looks to what
was left behind is fit for the kingdom of God.*

- *LUKE 9:62*

LIVE IN THE present, not the past. Look ahead, not behind. Jesus is very clear that if you want to be happy and holy you must set your hand to the plow, look ahead, and move forward. Farmers know plowing requires looking ahead; look back and you make crooked furrows. Jesus says that if we want to experience the kingdom of heaven in this life and the next, we must leave behind all our dashed hopes, troubling memories, and unfulfilled dreams. We must relinquish everything that holds us back in order to be free to move forward and experience the new life he has planned for us. *Let your eyes look straight ahead and your gaze be focused forward.* As we smoothly plow our way into our blessed future that is known only to him, Jesus walks with us, humming a familiar tune. With our hands gripping the wooden handles of the plow, we notice his hands are resting on top of our hands, guiding our furrows in the field of our dreams.

⌒

Pray: O Jesus, with every step I take, I gain confidence walking with you. Guide me forward in the path of love!

LOVE FORGETS WRONGS

❖ ❖ ❖

*Love isn't selfish or quick tempered. It doesn't
keep a record of wrongs that others do.*

- 1 CORINTHIANS 13:5

BELOVED, LOVE DOES not keep score of wrongs. You may
have noticed that some people have very good memories.
They can remember wrongs that people have committed against
them from years ago. Some people are so focused on offenses
that they carry grudges for a lifetime. These unhappy, unforgiving people carry a heavy burden indeed and they impose this
burden on others when they dredge up past offenses from the
graveyard of their minds. In contrast, love never keeps a record
or holds others accountable for the wrongs they have committed against it. Love forgives debts. *The Lord blesses people whose
sins are erased from his book.* If you love others, forgive them as
God has forgiven you. Certainly, if people have proven to be
abusive or dangerous you may justifiably separate yourself from
them or avoid them altogether, but you can still forgive them.
Instead of holding people accountable for their offenses as if
you were appointed to be their judge, jury, and executioner,
look beyond their sin to their potential in Christ.

⌣

Pray: O Lord, you are the only perfect judge of souls. Help
me forgive others and keep no record of their sins!

YOUR SINS ARE FORGIVEN

❖ ❖ ❖

Which is easier, to say to the paralytic, 'Your sins are forgiven,' or to say, 'Rise, pick up your mat and walk?'

- MARK 2:9

IF YOU HAD to choose one miracle, would you rather choose physical healing of all your ills, or spiritual healing of all your sins? One day a group of villagers lowered a paralyzed man through the roof to see Jesus in a crowded room. After forgiving the man's sins and healing his paralysis, Jesus asked the crowd which act was easier — clearly implying that forgiving a soul is more difficult than healing a body. Think about what Jesus is saying: healing a broken body is a great miracle, yet healing a wounded soul in an even greater miracle. If you are highly skilled doctor or nurse and you heal someone today, you have performed a miracle. But if you forgive someone's sins today, you have accomplished an even greater miracle. Far more miraculous than healing an earthly body, your forgiveness has healed a heavenly soul. One healing is temporary, the other is eternal. We are never more like God than when we practice his divine power of forgiveness. We most represent the face of Jesus to the world when we look at someone and say, "I forgive you."

⌣

Pray: O Jesus, I want to heal others in body and soul, but mostly I want to heal them with your power of forgiveness!

ACCEPTING YOUR CIRCUMSTANCES

❖ ❖ ❖

May it be done to me according to your word.

- LUKE 1:38

INSTEAD OF REJECTING or bemoaning your circumstances, accept them as God's will in your life. When the angel Gabriel appeared to Mary and informed her that she was to conceive by the Holy Spirit, she could have said no. She knew this unexpected pregnancy would jeopardize her engagement to Joseph and set her up for a scandal that might ruin her life. Yet she said yes. She accepted this news as the will of God in her life. Mary said yes. Instead of lamenting her circumstances, she rejoiced with faith and hope in God's perfect plan. *My soul proclaims the greatness of the Lord.* What unwelcome news or unhappy circumstances are you resisting today? What injuries, insults, or injustices are you suffering? Instead of complaining, accusing, and resenting, accept everything as coming from God for your good. Some things may appear as blessings in disguise, completely unrecognizable as being in your favor. Remember that God works in mysterious ways. He even allows evil sometimes in order to bring about a greater good. No matter what you are facing at the moment, have faith like Mary and say 'Yes!' *My spirit rejoices in God my savior.*

⌐

Pray: O Lord, give me the faith and freedom to accept
and rejoice in all my circumstances as your will in my life!

GOD INTENDED IT FOR GOOD

❖ ❖ ❖

Even though you intended to do harm to me,
God intended it for good, in order to preserve a
numerous people, as he is doing today.

- GENESIS 50:20

WHAT OTHERS MEAN for evil, God uses for good. When Joseph's brothers became jealous of him, they sold him as a slave to a passing caravan. Poor Joseph was battered, betrayed, and forsaken by those his own family! He must have felt miserable. But what his brothers had meant for harm, God intended for good. God redirected Joseph's life so that he saved countless people in Egypt from a famine and ultimately saved his own family too. When finally reunited with his brothers, Joseph lovingly forgave them and reconciled with them. Perhaps you, like Joseph, are suffering grievously as a result of an offense by others who meant harm. They may have been strangers or loved ones. Be patient, forgive them, and wait upon the Lord. What they meant for evil, God intends for your good and theirs too. God is at work this very moment rearranging, realigning, and renewing things behind the scenes to make everything turn out better than before. Soon you will see the marvelous outcome.

Pray: O Lord, I give you thanks for making all things turn out right in the end. I rejoice before I even see the results!

NO POWER OVER ME

❖   ❖   ❖

You would have no power over me
if it had not been given to you from above.

- JOHN 19:11

REMEMBER, BELOVED, NO one has any power over you. No earthly or spiritual beings have the power to harm you unless God gives it to them, and even then it is limited by what God allows to pass through his loving fingers to benefit you in some divine way. No stick will strike your head and no stone will break your bones unless God allows it to bring forth greater good in your life. When Pilate puts Jesus on trial and threatens to crucify him, Jesus calmly replies that Pilate has no power that is not given to him from above. In other words, Jesus trusts his Father's loving power even when it is lent temporarily to an unloving opponent. Jesus is so confident in his Father's perfect plan for his life that he trusts all creation to work in his favor. Jesus trusts his Father to work all things together for his good. In Jesus' eyes no one can cause him trouble that is outside the loving providence and miraculous healing power of his Father. When we imitate this trust in our Father, we too can live courageously, calmly, and fearlessly in the face of our enemies, and we discover the power to forgive them freely.

⌐

Pray: O Jesus, help me to live fearlessly, trusting that no one has any power over me except what is given by God.

WHY DO YOU OPPOSE ME?

❖ ❖ ❖

*Let me know why you oppose me. Is it a pleasure
for you to oppress, to spurn the work of your hands,
and shine on the plan of the wicked?*

- JOB 10:2

I F YOU ARE angry at God, listen to Job's story. Job was a good man, but God allowed Satan to deprive him of his wife, family, possessions and health. Covered with sores and sitting in a pile of ashes, Job cried out against God. *Why then did you bring me forth from the womb? I should have died and no eye have seen me. I should be as though I had never lived.* In his confusion and misery, Job questions God's motives and accuses God of taking pleasure in causing his suffering and rewarding the wicked. God patiently listens to Job's protests and then answers. *Where were you when I laid the foundation of the earth?*

Would you condemn me that you may be justified? Job is humbled by this reminder that he is a mere creature, beloved by the Creator of the Universe. Job repents and acknowledges God's superior wisdom: *I have uttered what I did not understand, things too wonderful for me.* If you are angry at God today, remember his ways are far above your ways. Trust your loving Creator to take care of you.

⌒

Pray: O Lord, forgive me for presuming to complain about my life. I trust you to make everything work out all right!

THE LORD RESTORES OUR FORTUNES

❖ ❖ ❖

The Lord restored the fortunes of Job when he
had prayed for his friends; and the Lord gave Job
twice as much as he had before.

- JOB 42:10

BELOVED, DO NOT doubt that God will restore your fortunes just as he did for Job. Pray for your friends and forgive your enemies. Then the Lord will open heaven and shower you with all that you feared was lost. It was not lost, only held by God in safekeeping to test your faith, galvanize your hope, and turn you more fully in love toward your Creator. He knows very well that nothing turns us toward him for help more effectively than when he allows us to be deprived of our usual comforts, familiar consolations, and cherished possessions. Left in darkness and doubt, we cry out for succor and relief as a baby cries for the presence of its mother. When God removes our normal delights and distractions, we fear we have been plunged into a terrifying abyss of utter darkness. God is teaching us to step out into the darkness and walk toward him, using the eyes of our heart to perceive the light of his love. *We walk by faith and not by sight.* Now we please God as a child pleases a parent, so he takes our hand again and rewards us with blessings beyond our imagination. *The Lord blessed the latter days of Job more than his beginning.*

⌣

Pray: O Lord, I trust you to restore everything I have lost and to bless my latter days more than my beginning!

THE REASON JESUS CAME

❖ ❖ ❖

*Jesus came into the world to save sinners —
of whom I am the foremost.*

- 1 TIMOTHY 1:15

HERE WE HAVE the whole point of Jesus' life: to save sinners and reconcile them with God. His entire mission is summed up by Paul, who writes that *Jesus came into the world to save sinners.* If we had not sinned, he would not have had to come to earth and die on the cross. But we did sin, and Jesus did come to save us by offering us forgiveness of our sins. Remarkably, Paul refers to himself as foremost among sinners. Rather than excusing or denying his guilt, he freely admits it. He could have swept it under the rug of history, but he chooses instead to acknowledge it to the whole world. His humble confession is a genuine sign of a broken heart and a forgiven soul. *I was once a blasphemer and a persecutor and an arrogant man, but I have been mercifully treated because I acted out of ignorance in my unbelief. Indeed, the grace of our Lord has been abundant, along with the faith and love that are in Christ Jesus.* When we are able to freely admit our sins, Jesus is faithful to forgive us. Instantly he heals us, embraces us, and gives us new life. Then we become living, breathing, loving examples of his mercy, and we can inspire others to ask for forgiveness too.

Pray: O Jesus, I know you forgive my sins when I confess them. Help me inspire others to trust in your mercy too!

WHY MUST I FORGIVE UNCONDITIONALLY?

❖ ❖ ❖

If we confess our sins, he is faithful and just,
and will forgive our sins.

- 1 JOHN 1:9

WHY DOES GOD require us to confess our sins in order to receive his forgiveness, yet he expects us to forgive others whether they apologize or not? It does not seem fair. Why do we have to forgive others unconditionally? The reason is that God wants us to learn to forgive others the same way he forgives us - unconditionally. Because God is love, it is his nature to offer love and forgiveness to everyone. But he loves us so much that he gives us free will to either accept or refuse his love. He does not force us to accept his forgiveness. He is not waiting for our repentance in order to forgive us; we need to repent in order to receive the forgiveness that he is always offering. That is why we are called to offer forgiveness to others even in the absence of an apology; God is calling us to be like him, to love as he does and forgive others as he forgives. He is calling us to be perfect in our love, as he is perfect in his love.

⌒

Pray: O Lord, teach me how to offer love and forgiveness to others the same way you do — unconditionally!

Sorrow Leads To Repentance

❖ ❖ ❖

You were made sorrowful to the point of repentance;
for you were made sorrowful according to the will of God.

- 2 Corinthians 7:9-10

W HILE YOU MAY be tempted to think that the suffering
you endure because of the sins of others is wasted, God
allows nothing to go to waste. The scars, wounds, and injuries
you carry in your body, mind, and soul may be precisely what
cause your trespassers to ultimately feel sorrow to the point of
repentance! For example, Both King David and Saint Paul were
convicted in their consciences and converted in their hearts by
the weight of the injuries they had caused others. They forged
their offensive chains of sorrow link by link, sin by sin, until
they were *made sorrowful to the point of repentance.* This shows
how sin contains its own punishment; it hardens the hearts of
sinners and separates them from God. So your injuries, painful
as they can be for a season in your life, may be precisely what
God is using to break your offenders' hearts and lead them to
repentance and eternal life. *For the sorrow that is according to*
the will of God produces a repentance without regret, leading to
salvation.

⌒

Pray: O Lord, I offer you all my injuries, knowing that you
can use them to lead others to repentance and salvation!

He Understands Our Weaknesses

❖ ❖ ❖

*We do not have a high priest who is unable to sympathize
with our weaknesses, but one who has similarly been
tested in every way, yet without sin.*

- Hebrews 4:15

MORE THAN YOU know, Jesus understands your suffering.
He is not aloof and uncaring because he experienced
all the same injuries, betrayals, and sufferings that we endure,
and he experienced them in the extreme. In his human nature,
Jesus experienced all the temptations, fears and anxieties we
face every day, so he is able to perfectly understand and sympathize with our weaknesses and help us in every circumstance.
Yet because of his divine nature, Jesus passed every test without giving in to sin, so he became the perfect example to show
us how to accept and embrace our suffering as the mysterious
will of our holy Father in heaven. And because he was without
sin, Jesus became the perfect living sacrifice to atone for the
sins of all humanity; when we offer our imperfections and sins
to Jesus, he accepts us, embraces us, forgives us, and washes
us clean in the waters of his perfect love. *So let us confidently
approach the throne of grace to receive mercy and to find grace for
timely help.*

Pray: O Jesus, it is wonderful to know that you intimately
understand my weaknesses and want to heal my sufferings!

HE LEARNED OBEDIENCE

❖　❖　❖

Although he was a Son, he learned obedience
through what he suffered and when he was made perfect,
he became the source of eternal salvation.

- HEBREWS 5:8

WHAT ARE YOU learning from your suffering? Jesus learned obedience: he learned how to accept his suffering as the mysterious will of his Father. Because of his divine nature, Jesus always obeyed his heavenly Father: *I always do what is pleasing to him*. But in his human nature, Jesus had to learn obedience by actually experiencing suffering. His willingness to obey his Father by suffering on the cross demonstrated the ultimate obedience. As a result Jesus was made perfect by his Father and the source of eternal salvation for all believers. We learn obedience the same way, not with words but in deeds, not in theory but in practice. We may easily promise to obey God and suffer for his sake, but we have not truly learned obedience until we have experienced suffering for his sake. When we endure suffering, God is teaching us obedience and making us perfect like Jesus. Beyond human understanding, God is also allowing us the mysterious privilege of participating in Jesus' suffering, helping him daily to redeem lost souls and bring them to eternal life. Do you believe this?

Pray: O Jesus, help me to learn obedience in my suffering, as you did, and joyfully offer it up to our Father in heaven!

SUFFERING WITH A JOYFUL HEART

❖ ❖ ❖

For the sake of the joy that lay before him
he endured the cross.

- *HEBREWS 12:2*

H OW WELL DO you suffer? What if you knew that your suffering had eternal significance and boundless rewards? We are all tempted to complain and resent our pain. Suffering appears as an unwanted intrusion into our lives. We naturally seek healing and relief, but sometimes we must endure suffering for an hour or a season. If we view our suffering as meaningless or as punishment from an angry God, then we will naturally be defiant and resentful. But if we raise our eyes to God, he will give us a different perspective; he helps us accept our suffering as a blessing in disguise, a rough cross made just for us and allowed by his perfect permissive will to share in the sufferings of Christ to offer forgiveness and reconciliation to lost souls everywhere. *God did the right thing when he made Jesus perfect by suffering, as Jesus led many of God's children to be saved and to share in his glory.* When we see this deeper meaning in our suffering and accept it as God's plan for our lives, we discover that our pain is actually a privilege. Jesus supernaturally empowers us to endure our cross, and he helps us to carry it with grace and joy for the sake of the glory that glows before us.

Pray: O Jesus, thank you for helping me to carry my cross as you carried yours, with gratitude and a joyful heart!

JOINING GOD'S FAMILY

❖ ❖ ❖

We are children of God, and if children, then heirs, heirs of God and joint heirs with Christ, if only we suffer with him so that we may also be glorified with him.

- *ROMANS 8:16*

Do you know that God wants you to be a member of his family? Your earthly family may be good or bad but it cannot compare with God's holy family, consisting of the Father, Son, Holy Spirit, all the angels and saints, and all believers throughout all time. It is one big happy family in which everyone shares perfect love eternally! As a beloved member of your new family, you are an heir just like Jesus to the kingdom of God, if only you accept your suffering with Jesus so that you may be raised by God to eternal life with him. *To all who received him, who believed in his name, he gave power to become children of God; who were born, not of blood nor of the will of the flesh nor of the will of man, but of God.* You will be transformed and entitled to inherit the same kingdom as Jesus, and your heavenly Father will delight in your presence as a loving parent delights in a child. *Beloved, we are God's children now; what we will be has not yet been revealed. What we do know is this: when he is revealed, we will be like him, for we will see him as he is.*

⌒

Pray: O Lord, I thank you for adopting me into your holy, loving, eternal family. Help me lead others to you too!

I Am God, You Are Not

❖　❖　❖

Be still and know that I am God.

- Psalm 46:11

BELOVED, THE BEGINNING of wisdom is understanding that God is God and you are not. When you discover that God is your Creator and you are his creature, you suddenly begin to see things clearly. When you realize that God is your loving Father and you are his cherished child, the scales fall from your eyes. All your troubles can be traced back to the bitter root of pride that entangles you and causes you to prefer your selfish will against the perfect will of our Father. Pride caused Satan to plunge from his position as the brightest angel, it caused Adam and Eve to fall by choosing to disobey God, and it causes us to stumble when we think we know better than God. We need to hear anew the words of God. *Where were you when I laid the foundation of the earth?* We need to understand God when he reveals his identity to us. *I am God.* He is the ground of our being, the way, the truth, and the author of life. Above all, we must know that God is love. And the love of God, like all true love, does not seek itself alone. Love reaches out beyond itself with tenderness, longing for what is best for the beloved, seeking always to heal and restore, forgive and forget, gather and embrace.

Pray: O Lord, my life is so much easier when I am still and contemplate your will. Bless me and keep me always!

FORGIVENESS OPENS HEARTS

❖ ❖ ❖

*All her sins are forgiven, and that is why
she has shown great love.*

- LUKE 7:47

LOVING PEOPLE HAVE been forgiven much, unloving people have been forgiven little. Do you know people overflowing with love? They have experienced the love and forgiveness of God. Now consider people who are unloving; they do not recognize their sins, so they have not yet humbled themselves to seek and receive God's forgiveness. *Anyone who has been forgiven for only a little will show only a little love.* You may be sure these loveless people are suffering greatly in their souls; they dwell in inner darkness, coldness, and solitude. They exist *incurvatus in se*, a latin phrase meaning "caved in on themselves." They live their lives inward for themselves, rather than outward for God and others. In contrast, contrite souls who confess their sins receive God's abundant forgiveness and life-changing love. Overflowing with God's mercy, they are easily able to turn outward and heal others with this same loving kindness. Love and forgiveness are twins, always born together.

⌒

Pray: O Lord, now that I am forgiven and renewed by your love, give me opportunities to show your love to others!

INCREASE OUR FAITH

❖ ❖ ❖

The apostles said to the Lord, "Increase our faith."

- LUKE 17:5

D O YOU NEED more faith today to be more loving, trusting, or forgiving? Did you know you can ask God to give you more faith? When the apostles heard Jesus instruct them to forgive others unconditionally, they felt so daunted and perplexed that they beseeched and implored him to increase their faith. Jesus assured them that even a little bit of true faith has great power. *If you have faith the size of a mustard seed, you would say to this mulberry tree, 'Be uprooted and planted in the sea,' and it would obey you.* Do you need more faith, hope, love, courage, grace, or joy? God is just waiting to hear you ask. If there is anything you want that accords with God's will in your life, you may rest assured that he wants to give it to you infinitely more than you want to receive it! So be bold and specific in your prayer requests; ask for what you want! If you don't get it right away, keep praying with perseverance, confidence, and expectation. You may be confident that if you pray for the virtues that you know God wants to give to you, soon you will be surprised at the abundance of gifts he bestows upon you in an unexpected hour.

⌒

Pray: O Lord, you know the desires of my heart.
Please increase my faith, hope, and love!

I Am With You Always

❖ ❖ ❖

I am with you always, even to the end of the age.

- MATTHEW 28:19

WITHOUT GOD YOU have nothing, but with God you have everything. God promises to be with you always, in every circumstance in your life, in good times and in bad, in sickness and in health, until the end of time, meaning forever. He will never leave you, betray you, or desert you. He your constant Companion and your ever-ready Friend. He is your always-present Comforter, Counsellor, Guide, Physician, Lover, Lord and Savior. Without him you can do nothing, but with him all things are possible. If you have everything yet lack God, you have nothing, while if you have nothing but God, you have everything. What do you wish to accomplish with God by your side? In what ways do you want to be confident and courageous? Knowing that God is with you always, and that you can truly live worry-free, anxiety-free, and fearlessly, what would you like to do today?

Pray: O Lord, thank you for being with me always! Guide me, forgive me, protect me, defend me, and befriend me!

MAKE GOD HAPPY

❖   ❖   ❖

There will be more joy in heaven over one sinner
who repents than over ninety-nine righteous people
who have no need of repentance.

- LUKE 15:7

D O YOU KNOW that you can make God happy or sad? You
may not realize it but the smallest choices you make today
can cause God to rejoice or weep over you. Jesus wept because
the people in Jerusalem refused to believe in him. On the other
hand, you can make God happy by trusting his promises and
walking daily in the footsteps of his Son. Of course God does
not feel sorrow or joy in the same way humans do because his
emotions are perfect. But he made us in his image, so he must
exhibit a perfect version of our flawed human emotions. And
sacred scripture is filled with references to Jesus feeling the
entire spectrum of our emotions toward those he encountered.
Think about it; since we are his beloved children, it makes sense
that our choices between good and evil cause God delight or
dismay. So let us consider how each of our decisions inclines
our hearts toward selflessness or selfishness, forgiveness or bitterness, and love or pride. God delights in you; make him a
happy Father today.

Pray: O Lord, I know what makes you happy. Help me make
choices today that reflect your loving delight!

REJOICE IN EVERY CIRCUMSTANCE

❖ ❖ ❖

Rejoice in the Lord always. I shall say it again: rejoice!

- PHILIPPIANS 4:4

I T IS EASY to be happy when things are going your way. But do you know how to rejoice in the midst of suffering? Paul teaches us how to do this. He explains how he learned to be content in all circumstances, with plenty or little, well-fed or hungry, in abundance or distress. His secret is deep faith in the love of his heavenly Father. *The Lord is near. Have no anxiety at all, but in everything, by prayer and petition, with thanksgiving, make your requests known to God.* Try this for yourself now; give thanks to God for all your blessings, but also be thankful for all your pains, heartaches, and sufferings. Trusting his promises to restore all your losses, say thank you to God aloud this very moment for all your disappointments, setbacks, and griefs. Now breathe deeply and repeat his words, *I can do all things through him who strengthens me.* This is the time to practice your faith and exercise your hope in God's promise that he is working all things together for your good. *Then the peace of God that surpasses all understanding will guard your hearts and minds in Christ Jesus.*

⌒

Pray: O Lord, I will rejoice and give you thanks for all the people and circumstances in my life today, I do rejoice!

Do Not Doubt

❖ ❖ ❖

Put your finger here and see my hands. Reach out your
hand and put it in my side. Do not doubt but believe.

- JOHN 20:27

IF YOU KNEW beyond a shadow of a doubt that all your injuries
would be healed, all your losses restored, and all your dreams
fulfilled, would you feel better? Would you be less angry, fearful, or sorrowful? Would you be more faithful, forgiving, and
loving? After Jesus was crucified and buried, he appeared to
his followers and they were astonished. They thought he was
dead! Thomas had doubts that were only dispelled when Jesus
invited him to feel his wounds. Do not doubt God's promises
that he will restore and renew everyone and everything you
have lost, so that your life will be unimaginably better than
before. Contemplate what he did for his Son by raising him
from the dead and restoring him to eternal life. This is the
essence of faith, the good news Jesus invites you to hear; if you
join your sufferings to his, willingly accepting your cross and
embracing it, as he did with his cross, you will be raised by the
Father to new life. *Jesus said to him, "Have you believed because*
you have seen me? Blessed are those who have not seen and yet have
come to believe."

Pray: O Jesus, I want to believe; help me to believe more. I
want to live my life with the utmost faith, hope, and love!

Proclaim The Good News

❖ ❖ ❖

*Go into all the world and proclaim the good news
to the whole creation.*

- MARK 16:15

THIS IS THE final instruction Jesus gave to his disciples, so imagine him saying the same thing to you. Like the disciples, you have been taught by Jesus and blessed by him. You know your sins are forgiven; you have been washed clean and given new life. Jesus has poured into your heart the love and mercy of God. Now you may overflow your abundance of new life to others. Having been healed deep in your inner heart, mind and soul, turn outward now and heal others. Tell everyone you meet about the good news of God's love and mercy. Tell others how God has changed your life for the better, how he has opened your eyes, softened your heart, and cleansed your soul. Even better, demonstrate this life-changing power of God that you have experienced by showing others genuine forgiveness. Let them experience God's love through you, let them hear his voice when you speak, and let them see the face of Christ in yours.

Pray: O Jesus, I want to show and tell everyone I meet
the wonderful healing power of your love and forgiveness!

GO FORTH IN JOY

❖ ❖ ❖

*For you shall go out in joy, and be led forth in peace; the
mountains and the hills before you shall break forth into
singing, and all the trees of the field shall clap their hands.*

- *ISAIAH 55:12*

A RE YOU TRULY joyful? The surest sign of someone who
knows the love and forgiveness of God is joy. If your heart
is filled with joy, you know God dwells in you. The joy of
knowing God is not giddy, silly, or frivolous; it is a profound
gratitude for God's mercy and a wholehearted inspiration to
love him that makes you sing praises of delight in the cathedral
of your soul. So when you go forth into the world every day,
go forth in joy. Of course, not everyone will appreciate what
you do and say because you bring the light of God's love while
some prefer darkness. But those kindred spirits who know God
as you do, and those lost souls who are still seeking the light
and yearning for the healing power of God's merciful love, will
together break forth in joyful singing at your presence, clap
their hands like the trees of the field, and lead you forth in
peace.

Pray: O Lord, I am so thankful to know you as I do!

THE POWER OF LOVE

❖ ❖ ❖

God is love.

- I JOHN 4:8

Love is the greatest power. We know that God is love and that he created the universe, so his love infuses and enlivens all people and all things, though it is often hidden. No one we know and nothing we do is beyond the reach or providence of God's love; there is no sin that love will not forgive, no wound that love cannot heal, no loss that love will not restore. Love bears all burdens, drive out fear, empowers us to lay down our lives for our friends and enemies alike, always reaches outward, and always seeks what is best for the beloved. Love is strong when it needs to be, rebuking, correcting, preserving, protecting, providing, and defending all life. Yet paradoxically love manifests itself in small, quiet ways that we mistakenly perceive as weakness. Love is born in meekness, humility, forgiveness, innocence, whispering, friendship, and reconciliation. Love is found everywhere, except where there is sin; in joy and sadness, celebration and mourning, birth and death. When we allow God's love to transform us, we become serenely truthful, quietly powerful, and secretly fruitful.

⌒

Pray: O Lord, I am overwhelmed by the power of your love. Make me a channel of your love to all people.

Made in the USA
San Bernardino, CA
09 February 2017